CORPUS OF THE ARAMAIC
INCANTATION BOWLS

CORPUS OF THE ARAMAIC INCANTATION BOWLS

by

Charles D. Isbell

WIPF & STOCK · Eugene, Oregon

Wipf and Stock Publishers
199 W 8th Ave, Suite 3
Eugene, OR 97401

Corpus of the Aramaic Incantation Bowls
By Isbell, Charles D
Copyright©1975 by Isbell, Charles D
ISBN 13: 978-1-60608-106-8
Publication date 8/18/2008
Previously published by SBL, 1975

TABLE OF CONTENTS

	Page
PREFACE	ix
ABBREVIATIONS AND SYMBOLS	xiii
INTRODUCTION	1
Text One (Montgomery 1)	17
Text Two (Montgomery 2)	19
Text Three (Montgomery 7)	21
Text Four (Myhrman, *Hilprecht Anniversary Volume*)	24
Text Five (Montgomery 5)	27
Text Six (Montgomery 27)	29
Text Seven (Gordon 11, *Orientalia*, X)	31
Text Eight (Montgomery 3)	34
Text Nine (Montgomery 14)	38
Text Ten (Montgomery 5)	40
Text Eleven (Montgomery 6)	42
Text Twelve (Montgomery 8)	44
Text Thirteen (Montgomery 17)	48
Text Fourteen (Gordon K, *Archiv Orientální*, IX)	50
Text Fifteen (Montgomery 9)	52
Text Sixteen (Montgomery 10)	54
Text Seventeen (Montgomery 11)	56
Text Eighteen (Jeruzalmi, pp. 64-75)	58
Text Nineteen (Gordon G, *Archiv Orientální*, VI)	60
Text Twenty (Montgomery 18)	64
Text Twenty-One (Montgomery 19)	66

	Page
Text Twenty-Two (Gordon, "An Aramaic Incantation," *AASOR*, XIV)	69
Text Twenty-Three (Montgomery 12)	71
Text Twenty-Four (Montgomery 16)	73
Text Twenty-Five (Montgomery 13)	75
Text Twenty-Six (Montgomery 15)	77
Text Twenty-Seven (Montgomery 20)	79
Text Twenty-Eight (Montgomery 21)	80
Text Twenty-Nine (Montgomery 22)	81
Text Thirty (Montgomery 23)	82
Text Thirty-One (Gordon 3, *Orientalia*, X)	83
Text Thirty-Two (Montgomery 24)	84
Text Thirty-Three (Gordon 1, *Orientalia*, X)	85
Text Thirty-Four (Montgomery 25)	87
Text Thirty-Five (Montgomery 26)	89
Text Thirty-Six (Montgomery 28)	91
Text Thirty-Seven (Montgomery 29)	92
Text Thirty-Eight (Montgomery 30)	94
Text Thirty-Nine (Gordon 2, *Orientalia*, X)	95
Text Forty (Gordon 4, *Orientalia*, X)	97
Text Forty-One (Gordon 5, *Orientalia*, X)	98
Text Forty-Two (Gordon 7, *Orientalia*, X)	100
Text Forty-Three (Gordon 6, *Orientalia*, X)	102
Text Forty-Four (Gordon 8, *Orientalia*, X)	104
Text Forty-Five (Gordon 9, *Orientalia*, X)	106
Text Forty-Six (Gordon 10, *Orientalia*, X)	107
Text Forty-Seven (Gordon A, *Archiv Orientální*, VI)	108
Text Forty-Eight (Gordon B, *Archiv Orientální*, VI)	110
Text Forty-Nine (Gordon D, *Archiv Orientální*, VI)	112

	Page
Text Fifty (Gordon E, *Archiv Orientální*, VI)	114
Text Fifty-One (Gordon F, *Archiv Orientální*, VI)	116
Text Fifty-Two (Gordon C, *Archiv Orientální*, VI)	118
Text Fifty-Three (Gordon H, *Archiv Orientální*, IX)	120
Text Fifty-Four (Gordon I, *Archiv Orientální*, IX)	124
Text Fifty-Five (Gordon J, *Archiv Orientální*, IX)	125
Text Fifty-Six (Gordon L, *Archiv Orientální*, IX)	127
Text Fifty-Seven (Gordon, "Two Magic Bowls in Teheran: The Aramaic Bowl" (*Orientalia*, XX)	129
Text Fifty-Eight (Ellis 3 and Jeruzalmi, pp. 52-63)	131
Text Fifty-Nine (Ellis 5 and Jeruzalmi, pp. 76-90)	133
Text Sixty (Yamauchi, "Aramaic Magic Bowls," *JAOS*, 85)	134
Text Sixty-One (Obermann I, *AJSLL*, LVII)	137
Text Sixty-Two (Obermann II, *AJSLL*, LVII)	138
Text Sixty-Three (Jeruzalmi, pp. 2-23)	140
Text Sixty-Four (Jeruzalmi, pp. 24-38)	142
Text Sixty-Five (Jeruzalmi, pp. 39-51)	144
Text Sixty-Six (Jeruzalmi, pp. 91-99)	146
Text Sixty-Seven (Jeruzalmi, pp. 114-126)	147
Text Sixty-Eight (Jeruzalmi, pp. 100-113)	148
Text Sixty-Nine (Jeruzalmi, pp. 127-139)	150
Text Seventy (Jeruzalmi, pp. 140-151)	152
Text Seventy-One (Jeruzalmi, pp. 152-158)	153
Text Seventy-Two (Jeruzalmi, pp. 159-163)	154
GLOSSARY OF ARAMAIC WORDS	155
INDEX OF PERSONAL NAMES	187
LIST OF QUOTATIONS FROM SCRIPTURE	195
BIBLIOGRAPHY	197

PREFACE

This dissertation is a collection of all the published Aramaic magic bowls. I am thus indebted to all the scholars who have previously worked on these bowls and wish to express my thanks to them in writing here. But two people in particular merit a special word of thanks for the help they have given me in my studies and in the preparation of this dissertation.

Dr. Harvey E. Finley of the Nazarene Theological Seminary (Kansas City, Missouri) was my first Semitics teacher and it was he who in large part inspired me to do further graduate work in the field to which he brings such devotion and mastery.

Dr. Cyrus H. Gordon gave patient and wise counsel as my thesis advisor and through three years at Brandeis, the inspiration of his teaching and scholarship have been matched by his friendship and fatherly interest in me.

I wish also to thank the University of Massachusetts for a special Faculty Research Grant allocation to cover the expense involved in the final typing of this manuscript.

Finally, I express appreciation and admiration for typist Judith Stark who learned the Hebrew alphabet in order to be able to type the Aramaic and Hebrew portions and did a superb job in all aspects of a difficult project.

לאשתי

ישלם יהוה פעלך ותהי משכרתך שלמה מעם יהוה
אלהי ישראל אשר באת לחסות תחת כנפיו (רות ב:יב).

ABBREVIATIONS AND SYMBOLS

AASOR	Annual of the American Schools of Oriental Research.
AJSLL	American Journal of Semitic Languages and Literatures.
AOR	Archiv Orientální.
BDB	Brown, Francis; Driver, S. R.; and Briggs, Charles A. A Hebrew and English Lexicon of the Old Testament.
BH	Biblical Hebrew.
Comptes-rendus	Comptes-rendus de l'Académie des Inscriptions et Belles-Lettres.
Dictionary	Jastrow, Marcus. A Dictionary of the Targumim, the Talmud Babli and Yerushalmi, and the Midrashic Literature.
Dictionnaire	Jean, Charles F., and Hoftijzer, Jean. Dictionnaire des Inscriptions Sémitiques de l'Ouest.
Discoveries	Layard, Austen. Discoveries In the Ruins of Nineveh and Babylon.
IDB	Buttrick, George Arthur (ed.). The Interpreter's Dictionary of the Bible.
JAOS	Journal of the American Oriental Society.
Jeruzalmi	Jeruzalmi, Isak. Les Coupes Magiques Araméenes de Mésopotamie.
JMIB	McCullough, W. S. Jewish and Mandaean Incantation Bowls.
JNES	Journal of Near Eastern Studies.
JPOS	Journal of the Palestine Oriental Society.
Judaism	Moore, George Foot. Judaism in the First Centuries of the Christian Era.
Mandaic	Yamauchi, Edwin Masao. Mandaean Incantation Texts.
Minoan	Gordon, Cyrus H. Evidence for the Minoan Language.

Nights	Burton, Richard F. *The Book of a Thousand Nights and a Night.*
PSBA	*Proceedings of the Society of Biblical Archaeology.*
RA	*Revue d'Assyriologie et d'Archéologie Orientale.*
Revue	*Revue des Études Juives.*
TSBA	*Transactions of the Society of Biblical Archaeology.*
UT	Gordon, Cyrus H. *Ugaritic Textbook.*
ZA	*Zeitschrift für Assyriologie und verwandte Gebiete.*
ZK	*Zeitschrift für Keilschriftforschung.*
(...)	Explanation.
[...]	Restoration.
{ ... }	Scribal Plus.
⟨ ... ⟩	Scribal Omission.
(?)	Uncertain Reading or Translation.
Inferior Point (א̣)	Uncertain Letter.

ʼ -- א	L -- ל
B -- ב	M -- מ
G -- ג	N -- נ
D -- ד	S -- ס
H -- ה	ʽ -- ע
W -- ו	P -- פ
Z -- ז	Ṣ -- צ
Ḥ -- ח	Q -- ק
Ṭ -- ט	R -- ר
Y -- י	Š -- ש
K -- כ	T -- ת

INTRODUCTION

Almost sixty years have passed since the publication of James A. Montgomery's definitive work on the Aramaic magic bowls, *Aramaic Incantation Texts From Nippur*,[1] a work which has been the starting point for every student of the bowls since its appearance in 1913. Professor Montgomery's student, Cyrus H. Gordon, was able to say in 1941 that Montgomery's book "remains the unrivaled authoritative work on the subject,"[2] an evaluation which would still be true today. But, although Professor Montgomery's 1913 book is the best, it is certainly not the only work on the subject.

Published in journals and periodicals of many different countries are "over one hundred complete texts plus numerous partial fragments."[3] These one hundred plus include bowls in Mandaic,[4] Syriac,[5] and what has been called "Jewish Babylonian

---

[1] James A. Montgomery, *Aramaic Incantation Texts From Nippur* (Philadelphia: The University Museum, 1913). Cited hereafter as Montgomery.

[2] *Orientalia* X, 1941, p. 116.

[3] William H. Rossell, *A Handbook of Aramaic Magical Texts* (New Jersey: Shelton College, 1953), p. 7. Cited hereafter as Rossell, *Handbook*.

[4] The definitive work on Mandaic texts is Edwin Masao Yamauchi's *Mandaean Incantation Texts* (Ann Arbor: University Microfilms, Inc., 1964), a dissertation done in the Department of Mediterranean Studies at Brandeis University under Cyrus H. Gordon. It contains a full introduction to Mandaic studies, a complete grammar of Mandaic (with chapters on Orthography, Phonetics, the Numerals, Pronouns, Nouns, Particles, Paradigms, Verbs, and Syntax), fifty-two texts transcribed into the Hebrew alphabet and translated into English, glossaries, and an extremely helpful bibliography. A revised edition is now published: *Mandaic Incantation Texts* (American Oriental Series 49; New Haven: American Oriental Society, 1967).

[5] The definitive work on Syriac bowls is Victor Hamilton's *Syriac Incantation Bowls*, a dissertation done in the Department of Mediterranean Studies at Brandeis University under Cyrus H. Gordon.

Aramaic."[6] The present dissertation is concerned only with those texts which were written in Aramaic, texts which have been described by Professor Gordon as follows:

> The texts under discussion come from Sasanian Babylonia before and after 600 A.D. These inscriptions are written spirally on terra-cotta bowls; usually on the inside of the bowl, sometimes on the outside, and sometimes on both sides.[7]

A complete bibliography of the previously published Aramaic bowls is unnecessary here, for that task has been handled by several other scholars,[8] but a word is needed about the exclusion of some, the inclusion of other texts among the seventy-two which comprise the bulk of this dissertation. Most of the publishers of texts failed to include either a photograph or a hand copy of the bowls they translated and explained. Their work is omitted in the present dissertation because of the fact that there is no way of checking their readings, and consequently their translations and comments. Only those bowls which could be read by photograph or by a facsimile have been included, and their number happens to total seventy-two.

---

[6]Rossell, Handbook, p. 7.

[7]Cyrus H. Gordon, Adventures In the Nearest East (London: Phoenix House Ltd., 1957), p. 161. Cited hereafter as Gordon, Adventures.

[8]Montgomery, pp. 13-22, cites all material known in 1913. Franz Rosenthal (Die aramäistische Forschung, Leiden, 1939) includes the bowls in his bibliographies of the various fields of Aramaic studies (pp. 34-35, 218-223, 233-235) and he omits only P. Lacau's article, "Une Coupe d'Incantation" in Revue d'Assyriologie, II, 1894, pp. 49-51. Edwin Masao Yamauchi (JAOS, 85, 1965, pp. 511-513) includes a "Survey of Research" done on the Aramaic bowls to the year 1965. These lists cite all the Aramaic bowls published with the exception of those handled by Isak Jeruzalmi in a Sorbonne dissertation (1964) entitled Les Coupes Magiques Araméenes de Mésopotamie. Material published since 1965 is included in the bibliography.

For the bowls published by Ellis in the volume by Layard, Discoveries in the Ruins of Nineveh and Babylon, Montgomery (followed by Rossell and Yamauchi) is incorrect in citing the pages as 509-523. Correct to 434-448.

Also, in the Yamauchi (JAOS 85 [1965] 512) citation of Halévy's article in Comptes-rendus, V, correct pages 228-233 to 288-298.

Three other Aramaic incantation bowls should be mentioned. In 1967, W. S. McCullough published two bowls inscribed in Aramaic and three in Mandaic.[9] Of the two Aramaic bowls, "Bowl B"[10] is "badly written" and "badly preserved," as McCullough notes[11] and little could be accomplished by repeating his work here. "Bowl A"[12] is very clear and legible, and there is little to add to McCullough's transcription, translation, or commentary on it. It does contain several proper names not attested elsewhere among the bowls as well as four new vocabulary words: חלד, "to gird, bind"; מרר, Afel-- "to afflict"; אוב, BH "ghost"; ירושלמאי, "the Jerusalemite."

The third bowl worthy of note was published by Stephen Kaufman.[13] The bowl does not contain an Aramaic incantation, but is "nothing more than a collection of quotations".[14] from Scripture or from the Targum to a Scripture verse.

Previous Publications Pertaining to the Bowls

The first Aramaic incantation bowls were published in 1853.[15] In the years following that first publication, a variety of opinions about the bowls have been expressed. Ellis, in 1853, declared of the seven bowls which he translated that "the subject of these inscriptions are amulets or charms against evil spirits, diseases and every kind of misfortune."[16] And Ellis was certain that the writers of the bowls were Jews, because "sometimes pure Hebrew sentences are found mixed with the Chaldee, especially in No. 5;[17] and the

---

[9]*JMIB*.

[10]*JMIB*, pp. 6-10.

[11]*JMIB*, p. 6.

[12]*JMIB*, pp. 1-5.

[13]S. A. Kaufman, "A Unique Magic Bowl From Nippur" (*JNES*, 32, 1973, pp. 170-174).

[14]Kaufman, "A Unique Magic Bowl," p. 171.

[15]In Layard's *Discoveries*, pp. 434-448, by Thomas Ellis.

[16]*Discoveries*, p. 435.

[17]Number fifty-nine in this dissertation.

words 'Halleluiah' and 'Selah' occur in nearly every one of them."[18] Layard adopted the view of Ellis about the Jewish authorship of the bowls, asserting that the Jews, "like the Chaldaeans, amongst whom they dwelt, appear to have been celebrated for their skill in the art of writing charms."[19]

As to the use of the bowls, Layard noted the conjecture of Ellis "that the writing was to be dissolved in water, to be drank (sic) as a cure against disease, or a precaution against the arts of witchcraft and magic."[20] But he justifiably raised the following objection to the theory of Ellis: "they could not have been used for that purpose, as the writing upon them is perfectly fresh, and it is essential that it should be entirely washed into the water to make the remedy efficacious."[21] And, having rejected the theory of Ellis, Layard added his own:

> As they were found at a considerable depth beneath the surface in mounds which had undoubtedly been used as place of sepulture, I am rather inclined to believe that they were charms buried with the dead, or employed for some purpose at funeral ceremonies, and afterwards placed in the grave.[22]

Such then were the views of Ellis and Layard in 1853. Sixty years later, Montgomery judged the views of Ellis to be "wild" and his facsimilies "unreliable."[23] In short, in the opinion of Montgomery, Layard's publication "did little more than attract the attention of scholars to a fresh field of philology and religious lore."[24]

---

[18] *Discoveries*, p. 435.

[19] *Discoveries*, p. 446.

[20] *Discoveries*, p. 447.

[21] *Discoveries*, p. 447.

[22] *Discoveries*, pp. 447-448. It is obvious that such a theory could not be true for all the bowls, as text two of the dissertation demonstrates. The first half of text two is written by "Kupitai" for the benefit of "'Abuna" while the second half is written by the same "'Abuna" for the benefit of "Kupitai." Two men would hardly be exchanging funeral incantations.

[23] Montgomery, p. 16.

[24] Montgomery, p. 17. Montgomery also cites in this place two articles by M. A. Lévy: *Über die von Layard aufgefundenen*

Some twenty-four years after the appearance of the volume edited by Layard, M. Halévy published some "Observations sur un vase Judéo-Babylonien du British Museum"[25] in which he noted two different opinions about the bowls among scholars:

> Les uns y voient des coupes à divination dont il est déjà fait mention dans l'histoire de Joseph (Genèse, xliv, 5); les autres supposent que ce sont des coupes consacrées et dont l'eau qu'elles renfermaient était censée imprégnée d'une vertu mystérieuse capable de guérir les maladies.[26]

The theory connecting the bowls with the divining cup of Joseph had been advanced in 1873 by one J. M. Rodwell, in an article entitled "Remarks Upon A Terra-Cotta Vase."[27] This idea Halévy rejected because the text of the inscription "porte un caractère plutôt prophylactique que curatif."[28] The second theory is that which had been given by Ellis in the Layard volume. Halévy deemed it equally false for two reasons:

> L'eau devait avoir pour effet d'effacer l'écriture à la longue. L'épaisseur du bord est telle, d'ailleurs, qu'on ne pouvait aisément se servir de la coupe pour boire.[29]

---

chaldäischen Inschriften auf Topfgefässen. Ein Beitrag zur hebräischen Paläographie u. z. Religionsgeschichte, published in 1885 in *Zeitschrift d. Deutschen Morgenländischen Gesellschaft*; and "Epigraphische Beitrage Zur Geschichte der Juden," published in 1861, in *Jahrbuch für die Geschichte der Juden*. Both articles treat bowl number one of Ellis, using his facsimile. Lévy's work was "the first scientific treatment of this new material" according to Montgomery (p. 17). However, his transcription of the bowl was very imperfect, as a comparison of his readings with those given in text eighteen of this dissertation will show.

[25]*Comptes-rendus*, iv, Vol. V, pp. 288-293. Halévy's article deals with the same bowl published in 1873 by J. M. Rodwell (*TSBA*, ii, 1873, pp. 114-118). Rodwell's attempts at decipherment were very unsuccessful, the fact which first prompted Halévy to take up the same text. In this dissertation, the Rodwell-Halévy text is number sixty-five.

[26]*Comptes-rendus*, V, p. 288.

[27]*TSBA*, II, 1873, pp. 114-118 and one plate.

[28]*Comptes-rendus*, V, p. 288.

[29]*Comptes-rendus*, V, pp. 288-289.

Having rejected the opinions of both Rodwell and Ellis,[30] Halévy proceeded to voice his own theory about the function of the bowls:

> Il paraît donc plus probable que ces vases étaient de simples amulettes, destinés à préserver la famille contre les démons et les maladies dont ces êtres étaient réputés les auteurs. En d'autres termes, c'étaient des talismans de famille.[31]

Halévy placed the approximate date of the bowl which he was editing "vers le neuvième siècle après notre ère."[32] Since the time of Montgomery the date has been pushed back by about two or three hundred years.[33]

The work of Halévy was followed in 1885 by the publication of an article entitled "Sur un vase judéo-babylonien de musée Lycklama de Cannes (Provence)"[34] written by Henri Hyvernat. Although he did include several points of interest in his article, "the photographic reproduction in Hyvernat's publication is not clear enough to warrant emendations of his

---

[30] Strangely, Halévy does not even mention Layard's own opinion about the funerary function of these bowls. Nor does he acknowledge the earlier works of M. A. Lévy, who, for example, in 1861, had already rejected Layard's idea and declared that the bowls were simply "Bannsprüche, welche schädliche Geister aus dem Hause vertreiben sollten" (*Jahrbuch*, II, p. 267).

[31] *Comptes-rendus*, V, p. 289.

[32] *Comptes-rendus*, V, p. 292. When the date of the bowls is set this late, room is made for the theory of Halévy about *Dallallah*. It is, he argued (pp. 292-293), composed of two elements: *Dall*, "porte" and *Allâh*, "Dieu." But by assuming that the element *Allâh* could have been represented by a pagan god during the Babylonian period, Halévy posits an original *Dall-Ani*, or "(petite) porte de Anou," the analogue of *Bâb-ili*, or "(grande) porte de Il." This name was later changed to *Dall-Allâh* by the Arabs, "au point de vue du monothéisme." Subsequent reading of this text, which is number sixty-five in the present dissertation, shows the reading of *Dall-Allâh* to be incorrect and Halévy's arguments unnecessary.

[33] Montgomery, pp. 102-105. He is followed by Gordon (*Adventures*, p. 161), Obermann (*AJSLL*, 1940, p. 2), Rossell (*Handbook*, p. 10), Yamauchi (*JAOS*, 85, 1965, p. 511), and McCullough (*JMIB*, pp. xi-xii).

[34] *ZK*, II, 1885, pp. 113-146 plus two plates.

transcription."[35] But in his work, Henry Hyvernat followed
Halévy in the citation of some Talmudic parallels to the
magic bowl which he published,[36] explaining such parallels in
the following terms:

> Les exilés de la Palestine n'acceptèrent donc jamais
> la religion de leurs conquérants et c'est pourquoi
> ils eurent plus d'une fois à souffrir leurs persé-
> cutions. Mais le sentiment du merveilleux se
> développa à l'excès chez eux et leur esprit con-
> tracta une tendance bien marquée à la superstition.
> Cette tendance présida à la composition des livres
> Talmudiques.[37]

In spite of the early recognition of such similarity between the bowls and certain parts of the Talmud, very little has been written beyond sparse comments by various men who have published some of the bowls. A full treatment of this subject would be extremely useful.

The phrase "the signet-ring of Solomon" occurs in Hyvernat's bowl[38] and evokes from him the following interesting explanation:

> Les légendes judéo-musulmanes nous parlent de quatre
> pierres précieuses qui furent données à Salomon par
> quatre anges envoyés de Dieu pour lui conférer la
> toute puissance sur la création. La première lui
> donnait l'empire sur les vent, la deuxième, sur les
> animaux; la troisième, sur la terre ferme et sur les
> mers; et la quatrième sur le monde des esprits. Une
> courte inscription gravée sur chacune d'elles rappelait
> à Salomon qu'il tenait de Dieu seul sa puissance mer-
> veilleuse. Le roi fortuné réunit ces quatre pierres
> et en forma le fameux anneau.[39]

---

[35]Cyrus H. Gordon in *Archiv Orientální*, VI, 1934, p. 331. Two parallel texts to the one treated by Hyvernat were published with facsimiles by Gordon (AOR, VI, 1934, pp. 331-334) and they are numbers fifty and fifty-one in this dissertation.

[36]Halévy's article in *Comptes-rendus*, V, 1877, p. 291, portrays the purpose of the *Kol Nidrê* prayer to be similar to that of some of the bowls. Cf. also the treatment of Hyvernat in ZK, II, 1885, pp. 117-119.

[37]ZK, II, 1885, pp. 118-119.

[38]And in many other bowls now known. Cf. the texts in the body of this dissertation for the frequent occurrences of forms of אעקתא/ן.

[39]ZK, II, 1885, pp. 124-125.

In concluding his article, Hyvernat spoke briefly about the purpose of the bowl, its "caractère paléographique,"[40] and its date. Concerning its purpose, Hyvernat proposed the idea that "c'était une croyance populaire chez les Juifs que l'on pouvait emprisonner les esprits nuisibles dans les vases."[41] This idea has been rejected by Gordon, who remarks aptly that "the last thing the ancients wished to do was to trap on their own property the demons which might subsequently escape and work mischief on the spot."[42]

Concerning the date of his bowl, Hyvernat, in viewing the opinions of several who had previously expressed themselves on the subject,[43] found himself at last in agreement with the conclusions of M. A. Lévy who had written "que son inscription ne saurait être antérieure à l'invasion arabe c.a.d. au VIIe siècle."[44] The main thrust of Lévy's arguments[45] depended upon the use of the Yodh as a *mater lectionis*, the use of א as well as of ה to indicate the emphatic state of nouns,[46] and especially on the final forms of ך, ם, ן, ף, and ץ at the end of words. These final forms were vestiges of an older alphabet, of Chaldean origin. As Hyvernat summarizes the argument, "Mr. Lévy croit . . . que l'absence ou la presence des lettres

---

[40]Hyvernat simply points out the fortunate circumstance of his bowl's letters being generally written the same way in each place they occur, a fact which gives his bowl an advantage over those in the British Museum (*ZK*, II, 1885, p. 139). He then includes (p. 146) "un alphabet calqué avec le plus grand soin sur l'original lui-même."

[41]*ZK*, II, 1885, p. 138. Montgomery (pp. 41-42) follows Hyvernat with modifications. His view will be treated in full on pages 13-15.

[42]Gordon, *Adventures*, p. 162.

[43]Among them Ellis and Layard.

[44]*ZK*, II, 1885, p. 141.

[45]Developed in full in his "Epigraphische Beiträge" cited in note twenty-four above.

[46]Although ה pointed to an earlier date, the repeated use of א seems to indicate a date somewhat earlier. However, as Montgomery (p. 27) has noted, Lévy had at his disposal "rather scanty epigraphical resources," i.e., only the one bowl. By 1913, Montgomery (p. 29) realized the fact that א was used more often than was ה in the bowls.

finales dans une inscription est un des criterium les plus certains d'antiquité ou de non-antiquité."[47]

Because the arguments of Lévy and Hyvernat were far different from a scholar named Chwolson, it was necessary for Hyvernat to note the views of Chwolson, and to cite his twofold objection to the opinion of Lévy. Reason number one was the following:

> Da wir aber keine älteren jüdischen literarischen Denkmäler als den Talmud aus Babylonien besitzen, können wir auch nicht wissen zu welcher Zeit diese Orthographie sich bei den babylonischen Juden ausgebildet hat.[48]

The second reason was because "jene Beschwörungen wohl von Ungelehrten und für Ungelehrte geschrieben wurden."[49] Chwolson, however, failing to follow those principles which he himself stated, had used his own ideas about paleography to date each of the five Ellis bowls to a different time,[50] and Montgomery was surely correct in opposing Chwolson on this issue, calling his methodology "*reductio ad absurdum.*"[51] Indeed, it is clear that Montgomery was thinking of both Lévy and Chwolson in his criticism of the use of paleography alone for dating purposes.

> It is hazardous to assign a date for these bowls on palaeographical grounds; it is impossible to relate the various variations of script to each other by a chronological scale. For instance, the contemporaneous character of many bowls at Nippur is shown by the recurrence of the same persons and families in the texts; indeed the same persons appear in texts of different dialects, yet these inscriptions differ greatly in script. But there is no reason, at least in the Nippur bowls, to assign them to different ages; from the interrelations between them, personal and phraseological, I am inclined to assign them to the

---

[47] *ZK*, II, 1885, p. 142.

[48] *ZK*, II, 1885, p. 143.

[49] *ZK*, II, 1885, p. 143.

[50] Cf. his arguments in *Corpus Inscriptionum Hebraicarum* (St. Petersburg, 1882), column 118 ff.

[51] Montgomery, p. 27.

same period. Indeed they might all have been written in the same year, so far as palaeography may say anything. The differences are chirographical, not palaeographical.[52]

From 1882 to 1901 the French savant Moise Schwab published some eighteen Aramaic bowls.[53] In general, Schwab's work was incredibly poor. In one text, "he failed to recognize seventy-three out of the hundred and ninety-three words," reading properly "less than forty different words including prepositions, pronouns, proper names, amens, selahs and other banalities."[54] In addition to his publication of readings which were incorrect, Schwab committed other blunders which make his work very difficult to use. First, he accompanied only one of his translation and explanation attempts with a facsimile,[55] so that most of the texts which he published cannot be checked.[56] Secondly, based on his erroneous way of reading the texts, Schwab made rather fantastic guesses as to the meaning of the texts.

The best example of Schwab's failure to comprehend the real nature and purposes of the bowls is seen in his theory that the texts were concerned with the practice of hydromancy.[57]

---

[52] Montgomery, p. 27.

[53] For a complete list of Schwab's bowl publications, see Montgomery, pp. 18-19.

[54] Gordon, *Orientalia*, X, 1941, p. 126.

[55] Cf. *Revue*, IV, 1882, p. 165, where Schwab collaborated with E. Babelon to present an article entitled "Un vase judéo-chaldéen de la Bibliothèque Nationale." But even this facsimile is not reliable enough to be used for checking Schwab's readings.

[56] Fortunately, other scholars have re-published many of the texts first presented by Schwab, and from their photographs or facsimiles his original readings can be judged.

[57] Cf. the title of one of his longest articles dealing with the texts, "Les Coupes Magiques et L'Hydromancie dans L'Antiquité Orientale" (*PSBA*, XII, 1890).
Note also that Schwab interpreted such biblical passages as Zechariah 13:1 and 14:8; Joel 3:18; Ezekiel 47:1-12; Proverbs 10:11, 13:14, and 16:22; Psalm 26:9-10; Isaiah 41:7 and 17; Jeremiah 25:15-27; and Matthew 20 and 26 as dealing with or referring to hydromancy (*PSBA*, XII, 1890, p. 293). And on the same page, he argues that "on reconnait aisement des allusions a des pratiques d'hydromancie dans les passages

In his text מיא[58] Schwab read the word "water" four times. However, an examination of the facsimile published earlier by Ellis[59] shows very clearly that in none of the four words is any form of מיא a correct reading;[60] and once the faulty readings of Schwab are rejected, his entire theory of hydromancy falls.[61]

In 1893 and 1894, Joseph Wohlstein published a series of five Aramaic bowls with translation and with commentary, but with no photographs or facsimiles.[62] Wohlstein's Einleitung[63] contained his opinion about several points. The contents of the bowls he described as follows: "Den allgemeinen Inhalt derselben bilden Beschwörungen und Verwünschungen gegen Dämonen und böse Geister, die Krankheiten oder sonstige Uebel am Körper und im Hause verbreiten."[64] Only one text among those which Wohlstein presented departed from the usual as far as content. "Eine Ausnahme davon bildet die Inschrift Nr. 2417, die keine Dämonenbeschwörung, sondern eine Bitte an die Geister gewisser Verstorbener enthalt und wahrscheinlich einem besonderen Gebiete des Aberglaubens angehört."[65] The writers

---

suivants du Talmud, ou l'on interprete et commente le texte biblique a la lumiere des usages contemporains." Biblical passages thus explained, according to Schwab's argument, include Genesis 42:9 and Proverbs 1:14.

[58]*PSBA*, XII, 1890, pp. 313-315. The text is number five in Layard's *Discoveries* and number fifty-nine in this dissertation.

[59]Layard, *Discoveries*, p. 448.

[60]Cf. text fifty-nine of this dissertation for corrections of both Ellis and Schwab.

[61]For other scholars who arrived at a rejection of Schwab's theory cf. Wohlstein (*ZA*, VIII, 1893, pp. 315-316); Montgomery, pp. 40-41; and Jeruzalmi, pp. 76-90.

[62]*ZA*, VIII, 1893, pp. 313-340 and *ZA*, IX, 1894, pp. 11-41. The title of the two-part article is "Über einige aramäische Inschriften auf Thongefässen des Königlichen Museums zu Berlin."

[63]*ZA*, VIII, 1893, pp. 313-327.

[64]*ZA*, VIII, 1893, p. 313.

[65]*ZA*, VIII, 1893, p. 314.

of the texts were Jews according to Wohlstein,[66] and the date of the bowls was sometime in the seventh century. In Wohlstein's own words, "sie alle der gleichen Zeit und zwar wahrscheinlich dem siebten Jahrhundert angehören."[67] It was concerning the purpose of the bowls that Wohlstein advanced a different theory. "Kein Zauberwerk," he said, citing page thirty-two of the book *Rasiel*, "kann ohne Zuhilfenahme eines Gefässes vollbracht werden."[68] Wohlstein felt that the Jews had long believed in the necessity of the writing down of an exorcism "um dem Zauberbann wirksam zu begegnen."[69] But why were food bowls the material chosen upon which to write these particular incantations.

There is now evidence from archaeology to show that the practice of writing incantations in ink on the inside of clay bowls was not limited to pre-Islamic Babylonia. "The praxis is similar in Crete and Babylonia; e.g., the Knossos magic bowls (II,1; II,2) were found inverted and under the floor as in Babylonia."[70] Thus a citation of Kabbalistic parallels by scholars such as Wohlstein and Lacau[71] does not accord with the facts. The Knossos bowls indicate that, although the Kabbalists may have fitted food bowls into their own way of thinking about certain magical practices, the origin of the Aramaic magic bowls is to be found in a practice that predates Jewish Kabbalism by several hundred years.

In 1895, Rudolph Stübe re-edited one of the texts which Wohlstein had published earlier,[72] but he added no new theory about the authorship, the date, or any of the purposes of the bowls.

---

[66]*ZA*, VIII, 1893, p. 318.

[67]*ZA*, VIII, 1893, p. 326.

[68]*ZA*, VIII, 1893, p. 325.

[69]*ZA*, VIII, 1893, p. 326.

[70]Cyrus H. Gordon, *Minoan* (Ventnor: Ventnor Publishers, 1966), p. 27, note 53.

[71]"Une Coupe d'Incantation" published in *RA*, III, 1894, pp. 49-51.

[72]*Jüdisch-Babylonische Zaubertexte* (Halle, 1895).

It was not until 1913 that a complete and accurate treatment of the Aramaic magical incantation texts was published, and the author was James A. Montgomery.[73] It is not necessary to repeat in this thesis all of the points which Montgomery presented so ably. His opinions were so well thought out that most of what he wrote in 1913 is still valid today. On one point, however, he was in error. That point concerns the purpose for which the bowls were written. He followed Hyvernat[74] in his view that the bowls were intended as traps for evil spirits and/or demons.[75] To support his view, Montgomery cited one of the thirty Aramaic texts which he transliterated and translated in the book.[76] The first words of the text are: מיטלי דמיכל מלאכין קדישין וכל רוחי בישתא: "Covers which are for containing holy angels and all evil spirits." This phrase shows, argued Montgomery, that the "conscious purpose of the bowl magic" was to contain or bottle up the demons in the bowls upon which the incantations were written. However, the very shape of the bowls themselves mitigates against such an assumption. All the bowls have wide, mouth-like openings and are not very deep at all.

Hyvernat had spoken[77] of Muslim legends which cited the power of Solomon to bottle up jinn as one of the parallels to the function which the bowls were to perform in the Aramaic magical praxis. But the parallel is a false one. In the "Tale of the Fisherman and the Jinni," Solomon is indeed reported to have shut up a jinni in a bottle.[78] But the word for "bottle" is Arabic "*kumkum*," which Burton describes as "a gourd-shaped bottle."[79] It is not a food bowl but a bottle.

---

[73] See above, page one.

[74] See above, page eight.

[75] Montgomery, p. 41.

[76] See Montgomery's text four, pp. 133-137. In this dissertation, the same text is number five.

[77] *ZK*, II, 1885, p. 138.

[78] Richard F. Burton, *Nights* (Burton Club, n.d.), Vol. I, p. 42.

[79] Burton, *Nights*, I, p. 42.

It does not have a wide mouth but a very small one, and the mouth is at the end of a long, slender neck.[80] In the tale itself, the jinni who reports about his being bottled at the hands of Solomon makes it clear that Solomon not only put him in the *kumkum* but that he also covered the *kumkum* over with lead.[81] It is clear that the magic bowls which contain the Aramaic inscriptions are ill-suited for such a procedure.

However, aside from the shape of the bowls, the texts themselves show clearly enough that the demons were not intended to be trapped in the bowls. First of all, if the demons were trapped, or if the author of the bowl hoped they were trapped, there would be no reason for them also to be "wholly bound and sealed and tied in knots."[82] Secondly, if the demons were to be trapped, why would the magician make provision against their further working of mischief? "If you sin at all against (my client) . . . I will enchant you."[83] And there certainly would be no reason at all for the magician to command demons to "go away" from his client[84] when he expected them to remain trapped inside the bowl on which he was writing; the exhortation would rather have been: "Do not escape from this bowl." But there is simply no text in which the magician exhorted the demons to remain trapped because that was not what he wanted to accomplish. He wanted to expel them, to get them as far away from the house and possessions of his client as possible.

One last point can be made about the idea of trapping the demons in the bowls. As Montgomery himself showed later in the same book, skulls were sometimes used instead of the

---

[80]A picture of a *kumkum* is given in Edward W. Lane's book, *The Modern Egyptians* (London: Ward, Lock and Co., Ltd., 1835), p. 185.

[81]Burton, *Nights*, I, p. 42.

[82]Cf. Text ten, line one.

[83]Cf. Text six, line six and line eight, and all parallel passages.

[84]Cf. Text twelve, line ten and Text thirteen, lines six and seven.

more common food bowls.⁸⁵ It was this fact which led Professor Gordon to posit the following theory:

> It is well known that a mass of superstitions and magical beliefs have always clustered around the dead and their skeletons, particularly their skulls; and these bowls, somewhat resembling the shape of the cranium, may have substituted the skulls that had been in use earlier.⁸⁶

Whether Gordon is correct or not, the finding of the skulls,⁸⁷ which could not have served as traps for the demons, shows the error of the Hyvernat-Montgomery theory.⁸⁸

---

⁸⁵Montgomery, pp. 256-257, comments upon one inscription written on the top of a human skull and adds the fact that a Professor Ranke had told him of two similar skulls in the Berlin Museum (p. 256, note one).

⁸⁶Gordon, *Adventures*, p. 162.

⁸⁷Besides the bowls and skulls, there is also a Mandaic magical incantation written on a lead amulet. For complete information about the amulet see Yamauchi, *Mandaic*, pp. 22-23. For Yamauchi's transliteration and translation of the text, cf. pp. 319-343. This amulet was first published by M. Lidzbarski, "Ein mandäisches Amulett," *Florilegium ou recueil de travaux d'érudition dédiés à M. Melchior de Vogue* (Paris: Imprimerie Nationale, 1909), pp. 349-373. Further lead amulets have been published by R. Macuch, "Altmandäische Bleirollen I," *Die Araber in der Alten Welt*, ed. F. Altheim and R. Stiehl (Berlin: W. de Gruyter, 1967), IV, 91-203; *idem*, V, 34-72.

⁸⁸Still, McCullough (*JMIB*, p. xiii) notes and then rejects Gordon's argument, concluding that Hyvernat and Montgomery are correct with respect to "most of the bowls."

TEXT ONE

הדין קמיעה דאפרה (2) בר ש[ברדוך] דתיהוי ביה (3) אסותא
לה[דין א] פרה בר שברדוך {ועים} (4) ולהדא בה[מנדוך] בח
סמא דתיהי לחון (5) אסותא להדין א[פרא] בר שברדוך ולהדא
בהמנדוך בת (6) סמא אמין א[מ]ין סלה הדין קמיעה דליליתא
דבת ביתלהון (7) להדין אפרא בר שברדוך ולהדא בחמנדוך
בת סמא (8) אשבעית עליכין כל מיני ליליתא בש[ום]זרעיתכין
דילדין. שידי (9) וליליתא לבני נורא סטין רי מרדין ועברין
על גזירתא דמריהון וי מן זיקא (10) פרח פרהין וי מחבלין
רי באתרשמכי מסאב המסין וירמסין וצלפין ומפגמין (11)
ומפגרין {ש} ומשגשין איצין ובלמין ומשגרין כמין רי . .
פוכתא ובתריכון (12) ובתריכון דחלין ומדחלין יסירין
למומתי ומידמין לבני אינשא לגברי בדמות נשי (13) ולנשי
בדמות גברי ועים בני אינשא שכבין בלילי' ובימא בשום
(14) שעש גש גשך כתבית עליכי ליליתא בישתא דכל שום
דאית ליכי אנחנא (15) כתבנא ושמיה יסיך אפרה אל עולם
ועד

TRANSLATION OF TEXT ONE

This is the amulet of 'Epra (2) the son of Ša[bor-
duk], that there may be (3) salvation[1] for th[is 'E]pra
the son of Šaborduk (4) and for this Bah[manduk] the
daughter of Sama, that there shall be for them (5) sal-
vation--for this 'E[pra] the son of Šaborduk and for this
Bahmanduk the daughter of (6) Sama. Amen. A[m]en.
Selah. This is the amulet against[2] the lilith which is
lurking in the house of (7) this 'Epra the son of Šaborduk and this Bahmanduk the daughter of Sama. (8) I adjure you, every species of lilith, in the name of your
offspring which demons and liliths bore (9) for the children of fire[3] who went astray. Woe, rebellers and
transgressors against the ban of their lord. Woe, from
the fast-flying (10) blast. Woe, destroyers. Woe,
B'TRŠMKY with unclean wounds. Woe, tramplers, scourgers,
mutilaters, (11) breakers, disturbers, squeezers, muz-
zlers, and dissolvers like water. Woe, . . PWKT' in

your place. (12) And in your place you are[4] fearful, terrified, and bound to my exorcism, you who appear to the sons of men--to men in the likeness of women (13) and to women in the likeness of men--you who lie with people during the night and during the day. In the name of (14) ŠᶜŠ GŠ GŠK I have written against you, evil lilith, whatsoever name you are using.[5] (15) We have written, and his name will heal you, 'Epra, for ever and ever.

NOTES ON TEXT ONE

[1] The meaning conveyed by the root אסי is primarily "to be strong, well" (Jastrow, *Dictionary*, p. 92). Therefore, "healings" and/or "Healer" would be as correct as "salvation" and/or "Savior." I have chosen the idea of "Savior" and "salvation" for these texts because the idea expressed so frequently, "if you *sin* (חטא) at all against (my client)" appears to warrant such a choice.

Another example of the twin ideas of "healing" and "saving" being expressed by one word is found in the New Testament usages of the word *sōzein*. Alan Richardson, writing on "Salvation" in *IDB*, 4, 169, notes three shades of meaning for the word: "deliverance from disease or from demon-possession"; "rescue from physical peril or from death"; and "salvation in the technical theological or specifically religious sense." It is clear that the word אסי carries at least the first two of these meanings in the Aramaic incantation texts.

[2] Lit., "of."

[3] Another possibility for the translation is "the children of light" (vs. "the children of darkness"), which could have Gnostic or Zoroastrian overtones in a context such as this.

Cf. also the Arabic name *Nûru-d-Dîn*.

[4] Or, "you will be."

[5] Lit., "is to you."

TEXT TWO

חוב אזלנא אנה פאבק בר כופיתאי בחילי דנפשי בקומחי גציצא
דפרזלא קרקפתי דפרזלא קומת דנורא (2) [דכיא] ולבישנא
לבושא דארמסא דביא וממללא וחילינא במן דברא שמיא וארעה
אזלית ופגעית בהון (3) בסני בישי ובעילדבבי מרירי אמרת
להון דאת מידעם חטיתון ביה באבונא בר גריבתא ובאיבא בר
זריתא אושפנא לכון באישפא (4) דימא ואישפא דליויתן תנינא
דאט מידעם {וותחטתו} חטיתון ביה באבונה בר גריבתא ובאיתחיה
ובבניה בי קשתא גיבנא לכון (5) ובי יתרא פשיטנא לכון חוב
‹אם› מידעם ‹חטיתון› בביתיה דפאבק ובקיניניה ובבל אינשי
ביתיה בי דידי אנה אבונה בר גריבתא או באיבא בר זויתאי
(6) מחיתנא עליכון שמתא וגזירתא ואחרמתא דאיתנה על
חירמון טורא ועל ליויתן תנינא ועל סדום ועל עמורא מיטול
למכבש דירי (7) אזלנא אנה אבונא בר גריבתא וכל רזי בישי
ולישן חומרי זידניתא אזלית ופגעית בהון בשידי ובדיוי
במבכלתא בישתא ויפתכרי וביסתרתא ניקבתא קימין סידרי
סדרין ורפדי מרפדין

TRANSLATION OF TEXT TWO

Again I am coming, I, Pabak the son of Kupitai, in the power of my own self, polished armor of iron on my body, my head of iron, my stature of [pure][1] fire. (2) I am clothed with the garment of Hermes, Dabya, and Mamlala;[2] and my power comes from the One who created heaven and earth. I have come and I have confronted (3) the evil haters and the potent adversaries. I have said to them: If you sin at all against 'Abuna the son of Geribta and 'Ibba the son of Zawita, I will enchant you with the spell (4) of the sea and the spell of Leviathan the sea-monster. If you sin at all against 'Abuna the son of Geribta, or against his wife and his sons, I will bend the bow against you, (5) and I will stretch the bow-string against you. Again, ⟨if you sin⟩ at all against the household of Pabak, against his possessions, or against all the people of his household, by my own power,[3] I, 'Abuna the son of Geribta--or against 'Ibba the son of Zawita--(6) will bring down upon you the ban, the prohibition, and the anathema which came down upon Mount Hermon and upon Leviathan the sea-monster and upon Sodom and upon Gomorrha. In order to subdue devils (7) am I coming, I, 'Abuna the son of Geribta, and all evil mysteries, and the tongue of impious pebble-charms. I have come and I have confronted them--the demons, the devils, the evil monsters, the idols,[4] and the female destroyers standing arrayed in rows and encamped in camps.[5]

NOTES ON TEXT TWO

[1]This word is added on the basis of the parallel passage in Text 6.4. Cf. also Text 7.2.

[2]Or perhaps, מְמַלְלָא, "The Talker."

[3]Lit., "hand."

[4]Or, "image-spirits," and so throughout the texts.

[5]Or, "row upon row and camp upon camp."

TEXT THREE

בישמך מרי אסותא (2) אסיא רבא דרחמי צארנא לך וחחימנא (3)
ומחחימנא לך נפשיה ביתיה וקיניניה דהדין יזידאד (4) בר
איזדנדוך בישמיה דאלהא רבא ובהחמא רבא דשדא אל (5) ובציצי
דצבאות ובזיווא רבא דקדוש דיזיעון ויזדעזעון ויפקון כל
שידי צ . . . . . (6) וכל סטנין תקיפין מין ביתיה ומין דירתיה
ומין כל פגריה דהדין יזידאד בר [איזדנדוך] (7) תוב צארנא
לך וחחימנא ומחחימנא לך נפשיה ו[ביתיה] וקיניניה ובית
מישכביה ד[יזידאד (8) בר] איזדנדוך בשום גבריאל ומיכיאך
ורפיאל ובשום [עסאל]^1 עסיאל מלאכה ואירמיס מריא [רבא]
(9) ואבהו רבא ואברכס רבא מנטרנא דרוחי טבאתא ו[מחז]לנא
דרוחי בישאתא מנטרנא ליכי נפשיה . . . . . (10) וקיניניה
דהדין יזידאד בר איזדנדוך ומחחימנא ליכי נפ[שה ביתה
ודי]רתה דהדא מירדוך בת באנאי דלא יחטון בכון כל . . . [בי]שין
(11) וכל סרנין אפיקי וכל ענקתא וכל קריתא וכל לוטתא וכל
יצערי וכל . . . . . וכל כורהני קשיי וכא סטני בישי וכל פת[כרי
וכל] חומרי זידנ[יתא] וכל מזיקי (12) תקיפי דמן תחית ידי
דילי מפיקנא להון מן הדין ביתא בשום פרנגיני בר פרנגין דמן
קדמוהי זע ימא ומן בתרוהי זיעין טורין [ביש]מיה דחה הה
[ורב]ישמיה (13) דבר משאאל דנזירתיה גזירתא ובר אינש על
מטרתיה לא עבר הא רזא הדין [לבטלא י]תכין רזי חרשי ומי.
מהראשי רזיפי וכוסי וקיט[ר]י ונידרי וענקתא ו[קריתא] ולוטתא
(14) ורוחי בי[ש]אתא וחומרי זידניאתא אפקא שידי ושידניאתא
ולילי וליליאתא ופגעי וס[טני בישי] וכל מזיקי בישי דמידמן
וכל אזלינין בישין בידמות שיקצא ורימסא ובדמות חית[א] ועפא
(15) ובדמות גברא ואיתתא ובכל דמו ובכל גיונין בטילו ופוקו
מין ביתיה ומי[ן] דירתיה ומין כוליה פגריה דהדין יזידאד בר
איזדנדוך ומין מירדוך איתחיה בת באנאי ומי[ן בני]הון ומין
בנחהון ומין כל אינשי ביתיהון (16) דלא תיחבלון בהון כל.
חבאלא בישא ולא תישנגון יתהון ולא תיפרדון יתהון ולא תיחטון
בהון ולא תיתהזון להון לא בחילמא דלליה ולא בשחרתא דיממא
מן יומא דנן ו[ל]עלם^2 אמן אסן סלה ועוד מומינא ומשבענא
(17) עלך יטרידך סרא רבא מפסיס גרמך ומעדי שורבתך ובשבעין
גברין דנקיטין שבעין מגלין חריפאתא למקטל בהון כל שידין
בישין ולשיציה בהון כל מבכלין זידנין מסחפין גונדין ורמי
על ערסיהון אמן אמן סלה הללויה

TRANSLATION OF TEXT THREE

In your name, Lord of salvation, (2) great Savior of love. I am binding to you and I am sealing (3) and I am doubly-sealing to you the life, house, and possessions of this Yezidad (4) the son of 'Izdanduk; in the name of the great God and with the great seal of Shadda El (5) and by the splendor[3] of Sebaoth, and by the great glory of the Holy One--that all demons depart and remove themselves and go out ..... (6) and all mighty satans, from the house, from the dwelling, and from all the body of this Yezidad the son of ['Izdanduk.] (7) Again, I am binding to you and I am sealing and I am doubly-sealing to you the life and [the house] and the possessions and the bed-room of [Yezidad (8) the son of] 'Izdanduk, in the name of Gabriel and Michael and Raphael, and in the name of the angel ᶜAsiel and 'Ermes the [great] Lord (9) and the great 'Abbahu and the great Abraxas, the guardian of good spirits and the [destr]oyer of evil spirits, I entrust[4] to you[5] the life ..... (10) and the possessions of this Yezidad the son of 'Izdanduk, and I doubly-seal to you[5] the li[fe, house, and dwel]ling of this Merduk the daughter of Banai, that there will not sin against you all [ev]il ... (11) and all (magic) circles, all necklace-charms, all invocations, all curses, all (shameful) losses, all ..... all dire[6] sicknesses, all evil satans, all id[ols, all] impi[ous] pebble-charms, and all mighty tormentors (12) which, under my own power, I send forth from this house in the name of Parnagin the son of Parnagin, before whom the sea trembles and behind whom the mountains tremble, [in the na]me of HH HH, [and in] the name (13) of Bar-Mešteel, whose ban is invoked[7] and whose guarding no one passes over. Lo, this mystery is [for annulling] you, mysteries, magic, poisoned water, eyebrows,[8] bowls, kno[t]s, vows, necklace-charms, [invocations], curses, (14) evil spirits, and impious pebble-charms. And now, demons, demonesses, lilis, liliths, plagues, [evil sat]ans, and all evil tormentors that appear--and all evil 'ZLYNYN[9]--in the likeness of vermin and reptile, in the likeness of beast and bird, (15) in the likeness of husband and of wife, and in every likeness and in all colors; cease and go away from the house, from the dwelling, and from the entire body of this Yezidad the son of

'Izdanduk, from his wife Merduk the daughter of Banai, from their sons and their daughters, and all the people of their household. (16) Do not injure them with any evil injury, or bewilder them, or scatter them, or sin against them, or appear to them, either in a dream of the night or in slumber during the day, from this day and forever. Amen. Amen. Selah. And I further charge and adjure (17) you. May the Great Prince frighten you away, the breaker of your bone and the remover of your rod.[10] And by the seventy men who grasp the seventy sharp sickles to kill all evil demons and to expel[11] all impious tormentors are they cast prostrate in troops and cast down upon their beds. Amen. Amen. Selah. Hallelujah.

NOTES ON TEXT THREE

[1]Cf. Text 4.4, where the correct form, עסיאל, is written.

[2]For וּלְעָלַם. וילעולם would also be possible in these texts.

[3]Lit., "rays of light."

[4]Lit., "guard."

[5]Lines 2, 3, and 7 of this incantation have the masculine form, לך. Here, however, the feminine form, ליכי is used.

[6]Lit., "hard."

[7]Lit., "banned."

[8]For this meaning of זיפא, pl. זיפין or זיפי, cf. Jastrow, *Dictionary*, p. 395.

[9]Perhaps a form of אָזְלָא, from the root נזל meaning "running waters, waves." Cf. Jastrow, *Dictionary*, p. 38.

[10]Or, "tribe."

[11]Shafel of יצא. Cf. Ezra 6:15 for this same word in the Shafel (שיציא).

TEXT FOUR

בישמך מרי חתמתא אסיא רבא דרחמי צארנא לכון[1] וחחימנא דכון[1]
גוי בר אספנז ומשכוי אתחיה בת סימוי וארדוי ברה וכל בני
ובנתא {אחין} להון וביתיהון כולי(י)ה בישמיה דאלהא (2) רבה
ובחתמא רבה דשדי ובציצי[2] דצבואת[3] דיז(ו)(ען) וייזדעזעון)
ויפקון כל שידי ודיוי וירורי ורוחי בישאתה וחומרי זידניתא
וכל שידין וכל דיוין מן כלי(י)ה הדין ביתא (3) ומן כל בני
אינשה דשר(י)ן בלי(י)ה תוב צארנא (ל)כון[1] ומחתימנא לכון[1]
גוי בר אספנז ומשכוי אתח(י)ה וארדוי בנה וביתא הדין כולי(י)ה
וביה מישכבה בשום גבריאל ומיכיאל (4) ובשום רפיאל ועסיאל
ובהרמיס מרי רבה בשום יהו ביהו[4] ואבהו רבה ואבכס(sic)
רבה מנטרנא דרוחי טבחא ומחבלנא (ד)רוחי בישתא ומנטרנא
לכון ומנחרנא לכון (5) ומחתימנא לכון גוי ומשכוי וארדוי
אילין ביתא הדין כולי(י)ה דלא יחטון בהון כל שידי וכל דיוי
וכל מבכלי וכל ליליתא ומבכלתא (6) וכל פתכרי ולוטתא וענקתא
וכל סטני קשיי וכל מזיקין בישין דמין ידי דילי מהנפיקנא
להון בשום פרנגין בר פרנגין דמין קדמוהי זעא ימא ומן
בתרוהי (7) טורין זעי(י)ן ובישמל(י)ה דבר משהאיל[5] דגזירתא
גזירא ובר אינש על מטרתיה לא עבר הא רזא הדין לבטלא יתכון
שידי ודיוי וליליתא (8) ומבכלתא ולוטתא וענקתא וקריתא
[ופתכ]רי ופתכרתא ופגעי וסטני וכל מזיקין דמידמן בידמות
שיקצא ורימסא (9) ובידמות חיתא ועופא ובידמות [אינשא]
ראחתא ובכל דמו ובכל גונין בטילו ופוקו מן גוי ומשכוי
וארדוי (10) אילין ולא היחטון בהון (ו)לא תיחבלון בהון
חבלא בישא ולא תידרון בביתיהון ולא תיתחזון להון (11)
לא בחילמהון דליליה ולא בשינתהון דיממא מן ירמא דין
ולעולם אמן אמן אמן סלה

TRANSLATION OF TEXT FOUR

In your name, Lord of sealing, Great Savior of love.
I am binding you and I am sealing you (for) Goi the son of
'Aspenaz, Maškoi his wife, the daughter of Simoi, 'Ardoi
her son, all their sons and daughters, and all their
household. In the name of the great (2) God, by the great
seal of Shaddai, by the splendor[6] of Sebaoth, that may
tremble and shake and go forth all demons, devils,

howlers, evil spirits, impious amulet-spirits, and all demons and all devils from this entire household (3) and from all the sons of man who are dwelling in it. Again, I am binding you and I am doubly-sealing you (for) Goi the son of 'Aspenaz, Maškoi his wife, 'Ardoi her son, this entire household, and the bedroom, in the name of Gabriel and Michael, (4) and in the name of Raphiel and ^cAsiel, and by Hermes my Great Lord. In the name of "Yahu-is-Yahu" and 'Abbahu the great, and Abraxas the great. I am placing a guard of good spirits and I am destroying evil spirits. I am guarding you and I am rebuking[7] you (5) and I am doubly-sealing you (for) these--Goi, Maškoi, and 'Ardoi--this entire household--so that they will not sin against them--all demons, all devils, all male monsters, all liliths, female monsters, (6) all idols, curses, necklace-charms, all hard satans, and all evil harmers which by my own power I am exorcizing for them in the name of Parnagin[8] the son of Parnagin[8] before whom the sea trembles and behind whom (7) mountains tremble; and in the name of Bar-Mešteel whose decree is set and no one crosses over his guard. Lo, this mystery is for bringing you to an end, demons, devils, liliths, (8) she-monsters, curses, necklace-charms, invocations, male [ido]ls, female idols, plagues, satans, and all harmers which appear in the likeness of vermin and reptiles, (9) in the likeness of animals and birds, in the likeness of [a husband] and a wife, and in every likeness and in every kind. Cease and go away from Goi, Maškoi, and 'Ardoi-- (10) these. You will not sin against them, you will not deal them an evil injury, you will not dwell in their house, and you will not appear to them (11) either in their dreams of the night or in their sleep of the day, from this day and forever. Amen. Amen. Amen. Selah.

NOTES ON TEXT FOUR

[1]But cf. Text three, which has both לך and ליכי.

[2]Cf. Text 3.5.

[3]For צבאות.

[4]Cf. Yah-b^e-Yah in Text 35.4.

⁵Perhaps the scribe intended to write משתיאל. In any case, the parallel text, 3.13, has simply משתאל.

⁶Lit., "rays of light." Cf. Text 3.5.

⁷For this meaning of נהר in the Pa^cel, cf. Jastrow, *Dictionary*, p. 896.

⁸This name may also be *Farangin*. Cf. Text 3.12.

TEXT FIVE

מיטלי דלמיכל מלאכין קדישין וכל {ו}רוחי בישתא וליש‌ן
חמרין זידני זידניתא אהשתא[1] כבישיתון אסיריתון אסירין
אסיריתון וחתימיתון בהדא מן ארבע (2) זוית ביתיה מיחטא
לא תיחטון ביה בפאבק בר כופיתאי ולא נסכלון ביה בכל
אינשי ביתיה ולא בליליא ולא (3) בימ‌מא מיטול דאסרנא
לכון באיסרא בישא ..... שרירא חוב אסרנא לכון באיסורא
דאסירי ביה אחנוך אחוי בישי תוב (4) אסרנא לכון באיסרא
בישא ומרירא תוב אסרנא [לכון באי]סורא דאתחסרו ביה שבעה
כוכבין ותרין עשר {מלויש̈ין}[2] מלויאשין עד יומא רבא (5)
דדינא ועד שעתא רבתי דפרקנא דראישיכון לא חי ..... לא
תיחטון בהון באבונא בר גריבתא ואכסולי לא נסכלון בהון
בכל אינשי ביתיה דפאבק (6) בר כופיתאי לא בליליא ולא
בימ‌מא מיטול דחתומ[י] מחת[ם] ביתיה וזרוזי מזרז ושורא
רבא דנחשא אחדרית ליה אנה דבעית נקטית ודשאילית נסבה
(7) אתון בתריה דאבונא בר גריבתא ובתריה דפאבק בר
כופיתאי

TRANSLATION OF TEXT FIVE

Covers which are for containing holy angels and
all evil spirits and the tongue of impious male and female pebble-charms. Now you are conquered, you are
bound, bound, you are bound and sealed in (each) one of
the four (2) corners of his house. You definitely will
not sin against him, against Pabak the son of Kupitai,
and they will not commit offense against him or against
all the people of his household, either during the night
(3) or during the day, because I am binding you with an
evil spell and a strong [seal]. Again, I am binding you
with the spell by which the evil brothers of Enoch bound
him. Again, (4) I am binding you with the evil and
strong spell. Again, I am binding [you with] the
[sp]ell by which are bound the seven stars and the
twelve zodiac-signs unto the great day (5) of judgment
and unto the great hour of the deliverance of your heads.
You will not ..... you will not sin against them, against

'Abuna the son of Geribta, and they will not commit offense against them, against all the people of the household of Pabak (6) the son of Kupitai, either during the night or during the day, because his house is [well]-sealed and well-armed, and I have surrounded it with a great wall of bronze. I grasp what I search for and I take what I ask for. (7) You (will be) behind[3] 'Abuna the son of Geribta and behind[3] Pabak the son of Kupitai.

NOTES ON TEXT FIVE

[1]For חשתא; the correct form occurs in Text 8.9.

[2]"In these texts, it is almost a rule to rewrite errors without erasing" (Gordon, *AASOR*, XIV, 1934, p. 143).

[3]Lit., "in the place of." But this is parallel to the rendition of the New Testament word in the phrase "get thee behind me, Satan" (cf. Matthew 16:23; Mark 8:33; and Luke 4:8), as Gordon has shown in *Orientalia* X, 1941, p. 276.

TEXT SIX

בישמך מרי אסראתה (2) אסיא רבא דרחמי אזילנא אנא יזידאד
(3) בר איזדנדוך בחילי דנפשי בקומתי גציצתא (4) דפרזלא
קרקפתי דפרזלא כולה קומתי דנורא דכיא ולבישנא (5) לבושא
דארמסא דביא ומללא וחלינא במאן דיברא שמיא וארעא אזלית
פגעית (6) בהון בסנאי בישי ובעילדבבי מריוי אמרית להון
דאם מידעם חטיתון ביה (7) ביתי⟨ה⟩ אנא יזידאד בר איזדנדוך
בי קשתא גאיבנא לכון ובי יתרא פשיטנא לכון תוב ⟨אם⟩ מידעם
חטיתון (8) ביה ביתיה {א}אנא מירדוך בת באנאי אשיפנא לכון
באישפא דימא ובאישפא דליויתן תנינא תוב ⟨אם⟩ מידעם חטיתון
(9) בידידי אנא יזידאד בר איזדנדוך מחיתנא עליכין שמתא
גזירתא ואחרמתא ד{א}איתנח על חירמון טורא ועל ליויתן תנינא
ועל סדום (10) ועל עמורה מיטול דלמיכבש דיוי אזילנא ורוחי
בישאתא ולישן חומרי זידניאתא אנא יזידאד בר איזדנדוך אזלית
פגעית בהון (11) בשידי בדיוי בליליאתא בישאתא בפתכרי דיכרי
באיסתראתה ניקבאתה כד קימין סידרי סידרי מרפדי מרפדי .....
עליהון ....

TRANSLATION OF TEXT SIX

In your name, Lord of salvation,[1] (2) Great Savior[1] of love.[2] I am coming, I, Yezidad (3) the son of 'Izdanduk, in the power of my own self, on my body polished armor of (4) iron, all of my head of iron, my stature of pure fire. I am clothed (5) with the garment of Hermes, Dabya, and Malala. My power comes from the One who created heaven and earth. I have come, I have confronted (6) the evil haters and the mighty foes.[3] I have said to them: If you sin at all against him, (7) his household, I, Yezidad the son of 'Izdanduk, by myself will bend the bow against you and by myself I will stretch the bowstring against you. Again, ⟨if⟩ you sin at all (8) against him, his house, I, Merduk the daughter of Banai, will enchant you with the spell of the sea and with the spell of Leviathan the sea-monster. Again, ⟨if⟩ you sin at all (9) against my beloved, I, Yezidad the son of 'Izdanduk will bring down upon you the ban, the prohibition, and the anathema which came down[4] upon Mount Hermon and upon Leviathan the sea-monster

and upon Sodom (10) and upon Gomorrha. In order to subdue devils am I coming, and evil spirits, and the tongue of impious pebble-charms. I, Yezidad the son of 'Izdanduk, have come, I have confronted them--(11) demons, devils, evil liliths, idols, female destroyers as[5] they are standing arrayed in rows and encamped in camps. ..... upon them .:...
.....

NOTES ON TEXT SIX

[1]For a discussion of אסי and its cognate forms, see Note 1 to Text one.

[2]I have not translated either this word or the plural form אסיאתא by an English plural. I believe the idea in both cases is intensity rather than plurality numerically.

[3]The phrase is a synonym of "enemy." It means literally "owner of (slanderous) talk."

[4]Lit., "rested."

[5]כד can also mean "when" or "since." Cf. Jastrow, *Dictionary*, p. 612.

TEXT SEVEN

אזלנא בחילא נפשא[1] ובקומתי (2) קצוצתא דפרזלא כולה
קומתי{ה} דינהורא (3) דכיה ובלישנא[2] לבושא דארמיט
ודדביה וממללא (4) והילינא בההוא דיברא שמיא וארעא
אזלית פגעית בהון בסוניתי[3] (5) בישי ובעלידבבי מרירי
אמרנא להון ואי לכון אם מידעם תעבדון להון (6) למאראי
בר איתי וקורדאס בר נאנאוך אשפנא עליכון באשפא רבא
דימא ובאשפא (7) דלייתהון חנינא חוב אם מידעם תאמרון
להון למאראי [בר אי]תי אראב[4] בר נונאוך בי קשתא (8)
גיבנא לכון וביתירא פשיטנא לכון תוף[5] אם מידעם תעבדון
לה[ו]ן למ[א]ראי בר איתי ולגורדאס[6] בר נאנוך (9) מחיחנא
עליכון גזירתא דישמיה ואחרומתא דאיתנח{י}{על{יכון}
[חירמון טו]רא וללייויתון חנינא ומיכבש (10) עיכורי[7]
אזילנא בחומרי בישאתא ובלישרן רוחי זדניאתא אזלית
פגעית [בהון ....]ין דקימא סידרא
סידרי (11) ומרפדי מ{מ}רפדי דכרנא עליתון שמא רבא
דמרי ביריאתא כל דקאים נפיל כל דניפל ..... מיטול
דמיכבש איכורי[7] אזילנא (12) בחומרי בישוחא ובלישרן
רוחי זדניאתא אזלית כבשחינון וכבשתינון ואסרתינון
וחתימ[נ]א ומחתמא .... ומי[ח]טא לא תיחטון ביה
{ו} ראסכולה לא (13) תסכלון ביה אם תיחטון ביה
ותסכלון ביה בפגריה בביתיה בימזיהון דמאראי בר איתי
ו[ד]גורדאס בר נאנאוך אסרנא עליכון באיסורא] דאיתסרו
שמיה וארעא (14) דחתימנא לכון תוף אם מידעם תעבדון
ליהון למאראי בר נאנאוך פקורדאס קידי ליה ולמאראי
ב]לר איתי ולגורדאס בר נאנאוך [..........] ודנהדמאו
תוף אם מידעם (15) תעבדון להון למאראי בר איתי
וגורדאס בר נאנאוך אסרנא עליכון באיסורא דאיתסרו
שבעה כוכ]בין ותרין עשר מלויאשין. עד יומא רבא דדינא
ועד שעתא רב]תא דפורקנא דראשכון לא תידלון (16)
ומחיטא לא תחיטון בהון בפגריהון וביתיהון ובדיר-
תיהון ובימזוניהו{ו]{ן אמיטול דחתים ומחתם [וזריז
ומזרז שירא רבה דנחשא אחדרית ליה אנה דבעית נקטית
ודשאי]ליתי בלישרן נציבית ואתון בתריה (17) דמאראי
בר איתי ו[קו]רד[אס ב]ר נאנאוך אתון כען אסיריתון
שידין וחתימיתון דיויין אסירין דיוין [..........
ח]עבדון באיסורא דאל שדי ובחותמא (18) דישלומר
מלכא בר [דויד ......[.....אמן ....
......

TRANSLATION OF TEXT SEVEN

I am coming in the power (of my) own self, and in my body (2) is a bar of iron. All of my body is of pure (3) light. I am clothed with the garment of Hermes, Dabya, and Mamlala, (4) and my power comes from the One who created heaven and earth. I have come and I have confronted the evil (5) enemies and the potent adversaries. I am telling them: Woe to you if you do anything to (6) Marai the son of 'Itay and Qurdas the son of Nanak. I am enchanting you with the great spell of the sea and with the spell (7) of Leviathan the sea-monster. Again, if you say anything to Marai the [son of 'I]tay (or) Qurdas the son of Nanak, I will bend (8) the bow against you and I will stretch the bowstring against you. Again, if you do anything [to M]arai the son of 'Itay or to Gurdas the son of Nanak, (9) I will bring down upon you the prohibition of heaven and the anathema which came down[8] upon [Mo]unt [Hermon] and upon Leviathan the sea-monster. To conquer (10) shrine-spirits am I coming with (?) the evil pebble-charms and with the tongue of impious spirits. I have come, I have confronted [them ....] which is standing arrayed in rows (11) and encamped in camps.[9] I am pronouncing against them the Great Name of the Lord of Creatures. Everything which stands falls. Everything which ..... in order to conquer shrine-spirits am I coming (12) with the evil pebble-charms and with the tongue of impious spirits. I have come, I have conquered them. Yes, I have conquered them and bound them. And seale[d and doubly sealed .... and] you will not commit a sin against him and you will not commit (13) offense against him. If you sin against him or commit offense against the body, against the household, against the sustenance of Marai the son of 'Itay or of [Gurdas the son of Nanak, I am binding you with the bond] with which heaven and earth have been bound, (14) wherewith I am sealing you. Again, if you do anything to Marai the son of Nanak (sic) and Qurdas .... to him. And to Marai the so[n of 'Itay and to Gurdas the son of Nanak ....] and which are destroyed. Again, if you do (15) anything to Marai the son of 'Itay and Gurdas the son of Nanak, I will bind you with the bond with which the seven stars/planets [and the twelve signs

of the zodiac have been bound unto the great day of judgment
and unto the great ho]ur of redemption, so that you will not
lift up your head (16) and you will not commit a sin against
them, against their bodies, against their house, against their
dwelling, and against their sustenance. Because it is sealed
and doubly-sealed, [fortified and doubly-fortified. I have
surrounded it with the great copper/bronze chain. I have
seized what I searched for and what I as]ked for with the
tongue I have taken. And you are behind (17) Marai the son
of 'Itay and [Qu]rd[as the s]on of Nanak. You are now bound,
demons, and sealed, devils. The devils are bound ....
[y]ou will do, with the bond of El Shadday and with the sealing (18) of King Solomon the son of [David .....] ..... Amen
....

NOTES ON TEXT SEVEN

[1] Note the absence of the ד. Cf. Text 2.1.

[2] For לבישנא.

[3] Cf. the correct form סני, of Text 2.3. If the word here
was intended to be a feminine form, the correct spelling
should have been סניאחא, the plural of סָנְיָא. However, the
masculine adjective which follows (בישי) would then be incorrect.

[4] Apparently an error for קורדאס. Note the different
spellings of נאנאוך which follow.

[5] Note חוב in line seven.

[6] Note קורדאס in line six.

[7] Both עיכורי and איכורי are clearly attested.

[8] Lit., "rested."

[9] Or, "row upon row and camp upon camp."

TEXT EIGHT

בשמך מרי אסוואתא אסיא רבא דרומי מזמן הדין איסרא ורזא
וחתמא שרירא לחתמתא דביתיה דהדין (2) ארדוי בר הורמיז-
דוך דיזח ויתרחק מיניה דיוא בישא וסטנא בישא דמיתקרי
צפעטסק[1] אבדה גברא דקטיל (3) גברא מילות איתחיה ואיתחא
מילות בעלה ורבנין ויבנן מין אבוהון ומין אימיהון
בימחא ובליליא אומואי מומינא לך ואשבועי (4) משבענא
עלך דלא תיקטול ית הדין ארדוי בר הורמיזדוך מילות
אחה איתחיה דלא תיקטול ית אחת בת פרכוי מילות ארדוי
בעלה (5) ולא תיקטול ית בניהון וית בנתהון בין דאית
להון ובין דהון להון מין יומא דנן ויעולם לא בליליא
ולא בימחא בישמיה דזעזוע[2] הסר הסר הסר פעספעטספע[3]
תמר תמר (6) תמר נקט זהזהזה הסר פעס חמר קק אסחו
יופת יופחיה מין אישחא יקידחא סקסין סין סין סקירן
סק[4] שמר קץ שמר ..... הדין הוא שמא רבא דמלאך מוחא
דחן[י]ל מיניה (7) וכד שמע יתיה דחיל יעריק ומיחבלע
מין קדמוהי[5] ומן קדאמיה[5] דהדין ארדוי בר הורמיזדוך
ידחול ויעיר[ויק] ..... מין אחת איתחיה בת פרכוי ומן
כל בניהון ומין (8) כל בנתהון דאיה להון ודהון להון
פוטשש אמן בשם סקסן סקסין קק אסחר יופת יופחיה מין
אישחא יקידחא סקירן ..... [הדין הוא] שמא רבא דמלאך
מוחא דחיל מיניה וכד (9) שמע יתיה דחיל יעריק ומיח-
בלע מין קדמוהי ומין קדמיה ומהדין[6] ביחא אף השחא
ביה בהדין שמא רבא דדחיל מ[יניה] ..... [מין קדם
דהדין ארדוי בר הורמיז]דוך ומין קדם אחת איתחיה בה
פרכוי (10) ומין קדם בנין ויבנן דאית להון ודהון
להון פוטשש אמן ובשום אסתר יופת יופת יופחיה מין
אישחא יקידחא סקסן סקסין סק ..... [הדין הוא שמא
ר]בא דמלאך מוחא דהיל מיניה וכד שמע יתיה (11)
דחיל יעריק ומיחבלע מין קדמוהי כין אף השחא בשום
הדין שמא רבא ידחול ויעריק ויפוק דיוא בישא דק
... (12) אחת איתחיה בת פרכוי ומין קדם כל בנין
ויבנן דאית להון ודהון להון פוטשש שנאמר[7] ויאמר
יהוה אל הסטן יגער יהוה בך הסטן יגער יהוה בך הבוחיר
בירושלם [הלא זה אוד מוצל מאש אמן אמן]

TRANSLATION OF TEXT EIGHT

In Your name, Lord of salvation, Great Savior of love. This spell and mystery and firm seal is designated for the sealing of the household of this (2) 'Ardoi the son of Hormizduk, that from him may move and depart the evil devil and the evil satan who is called ṢPᶜSQ, the mighty destroyer who kills (3) the man from beside his wife and the wife from beside her husband and sons and daughters from their father and from their mother, during the day and during the night. I verily make you swear and I verily (4) adjure you that you do not kill this 'Ardoi the son of Hormizduk from beside 'Aḥat his wife, that you do not kill 'Aḥat the daughter of Parkoi from beside 'Ardoi her husband, (5) and (that) you do not kill their sons and their daughters, either those they now have or those they will have, from this day and forever, either during the night or during the day. In the name of ZᶜZᶜZᶜ HSR HSR HSR PᶜSPᶜSPᶜ TMR NQT ZHZHZH HSR PᶜS TMR QQ 'STW YWPT YWPTYH, from the burning fire, SQSYN SYN SYN SQYWN SQ is his name, QS is his name. This is the great name of which the angel of death[8] is afraid, (7) and when he hears it, he flees away frightened, and is swallowed up before it. So from before this 'Ardoi the son of Hormizduk may he flee a[way] frightened ..... from 'Aḥat his wife, the daughter of Parkoi, and from all their sons and from (8) all their daughters, either those they now have or those they will have. PWTS͡S, Amen. In the name of SQSN SQSYN QQ 'STW YWPT YWPTYH, from the burning fire, SQYWN ..... [this is] the great name of which the angel of death is afraid, and when (9) he hears it, he flees away frightened and is swallowed up before it and before this household. Moreover now, in this great name o[f which] (the angel of death) is afraid ..... [from before 'Ardoi the son of Hormiz]duk and from before 'Aḥat his wife, the daughter of Parkoi (10) and from before the sons and the daughters they now have or will have, PWTS͡S, Amen. In the name of 'STW YWPT YWPT YWPTYH, from the burning fire, SQSN SQSYN SQ .... [This is the gr]eat [name] of which the angel of death is afraid, and when he hears it (11) he flees away frightened and is swallowed up before it. Therefore, now, by the authority of this great name, may the evil devil be fearful and flee away and go out, DQ ..... (12) 'Ahat his wife, the daughter of Parkoi and from before all the sons and the daughters they now have or will have, PWTŠŠ. According as it is said,[7] And YHWH said to Satan: May YHWH rebuke you, Satan, may YHWH who has chosen Jerusalem rebuke you. [Is not this a firebrand snatched from the fire?[9] Amen. Amen.]

NOTES ON TEXT EIGHT

[1] These five letters are together in the alphabet, although the first four are in reverse order here.

[2] The letters ז and ע are the equivalent of each other in *Athbash*.

[3] These three letters are together in the alphabet but are in reverse order in this text. For another example of the inversion of the letters ע and פ cf. Lamentations 2:16, 17; 3:46-51; 4:16-17.

[4] These two letters become חד, "One," in *Athbash*.

[5] Here and also in line nine below are two dialectical grammatical variants in the same sentence. For two different ways of indicating the same suffix in biblical Aramaic, cf. Daniel 2:32, where ראשה ("its head"), חדוהי ("its breast"), and מעוהי ("its belly") all occur in the same verse.

[6] The scribe started to write ומ to add yet another מין to the chain, changed his mind, wrote the ד over the מ, and finally completed the word הדין.

[7] שנאמר, like ככתוב in Rabbinic literature and καθὼς γέγραπται in the *Greek New Testament*, always introduces a quotation from Scripture.

[8] Painted on this bowl is a picture of "The Angel of Death." Its feet are shackled, its right hand is grasping a sword, and its left hand is grasping a spear. The text itself says that this angel has two evil jobs: it kills a husband from the side of his wife (or a wife from the side of her husband) and it also kills children from the side of their parents. An extremely interesting parallel to this idea is found in Text Fifty-Two of the Ugaritic poetry where the following passage

occurs: "Death-and-Evil sits; In his hand is the staff of privation, In his hand the staff of bereavement" (Cyrus H. Gordon, *Ugarit and Minoan Crete*, p. 94). I am indebted to my friend Dr. David Tsumura for calling this fact to my attention.

[9]Zechariah 3:2.

TEXT NINE

¹בישמך אני עושה יהוה אילהא רבא הדין כסא ניהוי²
לחתמתא להורמיזדוך בת מדוך אשבעית עלך מרס ..... (2)
[ב]ישא בשום אגרביס קדישא בשום מץ מץ בטוט סף סף יהוק³
יהוק³ דרחיק ית מרכבתיה עד ימא דסוף א ..... (3) דויד
מזמור ים סוף חוב אשבעית עליכון במן דאשרי שכינתיה
בחיכל נורא וברדא וכורסיה ..... (4) ...א מלכא רמא
הלליה הלליה יחוש יהוש אחושיה ובשום מיכאיל וגבריאל
המן ..... בציר ..... (5) בשמיה דשריאל בשמיה דסרפיאל
צוריאל וסרסמיאל ונדריאל (פני) פניאל נהריאל וכל זיקין
(6) ומז[י]קין בישין דאידכר שמיהון בכסא הדין וידלא
אידכרית שמיהון בכסא הדין יא (7) יא יחוש תבון חמן
ותרמון יחבין לגו נורא יקידתא וילשלהיבת אישתא (8)
אמ{ן} אמין אמן סלה

TRANSLATION OF TEXT NINE

I am acting in Your name, YHWH the Great God.
May this bowl be for the sealing of Hormizduk the
daughter of Maduk. I adjure ... . (2) [e]vil, in
the name of the Holy Agrabis, in the name of Yah Yah,⁴
in the name of SP SP YHWH YHWH who removed His chariot
to the Red Sea ..... (3) David the Psalm of the Red
Sea. Again, I adjure you by the One who caused His
Shekinah to dwell in the temple of light and hail and
His throne ..... (4) the exalted King. Hallelujah!
Hallelujah! Depart! Depart! May he be removed even
in the name of Michael and Gabriel the one who .....
(5) in the name of Sariel, in the name of Seraphiel,
Suriel, and Sarsamiel and Gadriel, Peniel, Nahriel.
And all blast-demons (6) and evil harmers whose names
are recorded in this bowl and whose names I have not
recorded in this bowl. Oh! (7) Oh! Depart! Sit
there! And you will be cast down while sitting inside the fiery flames and the flame of fire. (8)
Amen. Amen. Amen. Selah.

NOTES ON TEXT NINE

[1] There is no need for Montgomery's insertion of
בסא הדין at the beginning of the text. Cf. Texts 7.1, 3.1,
28.1, 27.1, and 19.1 for examples of texts which begin, as
this one does, with בישמך.

[2] Note the *Nun* preformative as in Syriac.

[3] Professor Gordon informs me in a private note that
"pious Jews still use ק to deform names of God (e.g., אלוקים
which is very common); and I've even heard קל for אל."

[4] Using the principle of *Athbash*, מץ becomes יה.
Cf. Montgomery, p. 184.

TEXT TEN

[אס]ירי אסירין והחימי וחתימין וקטירי קיטרין[1] ולחישי
לחיש⟨ין⟩ בשום תיעי[י]ן וחיחחמון ותירהקון מן ביתיה
..... ה דפרוך בר פושבי וניונדוך בת פושבי וית אבנדוך
בת פושבי וחינזח מינהון (2) כל לילי{ל}חא בישחא וכל
שידי ודיוי ואסרי ופהכרי ונדרא ולוטחא וקריחא וחרשין
בישין ועובדין תקיפין וכל [מינד]עם סניא אסיריחון
בשבעה איסרין וחחימיחון (3) בשבעה חחמין בישמיה דאל-
דדביה אבי פונן מרי ביזא וקללא אלנ ..... [אשב]עית עליכון
בשום הסר הגדול שחישמור ית פרוך בר פושבי וית ניונדוך בת
(4) פושבי מן עינא בישחא ומן סטנא תקיפא[2] ומן .....
ומישעירים בישביל דחמד הרבים בשום יהוה אח באח באח אמן
אמן סלה (5) על פי יהוה יחנו על פי יהוה יסעו את משמרת
יהוה שמרו על פי יהוה ביד משה ויאמר יהוה אל הסטן יגער
יהוה בך הסטן יגער יהוה (6) בך הבוחיר בירושלים הלא זה
אוד{ו}מוצל מאש אמן אמן סלה

Two Lines On Either Side of Figure In Center

(7) אמר אשר משה אמן אמן סלה

TRANSLATION OF TEXT TEN

[Who]lly bound and sealed and tied in knots and
charmed (are you) that you [g]o away and be sealed and
depart from the house ..... of Parruk the son of Pušbi
and Newanduk the daughter of Pušbi and 'Abanduk the
daughter of Pušbi, that there may depart from them (2)
all evil liliths, all demons, devils, spells, idols, the
vow, the curse, the invocation, evil black-arts, powerful practices, and every[thing] hateful. You are bound
with the seven spells and sealed (3) with the seven
seals in the name of 'Eldedabya 'Abi Ponan, the lord of
spoil and curse ..... I [ad]jure you in the name of the
Great Prince that you guard Parruk the son of Pušbi and
Newanduk the daughter of Pušbi (4) from the evil eye

and from the mighty satan and from ..... and from the many
satyrs in the path of the desire of the many,[3] in the name of
YHWH 'H B'H B'H. Amen. Amen. Selah. (5) According to
the command of YHWH they would encamp, and according to the
command of YHWH they would travel. The observance of YHWH
they kept according to the command of YHWH through Moses.[4]
And YHWH said to Satan: May YHWH rebuke you, Satan, may YHWH
who chose Jerusalem (6) rebuke you. Is not this a fire-brand
snatched from the fire?[5] Amen. Amen. Selah.

(7) What Moses said. Amen. Amen. Selah.

NOTES ON TEXT TEN

[1]For קטירין.

[2]Or, אקינא?

[3]Jastrow (*Dictionary*, p. 1438) cites a passage from the
Talmud (*K'thuboth* 8[b]) which substantiates such a translation
of the word רבים: רבים שתו רבים ישתו "many have drunk (the
cup of mourning), many shall drink." A further meaning of
the word is "community" or, more specifically, "the public"
(Jastrow, *Dictionary*, p. 1438). In Modern Hebrew, the word
means "plural."

[4]Numbers 9:23.

[5]Zechariah 3:2.

TEXT ELEVEN

כיבשא דכבשין להון לשידי ולדיוי ולסטני ולפיתכרי (2)
ודרוחי בישתא ולחומרי זידניתא ולגיסי וקיבלי וליליתא
דיכרי (3) וניקבתא דלוין עימהון דאדק בר האתוי ודאחת
בת חאתוי דלויןֹ עימהון ודשרין (4) בגובתיהון ודרבין על
איסכופתהון ומידמן להון בידמו דמו ומחן ורמן וקטלין
וכיבשא הדין (5) כבישנא להון ביומי בירזוי בכל שני ויומא
הדין מיכולהון יומי וירחא הדין מיכולהון ירחי ושתא הדא
(6) מיכולהון שני ועידנא הדין מיכולהון עידני ואזי)לֹ(נא
והברנא להון באיסכופת בתיהון דנא ושצארנא והתימנא עליהון
צירין פיתחיהון (7) וכל איגרהון וכיבשא הדין כבישנא
להון בשום הלין שבע מילין דישמיא וארעה כבישין בהון
בשום חדא גישמין ומרביל בשום (8) תינינתא גישמין ומרביל
בשום תליתיתא רוזביל בשום רביעיתא משבר בשום המישיתא
מורה בשום שתיתא ארדיבל בשום שביעיתא כיבשין דיבהון
(9) כבוֹישנאֹ) וֹעבד כזיא בהון חיתכבשין כל רוחי בישתא
והומרי זידניתא וליליתא דיכרי וניקבתא וגיסי וקיבלי
ומללתא ולא חיתחזין להון לאדק בר חאתוי ולאחת בת האתוי
(10)ולית לבניהוןֹ|ֹ לא בחילמא דליליה ולא בשינתא דימא
ולא תיקרבון לסיטרא דימינהון ולסיטרא דישמלהון וֹלא תיק־
טלון בניהון ולא חישילטון בכל קינינהון דאיתֹ (11) להון
ודהוי להון מן יומא דין ולעולם ומן דעל הדין כיבשא
ניבר והלין רזין לא מקביל ניפקא בי אזא וֹניצטרי בי
בינא וניזם במיזם נחשה ניזיל קליה בניגלי שמיא (12)
וניהוי דיריה בשבע שאול דימה ומן יומא דין וֹלעלם אמן
אמן סלה

TRANSLATION OF TEXT ELEVEN

A press which subdues demons, devils, satans,
idols, (2) evil spirits, impious pebble-charms, familiar-
spirits, counter-charms, and male and female (3) liliths
which are attached to 'Adaq the son of Ḥatoi and 'Aḥat
the daughter of Ḥatoi; which are attached to them, and
which dwell (4) in their archways and multiply upon
their thresholds and appear to them in various disguises,
and strike and cast down and kill. And this press (5)

am I pressing upon them during days, during months, during
all years, and this day of all days, and this month of all
months, and this year (6) of all years, and this time of all
times. And I am coming and enchanting them in the thresholds
of this their house, and I am binding and sealing them.
Their doors are bound (7) and all their roof. And this
press am I pressing upon them on the authority of these
seven words by which heaven and earth are subdued--on the
authority of the first word, Gišmin and Marbil; on the authority of the (8) second word, Gišmin and Marbil; on the
authority of the third word, Rahbil; on the authority of the
fourth word, Mašbar; on the authority of the fifth word,
Morah; on the authority of the sixth word, 'Ardibal; on the
authority of the seventh word, Kibšin--with which (words)
(9) [I am subdue]ing and .... through them may all evil
spirits, impious pebble-charms, liliths--male and female--
familiar-spirits, counter-charms, and words be vanquished,
and may they not appear to 'Adaq the son of Ḥatoi and to
'Ahat the daughter of Ḥatoi (10) and to their children,
neither in a dream of the night nor in sleep of the day.
May they not come near to their right side or to their left
side. May they not kill their children. May they not rule
over their possessions which they (11) now have or which
they will have, from this day and forever. And whoever
shall transgress against this press and does not receive[1]
these mysterious rites will burst open violently and split[2]
in the midst, and the sound of him will resound with the
resonance of brass melting in the spheres of heaven, (12)
and his dwelling place will be in the seventh Sheol of the
sea, even from this day and forever. Amen. Amen. Selah.

NOTES ON TEXT ELEVEN

[1] Or, "accept."

[2] Or, "be burst and be split."

TEXT TWELVE

בישמיה דמרי אסואתא מזמן הדין כסא לזותמתא דביתיה דהדין
ניונאי בר מאמי דתיזח (2) מיניה ליליתא בישתא בישמיה
דפרז יהוה אל ליליתא לילי דיכרא וליליתא ניקבתא ושלניתא
והטפיחתא (3) חליתיכון ארבעתיכון וחמי[שתיכון ערטילין]
שליחיתין[1] ולא לבישיחין וסעריכון ורמי אחור נביכון שמיע
עליכון (4) דאביכון פלחס שמיה ואימיכון פלחדד שמה שמעו[2]
וצותו[2] ופוקו[2] מין ביתיה ומין דירתיה דהדין ניונאי בר
מאמאי ומין רשנוי איתתיה (5) בת מארת ותוב לא תיתחז[ין]
להון בביתיה ולא בדירתיחרן ולא בבית מישכבי[הון] מיטול
דשמיע עליכון דאביכון פלחס שמיה ואימיכון (6) פלחדד
שמה מיטול דשמיע עליכון דשלח עליכון שמתא רבי יהושע
בר פרחיא אומית עליכון בריקא[3] דאביכון ביקרא דאימיכון
בשום פלחס אביכון (7) ובשום פלחדד אימיכון גיטא נחית לנא
מין שמיא ואישתכח כתיב ביה לשימועיכון ולהירודיכון בישמיה
דפלסא פליסא דהוא מתיב לכי גיטכי ופיטורכי גיטיכון (8)
ופטוריכין אנתי ליליתא לילי דיכרא וליליתא ניקיבתא
ושלניתא וזוטפיחתא הוי בשמתא ...[רבי] יהושע בר פרחיא
והכין אמר לנא רבי יהושע בר פרחיא (9) גיטא אתא לכי מן
עיבר ימא ואישתכח כתיב ביה דאביכין פלחס שמיה דאימיכין
פלחדד .... איתתיא ..... שמיע להון מין רקיעא
ולאכין (10) שימין בישי[ן] דודנא גד אב גדא שמעו וצותו
ופו[וקו מין ביתיה ומין דירתיה דהדין ניונאי בר מאמ]אי
ומין ר[שנוי איתתיה בת מארת ותוב לא תיתחזון להון (11)
לא בחילמא [דליליי]ה ולא בשחרתא [ד]יממא מיטול דחתימיתי
בעיזקתיה דאל שדי ובעיזקתא [דרבי יהושע בר] פרחיא ובשבעה
דקדמותיה אנ[חי לי]ליתא לי[לי דיכר]א וליליתא (12)
ניקבתא ושלניתא וחטפיחתא משבענא לכון באביר אברהם בצור
יצחק בשדי יעקב ביה שמו משר ביה זיכרו גבר וריכתא ומיה
.... מומינא (13) עליכון ד]תיסבון מין הדא רשנוי
בת מארת ומין ניונאי בעלה בר מאמי גיטכי וספר תירוכי[וכי
[ואיגרת] שיבוקי[י]כי ..... ח משלה ביד מלאכין קדישין
בהן ..... צבאות נורא בגלגלן רכובי אל פנים (14) עומדים
החיות מישתחוות באש כיסאו ובמים דיגלי אהיה אשר אהיה שב;
אין שמו חק שמו ..... שם ..... שמר ובמומתא דמלאכין
קדישין בחק .. אל מל[אכא] רבא ובעזריאל מלאכא (15)
רבא ובקבקבקיאל מלאכא רבא ובעקריאל מלאכא רבא עקריה
ענקתא בישאתא אף אנתי ליליתא [בישא]אתא קי[בלי] גיט[י]כי

וספר תירוכ[י]בי ואיגרת שיבוק[י]כי (16) . . . .
ותוב לא תיחדרון עליהון מין יומא דנן ולעולם אמן אמן
סלה חתימי עלוהי . . . . . ליליתא ב[וישתא] ורוחא בישתא
. . . . (17) על מרכביה יקר או תיקטלון . . . .
תיתרחקין מין הדא רש[נוי] בת מארת ויתקימון לח[יין]
אמן אמן סלה הללויה

TRANSLATION OF TEXT TWELVE

In the name of the Lord of Salvation. This bowl is
designated for the sealing of the house of this Geyonai the
son of Mamai, that there may flee (2) from him the evil
lilith in the name of the Scatterer, YHWH El. The liliths:
the male lilis and the female liliths, the ghost and the
ravager[4]--(3) the three of you, the four of you, and the
fi[ve of you]--you are stripped[1] [naked], and you are not
clothed. Your hair is disarranged and strewn[5] behind your
backs. It is announced to you (4) whose father's name is
Palhas and whose mother's name is Pelahdad. Hear, obey, and
come forth from the house and from the dwelling of this
Geyonai the son of Mamai and from Rašnoi his wife, (5) the
daughter of Marat. And again, you will not appear to them
either in his (sic) house or in their dwelling or in [their]
bedroom, because it is announced to you whose father's name
is Palhas and whose mother's (6) name is Pelahdad; because
it is announced to you that Rabbi Joshua the son of Perahia
has sent the ban upon you. I charge you by the honor of your
father, by the honor of your mother, in the name of Palhas
your father (7) and in the name of Pelahdad your mother.
A divorce-writ has come down to us from heaven and in it
there is found written for your advisement and terrification
in the name of Palsa-Pelisa who gives you your divorce-writ
and your writ of banishment--your divorce-writs (8) and your
writs of banishment. You, lilith--male lili, female lilith,
ban, and demon--may you be under[6] the ban of Rabbi Joshua
the son of Perahia. Even thus has Rabbi Joshua the son of
Perahia spoken to us: (9) A divorce-writ has come to you
from across the sea, and in it there is found written for
your banishment, whose father's name is Palhas, whose
mother's name is Pelahdad . . . . it is

announced to them from the firmament, even the ones who send[7] (10) the evil name. DWDN'.[8] GD 'B GD'.[9] Hear, obey, and go forth from the house and from the dwelling of this Geyonai the son of Mamai and from Rašnoi his wife, the daughter of Marat. And again, do not[10] appear to them (11) either in dream [by nigh]t or in slumber [by] day, because you are sealed with the signet-ring of El-Shaddai and with the signet-ring [of Rabbi Joshua the son of] Perahia and by the Seven which are before him. Yo[u, li]lith--[male] lil[i], female lilith, (12) ghost, and ravager--I adjure you by the Mighty One of Abraham, by the Rock of Isaac, by the Shaddai of Jacob, by Him Whose name is "Righteous," by Him Whose memorial is strong .... I adjure (13) yo[u to] turn away from this Rašnoi the daughter of Marat and from Geyonai her husband, the son of Mamai. Your divorce-writ and document of abandonment [and letter of] dismissal .... sent by the hand of holy angels ..... the hosts of the fire of the spheres, the chariots of El-Panim (14) are standing (ready), the beasts worshipping at the fire of his throne and in the water, in which is revealed "I-am-who-I-am," His name. His name is not inscribed ..... and by the adjuration of holy angels ..... by ... El the great an[gel], by ᶜAzriel the great angel, (15) by Qabqabqiel the great angel, and by ᶜAqriel the great angel, I uproot the evil necklace-spirits. Indeed, you [ev]il liliths, counter-[charms], your divorce-writ and your document of abandonment and your letter of dismissal (16) .... And again, you will not return to them from this day and forever. Amen. Amen. Selah. Sealed against him ..... e[vil] lilith and evil spirit (17) upon his chariot ..... or kill ..... you will go far from this Raš[noi] the daughter of Marat. May they be preserved for l[ife]! Amen. Amen. Selah. Hallelujah!

NOTES ON TEXT TWELVE

[1]For this meaning of the root שלה. cf. *BDB*, p. 1020. Cf. also the Arabic root سلا. Jean and Hoftijzer, *Dictionnaire*, p. 302, cite the noun שלחא from Palmyra which they define as "dépouille" or "peau."

²ū instead of î to agree with the plural forms in line three.

³For בִיקְרָא.

⁴Cf. Montgomery, pp. 157-158 and p. 191. I believe the correct form should be חֲטִיפְתָּא, from חטיף, "to seize, snatch, rob" (Jastrow, *Dictionary*, p. 450). Cf. also Text 13.4.

⁵Lit., "thrown."

⁶Lit., "in."

⁷The root לאך is normally used as a verb only in Ethiopic (cf. *BDB*, p. 521) and in Ugaritic (cf. *UT*, p. 426).

⁸דודנא, "our friendship?"

⁹גַּד אַב בְּהָא. Perhaps "Grow (from the root נגד), father of (good) luck!" Cf. Jastrow, *Dictionary*, p. 210.

¹⁰The negative imperative here is לא followed by the imperfect. The best-known examples of the same construction in Hebrew are found in Exodus 20.

TEXT THIRTEEN

דין יומא מכל יומא שני ודרי (2) עלמא אנה כזמיש בת מהלפתא
שביקוילןת (3) ופטירית ותרכיא יהיכי אנתי לילי/הא לילית
דברא (4) שלניחא וזוטיפתא {אנה}[1] תלחיכין ארבעתיכין
וחמישתיכין (5) ערטיל שלהתין ולא לבישחין סתיר סעריכין
מיעל גביכין (6) שמיע עליכין דאימכין פלחן שמה ואביכין
{פ}לחדד ליל{י}תה שמעו ופקו ולא תסיסון (7) {לא} לכל{ו}מיש
בת מחלפתא בביתה פק אחין כל מן ביתה ומן דירהה ומן כלתא
ומארתשריה (8) בנה גדרת עליכין בשמתא דשלוו עליכין יהושע
בן פרוחיה אומיתי עליכין ביקרא דאביכין (9) וביקרא
דאימכין וסיב לכין ניטיכין ופיטריכין גיטכי ופיטוריכי
{דאת שלהתן} בשמתא דשלח (10) עליכין יהושע בן פרחיה
דהכדין אמר לכא יהושע בן פרוחיה גיטה אתא לכא מעבר ימא
אישתכח כתיב דאימיכין (11) פלחן שמה ואבלי{כין פלחדד
ליל{י}חא פמטו ופקו ולא תסיסון לה לכומיש בת מחלפתא
לא ביתה ולא {ב}בדירתה אסריח (12) וחתמיח בעיזקתא
דאל שדי ובעיזקתא דיהושע בן פרוהיה אסיא אסותא ופטרתא
מן שמיא לאבא וליזדיד ולהוניק בני כזמיש (13) בטילן
ומבלטן[2] כל מבכלחא דפירקין להון בשמתא {להון} אמן אמן
סלה

TRANSLATION OF TEXT THIRTEEN

This day more than every day, years, and generations of (2) the world, I, Komeš the daughter of Mahlapta, have forsaken, (3) separated, and banished you, you lilith, lilith of the desert, (4) ghost, and ravager.[3] The three of you, the four of you, the five of you (5) are stripped naked and you are not clothed. Your hair is disheveled behind your backs. (6) It is announced to you, whose mother's name is Palhan and whose father's name is [Pe]lhdad--hear, liliths, go away, and do not bother (7) Komeš the daughter of Mahlapta in her house. Go away, all of you, from her house, from her dwelling, and from the daughter-in-law, and from 'Artašriha (8) her son. I have fenced you in with the ban which Joshua the son of Perohia sent against you. I adjure you by the

honor of your father (9) and by the honor of your mother--take
your divorces and your separations, your divorce and your separation from[4] the ban which (10) Joshua the son of Peraḥia has
sent against you, for thus has Joshua the son of Peroḥia
spoken to you: A divorce has come to you from across the sea
(in which) there is found written (a divorce) of you liliths
whose mother's (11) name is Palḥan and whose father's name is
Pelḥadad. And flee,[5] go away, and do not bother Komeš the
daughter of Mahlapta either in her house or in her dwelling.
I have bound (12) and I have sealed with the signet-ring of
'El-Shaddai and with the signet-ring of Joshua the son of
Peroḥia the savior. Salvation and separation from heaven for
'Aba, for Yazdid, and for Honiq, the sons of Komeš. (13)
Abolished and annulled are all monsters which are removed from
them[6] by the ban. Amen. Amen. Selah.

NOTES ON TEXT THIRTEEN

[1]The scribe started to write אנתי ("you," feminine singular), realized it was extraneous, and then continued without
correcting his error.

[2]For ומבטלן.

[3]Cf. Text 12.2 and Note four on Text twelve.

[4]For this translation of ב, cf. *UT*, p. 370: "'from' is
common . . . in accordance with an Egypto-Semitic feature
whereby prepositions meaning 'in' or 'to' tend to connote also
'from.'"

[5]This is an imperative form of מוט, with prefixed con-
junction פ (cf. Rossell, *Handbook*, p. 144). The word would
normally be written מוטו, but cf. פקו immediately following,
which should be written פוקו.

[6]For this translation of ל, cf. *UT*, p. 425. Cf. also
Note four above.

TEXT FOURTEEN

מזמן הנא [כסא לחת]מתחרון דהלין בר שרקוי וניונדוך איתחיה
בה כפנ(לא)י וזדנוי בריה דיתחחמון ברחמי שמיה מחרימנא
וגזר[נ]א (2) ומקימ[נ]א ..... ליליתה ומבכלתא ושידין
ושובטין ופגעין וסטנין וחילמין בישין וס{ט}טנין תקיפין
ולילי דיכרי וליליתא (3) ניקב[ח]א [תל]חיכ׃ן[1] ארבעתלי<כון
המ(י)שת(י){כון ערטיל שליחיתון ולא לבישיתון סתר סעריכון
רמי על כרב[יכון (4) שמיע על[יכון דאבוכ:ן פלוס שמיה
ואימכון פחלדד ליליתא אתון לא תיתהזון [להלין בר] (5)
שרקוי ולנ<י<ונדוך בת [כפנאי] כפנאי ולזדוי ברה לא
הברא בימטא (6) ולא צותא בליליה לוט[ח]ע(sic) במומת
בר מיט ובר (7) מומא אמן אמן סלה הלליה שריר

TRANSLATION OF TEXT FOURTEEN

This [bowl] is designated [for the sea]ling of
HLYN the son of Šarqoi, and Newanduk his wife, the daughter of Kapnai, and Zadoi his son--that they may be sealed
by the mercies of heaven. I ban and I decree (2) and I
confirm (the ban against) liliths, monsters, demons,
bands (of spirits), plagues, satans, evil dreams, powerful satans, male lilis, and female (3) liliths--the three
of you, the four of you, the five of you--you are
stripped naked, and you are not clothed. Your hair is
disheveled and strewn[2] over your ba[cks. (4) It is announced to] you whose father's name is Palḥas and whose
mother's name is Lilith Pahladad: You! Do not appear
[to HLYN the son of] (5) Šarqoi, to Newanduk the daughter
of Kapnai, or to Zadoi her[3] son. (There is) no company
by day (6) and no society by night. The curse is in the
oath of the cripple and (7) the maimed. Amen. Amen.
Selah. Hallelujah! Reliable.

NOTES ON TEXT FOURTEEN

¹I have read כון "you" (masculine plural) throughout this text instead of כין "you" (feminine plural) because these pronouns refer to both male and female (cf. lines two and three) and because of the verbal form תיחחזון in line four, which, if it were feminine, should be written תחחזן and not תיחחזין.

²Lit., "thrown."

³The text is clearly ברה here but בריה in line one.

TEXT FIFTEEN

פורא רמינא ו[נ]שקי[נ]א ועובדא (2) עבידנא זהוא הוה במיה
..... דרבי יהושע (3) בר פרחיא כתבנא להון גיטי לכל
ליליתא דמיתחזין להון בהדין ‹ביתיה› (4) דבבנוש בר
קיומ[תא] ודסרדוסת בת שירין-אינתתיה בחילמא דליליה
ובשינתא (5) דיממא {ד}גיטא דפי[טורין] [ד]שבוקין בשום
אות מתוך אות ואותיות מתוך אותיות (6) ושום מתוך השימות
ינקב מתוך [הנקבים] דיבהון איתבלעו שמיא וארעה טוריא
איתעקרו ורמתא בהון איתמסי (7) אה שידי חרשי ודירי
ולטבי ליליתא בהון אבדו מן עלמא בכין סליקית עליהון
לימרותא ואיתיתי עליכון (8) מחבלא להבלא יההון ולאפפא
יתכו[ו]ן מ[ן] בתיהוין ומן דירתיהון ומן איסקופתהיהון ומן
כל כת ..... אתר בית מישכביהון דבאב[נ]ו[ש בר קיומת[אן]
(9) ודסרדוסת בת שירין אינחתיה ותוב לא היה[חזון להון]
לא בחילמא דליליו[ה ו]לא בשינ[תא דיממא]..... פטרנא
יהכון (10) ..... ואגרת שיבו[קין] ..... כדה בנה
[ואדם]

Exterior

(11) אני לישמך עשיתי יהוה אלהים צבאות גבריאל ומיכאל
ורפאל חתומך על הדא חתמתא ועל הדא איסקופתה אמן אמן

TRANSLATION OF TEXT FIFTEEN

I deposit and si[nk do]wn the bowl (2) and I perform the praxis and it is in the ..... of Rabbi Joshua (3) the son of Perahia. I am writing divorces for them, for all liliths which appear to them--in this ‹house› of (4) Babanoš the son of Qayom[ta] and of Saradust[1] the daughter of Širin, his wife--in dream by night and in sleep (5) by day. The divorce of se[paration] and dismissal is in the name of (one) letter out of the middle of (another) letter and (several) letters out of the middle of (several other) letters (6) and (a single) name out of the middle of (many) names and (a single) perforation[2] out of the middle of (many) [perforations] by which heaven and earth are swallowed up and mountains are uprooted, and by which[3] high places are melted. (7) Ah, demons, black-arts, devils, and no-good-ones, liliths. Perish by them from the world. At this juncture,[4] I have come up against them with authority, and I have caused the destroyer (8) to go against you to destroy them and to bring yo[u] forth [fr]om their house, from their dwelling place, from their threshold, and from all ..... the place of the bedroom of Baba[no]š the son of Qayomt[a] (9) and of Saradust the daughter of Širin, his wife. And again, you will not appe[ar to them] either in dream by nigh[t or] in sle[ep by day] ..... I am dismissing you (10) ..... and a letter of dismis[sal] ..... according to the law of the daughters of [mankind].

Exterior

(11) I have acted for your name, YHWH, Elohim, Sebaoth, Gabriel, Michael, and Raphael. Your seal is on this sealing and on this threshold. Amen. Amen.

NOTES ON TEXT FIFTEEN

[1] On Saradust, cf. Montgomery's Text nine and his commentary there.

[2] נקב. Cf. Jastrow, *Dictionary*, p. 930 and also *BDB*, p. 666.

[3] Lit., "them."

[4] Lit., "after this." Cf. Jastrow, *Dictionary*, p. 647.

TEXT SIXTEEN

דנא קמיעה לאסותה דהדא ניונדוך בת כפני וכפני בעלה בר
שרקוי וזדו‹י› ברה וביתה ואיסקופתה כולה בשום יה יהו
אה ..... (2) החים ומהת[ם בי]חה הדין ואיסקופתה הדא
אינחור זורא ויה הירא בישמיה דללזריון ושבייאל וגבריאל
ואילי[אל] ..... (3) ומחתמין הל[ין] זדוי וניונדוך בההוא
חתמא דווחמה אדם קדמאה לשת בר‹י›ה ואיתנטיר מן ש[ידין]
(4) ומן דיוין ומן מבכלין ומן סטנין חוב זחימין ומחחמין
הלין ‹כפני›[בר] שרקוי וניונדוך אינתת‹י›ה בת   (5)
כפני וזדוי ברה בההוא חתמא דחחמא נח לחיבותה מן מיה
דטופנא (6) [ויזדחון] ויבטלון ויפקון ויתרחקון מינהון
ומן ביתהון ומן ד[ירחיהון] (7) ומן ב[ית] משכביהון מן
יומא דין ולעולם אמן אמן

TRANSLATION OF TEXT SIXTEEN

This amulet is for the salvation of this Newanduk
the daughter of Kapni, Kapni her husband, the son of
Šarqoi, Zado[i] her son, her house, and all of her
threshold, in the name of Yah, Yahu, Ah ..... (2) Sealed
and doubly-seal[ed] are this [ho]use and this threshold
'YNHWR HWR' and Yah HYR' in the name of LIZRYWN and
Šabyiel, Gabriel, and 'Eli[el] ..... [Sealed] (3) and
doubly-sealed are the[se]--Zadoi and Newanduk--with
that seal with which the First Adam[1] sealed his son Seth
to protect him from d[emons], (4) from devils, from monsters, and from satans. Again, sealed and doubly-
sealed are these--‹Kapni› [the son of] Šarqoi, and
Newanduk his wife, the daughter of (5) Kapni, and Zadoi
her son--with that seal with which Noah sealed the ark
from the waters of the flood. (6) [May they fly away]
and cease and go forth and get far away from them, from
their house, from [their] dw[elling], (7) and from
their b[ed]room, from this day and forever. Amen.
Amen.

NOTE ON TEXT SIXTEEN

[1] Cf. I Corinthians 15:45. Could this scribe have been a Christian?

TEXT SEVENTEEN

אסותא. מן שמיה להדא ניונדוך בת כפני דתיחסי (2) ברחמי שמיה מן ליליי<חא ומבכלתא אמן ותוב חיזח ותיחבטל (3) ותיתרחק מינה מן ניונדוך בת כפני ל<י>ליתא ומבכלתא ושערתא ועקרתא (4) ותכלתא בשום מאן דאחיד להון לשידי [ולדיוי] וליליתא ובשום אהיה אשר אהיה אילסור[1] (5) בגדנא מל{י}כיהון וש[ליטי]חון מלכיהון דש[וידי ודיוי ש[ליט]א רבא דליליתא] אשבעית עליכי חלבס ליליתא (6) בת ברתה דרזני ליליתא ד[יתבא] בביתה ודירתה דניונדוך [בת כפני וש[קפא דרדקי ויד]ודדקתא משב[ענא עליכי] (7) דתיחמחין בטורפס ליבבכי ובמורניתיה דק[תרו]ס דחוא שליט ..... [עליכי] הא כתבית ליכי והא פטריח [יתיכי מן ניונדוך בת כפני] ..... [כמא שידי] (8) דכתבין גיטי לינשיהון ולא ח[דרי]ן עליהון שקולי גיטיכי מן ני<ו>נדוך בת כפני ולא תיחחז[י]ן ל[ה לא בליליה ולא בימטא ולא תשכבין [עימ[ה ולא (9) תיקטלין יח בנה ובנתה בשום ממינתש שמר די חבנזיג יו ידיד יט יט יט בעיזקחה דציר וגליף עלה שם מפורש מן יומי עלמא ימי ששה ימי בראשית

TRANSLATION OF TEXT SEVENTEEN

Salvation from the heavens for this Newanduk the daughter of Kapni that she may be saved (2) by the love of the heavens from liliths and monsters. Amen. Amen. And again, you will fly away and cease (3) and get far away from her, from Newanduk the daughter of Kapni, lilith, monster, fever,[2] barrenness, (4) and abortion;[3] in the name of the one who is holding the demons, [the devils], the liliths, and in the name of "I-am-who-I-am." For the binding of (5) Bagdana their king and their ru[ler], the king of dem[ons and devils, and the great] ru[ler of liliths]. I adjure you, Lilith Halbas, (6) granddaughter of Lilith Zarni [dwelling] in the house and the dwelling of Newanduk [the daughter of Kapni and s]haking boys and [gi]rls. I adju[re you] (7) that you be struck in the membrane of your heart and with the spear of Qa[tro]s who rules [over you].

Lo, I have written for you and lo, I have separated [you from Newanduk the daughter of Kapni] ..... [as demons] (8) who write divorces for their wives and they do not re[tur]n to them. Take your divorce from Newanduk the daughter of Kapni and do not appear [to] her either by night or by day, and do not lie [with] her, and do not (9) kill her sons and her daughters. In the name of Memintaš the guardian of Habgezig. Yo is Beloved. Yat. Yat. Yat. By the seal on which has been carved and engraved the Ineffable Name from the (first) days of the world, the days of the six days of Creation.

NOTES ON TEXT SEVENTEEN

[1] The correct form of this phrase is אֶל אִיסוּר, attested in Texts 18.4 and 20.4. Text 22.2 reads עַל אִיסוּר. Text 19.2 reads אֱלִיסוּר, the phonetic spelling of אֶל אִיסוּר.

[2] Professor Gordon informs me in a personal note that this word is "the female counterpart of 'satyr' = 'hairy demoness.'" "Fever" is the definition given by Rossell (*Handbook*, p. 152) along with the citation of an Arab cognate, سَعَر.

[3] תִּכְלְתָא for תִּכְלָא Cf. Jastrow, *Dictionary*, p. 1668.

TEXT EIGHTEEN

הדין גיטא לשידא ול[דיו]א ולסטנה ולניריך (2) קל גריש
לאביטור אולד ..... ס וליליתא דיבטלון מן (3) בהמנדוך
בת ניונדוך ומן בהרד[1] בר איספנדרמיד ומן ביתה כול<י>ה
(4) אל איסור בגדנא מלכיהון דשידי ודדירי שליטא רבא
דליליתא משבענא על<י>כי חבסלס[2] (5) ליליתא בת ברחה
דזרני[3] ליליתא אם דכר אם ניקבה משבענא עליכי דת[ו]חמחין
בטורפס לילב[לי]כון ובמורניתא דתיקס[4] (6) גברא הוא שליט
עליכון דירי ולילי[לי]חא הא כתבית בכתבא הא בטלית יתכון
מנה ומן ביתה דבהמנדוך בת ניונדוך (7) ומן ברה כמא
דכחבין שידין גיטין ויהבין לינשיהון ותוב לא חדרין
עליהון שקול<ו>גיטיכון וקבילו פ[5] מכתבין ופוקו (8)
וקאמו[6] ועירוקו ואזילו מן ביתה דבהמנדוך בת ניונדוך
בשום היגוי וחיה וטטס אחינר בהיכל לחמית דתיקס[4] גברא
ובעיזקתיה דשמולו (sic) (9) דעלוהי שם מפל<ו>רש רבה אמן
אמן אמן סלה

TRANSLATION OF TEXT EIGHTEEN

This divorce is for the demon, for the [devil], for
the satan, and for Nirik.[7] (2) Hark! It expels 'Abitur
..... and the liliths that they cease from (3) Bahmanduk
the daughter of Newanduk and from Bahrad[1] the son of
'Ispandarmid, and from all her house. (4) For the binding of Bagdana the king of demons and devils, the great
ruler of liliths. I adjure you, Lilith (5) Habsalas,[2]
granddaughter of Lilith Zarni,[3] whether male or female,
I adjure you that you be struck in the membrane of your
heart and with the spear of the mighty Tiqas[4] (6) who is
the ruler over you, devils and liliths. Lo, I have
written in writing. Lo, I make you cease from her and
from the house of Bahmanduk the daughter of Newanduk (7)
and from her son, as demons write divorces and give
(them) to their wives and furthermore, they do not return to them. Take your divorce and accept the writings
and go forth, (8) Q'MW,[6] run away, and go from the house
of Bahmanduk the daughter of Newanduk, in the name of

HYGWY .... of the mighty Tiqas[4] and of the signet-ring of Solomon (9) upon which is the Great Ineffable Name. Amen. Amen. Amen. Selah.

NOTES ON TEXT EIGHTEEN

[1]Or perhaps בהרם.

[2]Habsalas is plainly written here, but cf. also Halbas in Text 17.5 and Text 20.5 and Hablas in Text 19.3 and 11.

[3]"Zarni" (זרני) is clear here and in Text 17.6 and Text 20.5. The variant "Zarnai" (זרנאי) is attested in Text 19.3 and 11.

[4]In some parallel texts, the name is Qatros (cf. Text 17.11 and Text 19.4 and 11). In Text 20.7, there is another variant which begins סק-. Unfortunately, a break in the text prevents a proper reading of the full form of the name which the scribe intended to write there.

[5]An extraneous letter.

[6]The letters are clearly attested, but the word is difficult to read. Parallel passages offer little help, for they either have no word following פוקו (e.g., Text 17.8) or a word which is clearly unrelated to the letters in this passage (e.g., לא<חעקרי in Text 19.7). The letters are too clearly written to permit emendation to קדחי as in Text 20.9.

[7]Probably the pagan god "Nirig" = "Nergal."

TEXT NINETEEN

בישמך מזדואי בת אמא סלמא ברלא בר אימא [בע[ל]ה] (2) בשמוך
אני ע[ו]שה אסותא מן שמיא מזדואי בת אימא סלמא בירל<א>
בר אמא בעלה דיחון ויהק<ימו>ן לה בנתי ובבני בננ[1]י ולא
חינעון בהון כל {מעם}[2] מדעם ביש בעלמה בש<ו>ס א ואהיא
אשר אהיא אליסור בוגבנא (3) {דמלכא} מלכיהון דש<י>די
ודיוא ושליטא רבא דליליתא אשבעת עלכי {ח[ב]לס} חבלס
לילי'תא בת ברתה דזרנאי ליליתא{תא} דשריא על איסקבת
בית{י}ה דהדא מזדואי בת אימא סלמא ודהד{י}ן בירלה בר
אימא אמן (4) דימליא עמקי מחיא שקפא ורמיא וחנקא וקטלא
ורמיא [ו]דרדקא ודרתקתא נלמר מצי ומר מיציתא[3] אשבעת
עלכי דחמחין בטופרי ליבכי {ובמרניתיה} ובמרניתה דקתרוס
גוברא וחתיעקרין ותוב (5) תיבטל<יי>ן ותתר<ח>ק<יי>ן מן
הדא מזדואי בת אימא סילים (sic) מן הדין בעלה בירלא בר
אימא אמן מן בניהון ומ<ן> בנתה<ו>ן דיתי ליהון ודהוי
ליהון ומ<ן> ביתהיהון מן כולה דל<י>רתיהון ומן כולה
אסק<ב>תיהון הא כתבל<י>א ליכי הא פטר[ית] יתיכי (6)
והא שביקת[4] יתיכי והא תריכת[5] יתיכי בנט פיטורין ואמן
מירלב פוקי .ת.טעו עיריק ל כי<מ>א דכתבין ויהבין שידי
ודיוא גיטי ל<י>נ[ש<י>הון ותוב[ו]ר] לא חדרין עליהון
במותימיהון אף אנתי לילית<א> בישתא (7) לילי {ב}דיכרא
ליל<יתא> נקבתא והנקתא וברתא[6] ושלנית<א> ועת[י]ק[ת]א
וחללתא שיק<ו>לי ניטיכי וספר חיר<ל<ו>כ<י>כי ואגרת
שיבוקיכי ועקרי ועקדח ופ<ו>קי ול<א>תעקרי מן הדא מזדואי
בת אימא סילים מן בעלה בירלה (8) בר אימא אמין מן בנה
מן בנת{י}ה ומן כולה ד<ל<רח{י}ה ולא תיתחזין להון לא
בחזו<י> דימא ולא בהרהרי ליליא ולא בידמות גברא
ויתיתא ולא כל מ.דמת מחת ולא תיק<ר<בין ליהון ל<לא>
תיפנ<ע<ין (9) בהון ולא תיכל<י<ן ב{יהב}ני ובנתי
ובנתיהל<ו>ן דיה לוהן (sic) וידהוי לוהן (sic) [לוהן}
מיחתם בחתמ[א] רבא דקדוש חתים על גיטכי קדוש יה קדוש
הוא צבואות שמו יה יה יה יה אהיא אשר אהיא נ<רא
וקדל<ו>ש אמן (10) אמן אמן סלה תלא כבל תלא ביחון
חלא יר<ו>של<יס הרים סב<יי<ב לא {מעתה} ואהיה סב<יי<ב
לעמר מעתא ועד עלם וזביבה מרחמת ישראל {קבלין} קיביליך
{אב} אסקיך לתבוהא בשרא בהל<י>רה אוכלי<כ>ך והמרה (11)
בחל<י>רה אשקיך תח<ו>{ב<ו>} אוסותא מן שמ<יא [ה}להדא
מזדואי בת אימא סלמא מתסי כרה בישל<ו>ס א אשבעת

עלי<כי חבלס ליליתא בת ברתה דזרנאי ליליתא מחיא
ושקפא וקטלא אשבעת עלי<כי מ..אס חי..פו. בטופרי ליבכי
ב<מ<רנ<י<חה דקחר<ו<ס גברא הָא כתב<י<ת לי{ך}כי הא
{פ}פטר<י<ת. יחי{ת}כי כימא דבבין וי̈לין שידי גיטי
ל<י<נשיהון ותוב<ו<} לא חדרין עליהון כען שיק<ו<לי
גיטכי וקבילי מומתיכי ויפרח (12) ויקדח ופל<ו<קי מן
בית{י}ה מן דל<י<רת{ת}ה מן אסק<ו<בתה מן {ארי} ארבע{י}
מיצעתה דבית{י}ה <ו<מן פגרה <ד<מזדואי בת אמא סלמא
אמן אמן סלה

TRANSLATION OF TEXT NINETEEN

In Your name. Mazdewai the daughter of 'Imma Salma
(and) Beryl the son of 'Imma, [her husba]nd. (2) I am
acting in Your name. Salvation from the heavens.
Mazdewai the daughter of 'Imma Salma, Beryl the son of
'Imma, her husband--that sons and daughters may live and
be esta<blish>ed for her, and that nothing evil at all
shall touch them. In the name of the Lord[7] and "I-am-
who-I-am." For the binding of Bagdana (3) the king of
the demons and the devils, and the great ruler of the
liliths. I adjure you, Lilith Hablas, granddaughter of
Lilith Zarnai, who dwells on the threshold of the house
of this Mazdewai the daughter of 'Imma Salma and of this
Beryl the son of 'Imma. Amen. (4) (You are) the one who
fills deep places, strikes, smites, casts down, strangles,
kills, and casts down boys and girls, male and female
foetuses(?). I adjure you that you be struck in the membrane of your heart and with the lance of Qatros the
mighty. And you will be uprooted. And again, (5) you
will cease and go fa<r a>way from this Mazdewai the
daughter of 'Imma Salma, from this Beryl the son of 'Imma,
her husband--Amen--from their sons and daughters whom
they now have or will have, from their house, from all
their dwelling, and from all their threshold. Lo, I
have written (a divorce) for you. Lo, I have dismis[sed]
you. (6) Lo, I have forsaken you. Lo, I have banished
you with a writ of divorce. And Amen. ....
... As demons and devils write divorces and give them to
their [wiv]es and furthermore, they do not return to them

in their residence. So, you evil lilith--(7) male lili or
female lili⟨th⟩--strangler, daughter, ghost, ol[d-o]ne, and
profane--take ⟨your⟩ divorce, your document of banishment,
and your letter of dismissal. Flee! Go away! Go forth!
Go completely away from this Mazdewai the daughter of 'Imma
Salma, from her husband Beryl (8) the son of 'Imma--Amen--
from her sons, from her daughters, and from all her dwelling.
And do not appear to them in visions by day or in "impure
fancies" by night--in the likeness of either man or woman, or
any .... Do not come near to them, do not hurt (9)
them, and do not devour their sons and their daughters, whom
they have or will have. Sealed with [the] great seal of the
Holy One. Sealed upon your divorce. The Holy One, Yah, the
Holy One is He. The Hosts is His name. YH. YH. YH. YH.
"I-am-who-I-am," awful and holy. Amen. (10) Amen. Amen.
Selah. TL'. KBL. TL' in them TL'. As mountains encircle
Jerusalem, so the Lord encircles His people from now and forever.[8] Beloved and pitied are you,[9] Israel. I will receive
you. I will bring you up to the ark. I will feed you choice
meat, and I will give you (11) choice wine to drink. Again,
salvation from the heavens for this Mazdewai the daughter of
'Imma Salma. Saved .... in the name of the
Lord. I adjure you, Lilith Hablas, granddaughter of Lilith
Zarnai, striker, smiter, and killer. I adjure you (that you
be struck) in the membrane of your heart and with the ⟨la⟩nce
of Qatr⟨o⟩s the mighty. Lo, I have written (a divorce) for
you. Lo, I have dismissed you. As demons write divorces and
give (them) to their wives and furthermore, they do not return to them. Now, take your divorce! Receive your adjuration! Fly off! (12) Go away! Go forth from the house,
from the dwelling, from the threshold, from the four (walls),
(from the) center of the house, from the body ⟨of⟩ Mazdewai
the daughter of 'Imma Salma. Amen. Amen. Selah.

NOTES ON TEXT NINETEEN

[1]The expression here is quite abnormal. Normal forms
would be בניך ובנן and these forms do occur in Text 49.12.

²"The scribe first omitted the ד of מדעט and then without erasing, rewrote the word. Rewriting without erasing errors is very common in these inscriptions, probably because the scribes feared that the bowls would not be bought, if prospective buyers suspected them of being ineffective due to erasures" (Gordon, *AOR*, VI, pp. 471-472). It is also obvious from such occurrences that most of the clients were unable to read.

³Cf. Gordon's note on this phrase in *AOR*, VI, p. 472.

⁴For שבקיח.

⁵For חרכיח.

⁶Or, ברחא.

⁷Lit., א. For an example of a single letter used as a name of God, cf. Revelation 22:13: ἐγὼ τὸ Ἀλφα καὶ τὸ Ω, ὁ πρῶτος καὶ ὁ ἔσχατος, ἡ ἀρχὴ καὶ τὸ τέλος. Cf. also Isaiah 44:6: אני ראשון ואני אחרון.

⁸Psalm 125:2.

⁹Note participles with pronominal suffixes!

TEXT TWENTY

ברחמי שמיא אסותא [לנפשא ו]לביתא דאפרה בר איהי וכל (2)
שום דאית ליה דיתקימון [ליה בנין] מן איצפנדוי איתת[י]ה
ויחון (3) ויתקימון ולא יגע בהון כל מזיק [בהדין] עלמא
בשום אהיה אשר אהיה (4) אל איסור בגדנא מלכא מלכיהון
דשיד[י ודיוי ושליטא] רבא דליליתא אשבעית (5) עליכי
בחלבס ליליתא בת ברתה דזרני לי[ליתא דיתבא] על איסקופת
באבה דא (6) ודאביא ..... ודמחיא וטרפא וחנקא ואכלא
דרדקי ו[דרדקתא] .... (7) מר מוצה [ו]מר מוציתא¹
אשבעית עליכי דחי[לת]מחין בט[ו]רפס ליליבכי ובמורניתא
דסק² ..... [גבד]א דהו[לא] שליט על שידי ועל דיוי ועל (8)
פתכרי {ול} ועל ליליתא הא כתבית לכין גיטא והפטרית
ית[כין כמא כתבי]ן שידי גיטא לינשיהון ותוב (9) לא
חדרין עליהו[ן] שקול גיט[י]כין וקביל מומחכין וקדחו
ועי[וריקי מן בי]תא הדין דאפרא (sic) בר איוי (sic)
ולא תיתחזין (10) ליה עוד לא לה לאיצפנדוי איתתיה ולא
תינעון ולא תיקר[בון להון ולבנין] דאית להון לא בחילמה
דליליה (11) ולא בחילמא דיממה בשום מתחמן יאבגביג דידי
טדטי ..... ב[עיזקתא דציר וגליף עלה שם] מפורש מן יומי
עלמא (12) ומן שישת ימי בראשית אמן אמן סלה הלליה

TRANSLATION OF TEXT TWENTY

By the love of the heavens, salvation [for the life and for] the house of 'Epra the son of 'YHY, and every (2) person[3] who belongs to him, that [his children] may be established--from 'Ispandoi his wife--and may live (3) and be established, and that no harmer [in this] world may touch them, in the name of "I-am-who-I-am." (4) For the binding of King Bagdana, the king of demon[s and devils and] the great [ruler] of liliths. I adjure (5) you by Lilith Halbas the granddaughter of Li[lith] Zarni [who is sitting] upon the threshold of B'BH D' (6) and lurking ..... and who smites and knocks down and strangles and devours boys and [girls] .... (7) male and female foetuses(?). I adjure you that you be

struck in the membrane of your heart and with the spear of the
[mighty] SQ ..... who is the ruler over demons, over devils,
over (8) idols, and over liliths. Lo, I have written to you
the divorce and I have separated y[ou. As] demons [writ]e
divorces for their wives and furthermore, (9) they do not return to them. Take your divorce and accept your adjuration
and flee and run [away from the ho]use of this 'Epra the son
of 'YYY and do not appear (10) to him any more, nor to
'Ispandoi his wife. Do not touch and do not come [near to
them or to] their [sons] either in a dream of the night (11)
or in a dream of the day, in the name of MTHMN Y'BGBYG DYDY
TDTY .... by [the signet-ring upon which has been carved
and engraved the] Ineffable [Name] from the (first) days of
the world, (12) even the six days of Creation. Amen. Amen.
Selah. Hallelujah!

NOTES ON TEXT TWENTY

[1]Or, מרמיצי ומרמיציחא. Cf. Text 19.4 and the Note there.
The translation "male and female foetuses" both here and in
Text 19.4 was suggested by Professor Gordon. Cf. especially
Text 22.5.

[2]On this form of the name which is normally written
"Qatros," cf. Note four on Text 18.

[3]Lit., "name."

TEXT TWENTY-ONE

בישמך מרי אסואתא אסיא רבא (2) דרחמי אסירא והיתמא ומחתמא
כולה (3) קומתיה רבית מישכניה דהדין משרשיה דמיתקרי (4)
דהבאי בר מחלפתא בשיבעא איסרין דילא מישתרין ובתמניה
חמין (5) דלא מיתברין בשמיך מריא איבול מלכא רבא דאלהי
ובשמיך מרתין איבולית (6) מלכתא רבתא דאיסתראתא ובשום
טילאכטיל מריא רבא דבגדני ובשום סחנודמוך (7) ובשום
איבול בר פלג ובשום אנגרוס ובשום מריא מלילא ומרגלא
וארמסא ובשום אזפא ועליים (8) ובשום נקדרוס מרי בוניוב
הואתא ובשום סרפיאל מרי דינא ורימזא ובשום שיתין אלהי
דיכרי (9) ותמני איסתראתא ניקבאתא ובשום ארדיסבא סבתא
קשישא קשיש מין כנואתיה ובשום אנד מריא רבא דמיתנחישי
(10) ואניזקי רמין לעיל פרזלא רנחשא ומתקנא ליה {סיליתיה}
סיליתא דאברא ושבעא כומרי רמי דבגדנא ובשום בגדנא בר
חבאל (11) וסופרזיא קחשן ועלימון ובשום פליני ומנדינס
ומנירנש נגגיל ובשום אירס בר חנס ובשום אברכס ובשום
אגוריאל דרחמי לא אית ליה (12) ובשום ארזן וכרין רוס
ברוס חרוס דעלתרוס ובשום במאיל לאריאל שדר שקול לשליטא
רבא דקדמוהי ובשום חעונ....... ובשום מריא איבול (13)
מלאכה רבא ד[1]זעקי ובשום אילהא גיברא ומריא רבא דבגדני
ובשום אריון בר זנד אתון אסירי וחיליצי וזריזי עא כל
שידי דירי וסטני בישי איסרא (14) וכסא הדין שרירא וחתמיה
קיימי עליהון דאינש מין איסוריה לא נפיק ומן תחות ידוהי
[לא] שיר בישמיהון דהלין איסרי ניתסר המן שידא ודנחיש
וליליתא בישהא (15) דאית בפגריה [דה]דין משרשיה דמיתקרי
דהבאי בר מחלפתא באיסרין בארבעה וחיההין בשמיא הוב
אסירין באסרא וחת<י>מין בתינא בר מין פגריה דהדין משרשיה
(16) דמיתקרי דהבאי בר מחלפתא אמן תוב אסירי עידא ודירא
ודנחיש וחומרתא ופתכרא דאית על פגריה דהדין משרשיה ד-
מיתקרי דהבאי בר מחלפתא באיבול וחתים (17) באיבולית תוב
אסיר בשינאס ומנא וחתים בנורא תוב אסיר באלהי גבדי וחתימין
באריון בר זנד תוב אסיר בעיזקת בית חנון וחתימין במכילא
רבא דזעוזא תוב אסירין באלהא שרירא וחתמין בשליטא רבא
(18) דקדמוהי בר מין פגריה דהדין משרשיה דמיהקרי דהבאי
בר מחלפתא בשום פטירגינוס אוקינוס שונקא קוסא קפא אזזיאל
דריסק ופרס ובשיס ברקפת ..... סר בתרה ליליבי מיתדבך
ובשום א.כא עלינא (19) דעלם אלהי באידכור יתון עילך

מלואשית דהדין משרשיה דמיתקרי דהבאי בר מחלפתא ניתחחם
מין בינתא דראשיה ועדמא טורפא ריבליה בחיבי סוטיא .....
לבא לא ניהון ולהדין ביתא דמשרשיה (20) דמיתקרי דהבא (sic)
בר מחלפא (sic) לא ניעלון ולא ניקרבון ליה ולא ניתחזון
[ליה לא בליליה] ולא ביממא מין יומא [דנן ולעלם]
....

TRANSLATION OF TEXT TWENTY-ONE

In Your name, Lord of salvation, great Savior (2) of love. Bound, sealed, and doubly-sealed is the entire (3) body and dwelling of this Mešaršia who is called (4) Dahabai[4] the son of Mahlapta, by the seven bonds which are not loosened and with the eight seals (5) which are not broken. In your name, Lord 'Ibbol, great king of the gods. In your name, Lady 'Ibboleth, (6) great queen of the goddesses. In the name of Ṭilaktil the great lord of the Bagdani. In the name of Sahnudmuk; (7) in the name of 'Ibbol the son of Palag; in the name of 'Angaros; in the name of the Lord, the Word, the Leader, and Hermes; in the name of 'Azpa and ᶜAlim; (8) in the name of Naqderos the lord of Biniwab HW'T'; in the name of Seraphiel the lord of judgment[3] and gesture; in the name of the sixty male gods (9) and the eighty female goddesses; in the name of 'Ardisaba the venerable, the elder, the eldest of his colleagues; in the name of 'Anad the great lord of sorcerers (10) and injurers ..... thrown over (him) are iron and bronze, and attached to him are bread-baskets of lead and the seven exalted priests of Bagdana; in the name of Bagdana the son of Ḥabal; (11) .... in the name of Palnini and Mandinas and Menirnas, Naggil; in the name of 'Iras the son of Hanas; in the name of 'Abraxas; in the name of 'Agzariel who has no love; (12) in the name of 'Arzan and Karin--Ros, Beros, Teros of Alteros; in the name .... in the name of lord 'Ibbol (13) the great king of the blast-demons; in the name of the mighty God and the great lord of the Bagdani; in the name of 'Arion the son of Zand are you bound, armed, and equipped against all demons, devils, and evil satans. This bond (14) and this bowl is certain and its seals are established against them from whose bond no one gets loose[4] and from under whose control [no] (one) escapes.[5] In the name of these bonds, the demon Danḥis, and the evil lilith (15) which are in the body of [th]is Mešaršia who is called Dahabai the son of Mahlapta, are bound by bonds in earth and by seals in heaven. Again, (you are) bound with the bond and sealed a second time away from the body of this Mešaršia (16) who is called Dahabai the son of Mahlapta. Amen. Again, bound are the demon, the devil, Danḥis, the amulet-spirit, and the idol which are on the body of this Mešaršia who is called Dahabai the son of Mahlapta, by 'Ibbol, and sealed (17) by 'Ibboleth. Again, (you are) bound by Šinas and Mana and sealed by fire. Again, (you are) bound by the mighty gods and sealed by 'Arion the son of Zand. Again, (you are) bound by the signet-ring of the house of Hanun and sealed by the great retribution of Zeus. Again, (you are) bound by the steadfast God and sealed by the great ruler (18) who is before him, away from the body of this Mešaršia who is called Dahabai the son of Mahlapta. In the name of Patragenos, Okeanos,[6] Šunqa, Qosa, Qapa, 'Azaziel .... behind her(?) .... and in the name .... against us. (19) Of eternity. The gods .... he will set his zodiac signs against you, that this Mešaršia who is called Dahabai the son of Mahlapta might be sealed from the top of his head to the toes of his feet. .... they shall not be. And into this house of Mešaršia (20) who is called Dahabai the son of Mahlapta they shall not enter. They shall not come near to him and they shall not appear [to him either during the night] or during the day, from [this] day [and forever]. ....

NOTES ON TEXT TWENTY-ONE

[1]Or, שׁפי.

[2]"Goldsmith."

[3]Or, "religion." Cf.

[4]Lit., "goes away."

[5]Lit., "leaps."

[6]"Ocean."

TEXT TWENTY-TWO

אפיכן לוטתא על בורזין בת מחיא על איסור (2) בגדינא
{ו}מלכ<יה<ון דדיוא ושליטא רבה דל<י<ליתא אשבעית (3) עלכי
חבלס ליליתא בת ברתה דלז<רני {לי}לילית דשריא על (4)
אסכופת ביתה דמחישי בת דודי {ו}מחיא וסרפא דרתקא ודרתקתא¹
(5) מרמיצי ומרמציתא² אשבעית עלכי דתמחן בטפרס ל{ל}בכי
ובמראנית<י<ה דקתרוס נוברא הא כתבית (6) ליכי {והא} והא
תארכית יאתכי כמא דכתבין שידי גיטא לנש<י<הון ותוב לא
חדרין ושקולי (7) נסכי וקבלי מומתכי וקדחי ועקורי ופוקי
מן ביתה ומן גובה דמחישי בת דודי בשום רת מחץ מחץ מחץ
(8) שם מפורש מיששית ימ<י< בר<א<ש<י<ת הלל<ו<יה לישמך
הלליה למלכותך צבירת צבירת יודגא יודבא צבירת צבירת
יודגא יודבא צבירת צבירת יודגא (9) יודבא לישמך אני
עש<י<תי אמן

TRANSLATION OF TEXT TWENTY-TWO

Overturned are the curses upon Burzin the daughter of The Smiter, upon Prince (2) Bagdina, the king of the devil(s) and the great ruler of the liliths. I adjure (3) you, Lilith Hablas, the granddaughter of Lilith Zarnai who dwells on the (4) threshold of the house of Mehiṣai the daughter of Dodai, smiter and burner of boys and girls, (5) male and female foetuses(?). I adjure you that you be struck in the membrane of your heart, and with the spear of Qatros the mighty. Lo, I have written (a divorce) (6) for you and Lo, I have expelled you. As demons write divorces for their wives and furthermore, (they) do not return. Take (7) your divorce, receive your oath, flee, take flight, and go forth from the house and from the back of Mehiṣai the daughter of Dodai. In the name of RT MHS[3] MHS MHS, (8) the Ineffable Name from the six days of Creation. Hallelujah for Your Name! Hallelujah for Your Kingdom! SBYRT SBYRT YWDG' YWDB' SBYRT SBYRT YWDG' YWDB' SBYRT SBYRT YWDG' (9) YWDB' I have acted for Your name. Amen.

NOTES ON TEXT TWENTY-TWO

[1] Gordon notes that "in both cases ה is dissimilated from ד" (*AASOR*, 14, 1934, p. 143).

[2] The letters which form this phrase are more clearly written in this text than in any parallel passage. Cf. Texts 20.7 and 19.4.

[3] By *Athbash*, the name מחץ becomes יסח, a common spelling of the proper name יוסף. This name is borne by several Tannaim and Amoraim, and is also attested as "a disguise of one of the Divine Names" (cf. Jastrow, *Dictionary*, p. 570). That is obviously its function here.

TEXT TWENTY-THREE

אסותא מן שמיא לדדבה בר אסמנדוך ולשרקוי (2) בת דאדה
איתתיה ולבניהון ולבנתהון ולביתיהון (3) ולקיניניהון
דיהון להון בנין ויהון ויתקימון ויתנטרון (4) מן שידי
ומן דיוי ומן שובטי ומן סטני ומן לוטתא ומן ליליתא ומן
מבכלתא דמיתחזין (5) להון מומינא עלך מלאכה דנחית מן
שמיא כד גביל בדמת קרן ליה זיף זליף (6) מלאכה דעביד
רעותא דמרוהי ועל כיבשי מרוהי מסגי שאר ומישתבח בישמיא
(7) שאר ותושבחתיה בארעה סמר ויתמלאון ציצית דקימ[ין]
ומטהרין מן יומי עלמא וניגריהון (8) לא מיתחזין ברקדיהון
ליה לעלמא כוליה ויתבין וקימין באתרהון נשפין כי זיקא
ברקין כי כרקא (9) אינון יבטלון וישמתון כל ניסי וקיבלי
ואנקי ולוטתא וקריתא ושיקופתא ואשלמתא ומללתא ושידי
(10) ודיוי ושובטי ולליתא ופתכרי ומבכלתא וכל מידעם
ביש דיזהון ויפקון מן דדבה בר אסמנדוך ומן שרקוי (11)
בת דאדה איתתיה ומן חוניק ומן יסמין ומן כופיתי ומן
מהדוך ומן אברהם ומן פנוי ומן שילי בני שרקוי ומן
ביתיהון ומן (12) קיניניהון ומן דירתיהון כולה דשרן בה
מן יומא דנן ולעולם בשום יהוה צבאות אמן אמן סלה יהוה
ישמורכה מכול רע ישמור את נפשך

Exterior

(13) דאידרונא דאיספלידא

TRANSLATION OF TEXT TWENTY-THREE

Salvation from the heavens for Dadbeh the son of 'Asmanduk and for Šarqoi (2) the daughter of Dada, his wife, and for their sons and their daughters and their house (3) and their possessions, that they may have sons, that they may live and be established and be protected (4) from demons, from devils, from bands (of spirits), from satans, from curses, from liliths, and from monsters which appear (5) to them. I adjure you, O angel

which comes down from heaven--as it is kneaded in the shape
of a horn on which honey is poured--(6) the angel which does
the will of his lord and which walks upon the steps of his
lord, $šâ'û$,[1] even the one praised in heaven, (7) $šâ'û$,[1] and
his praise is in the earth, *semu*. They are filled with glory
who endu[re] and remain pure from the days of eternity. Their
feet (8) do not appear in the dances for the entire world.
They sit, they stand in their place, they blow like the blast,
they flash like the lightning. (9) These will frustrate and
and ban all familiars, counter-charms, necklace-charms,
curses, invocations, knockings, rites, words, demons, (10)
devils, bands (of spirits), liliths, idols, monsters, and
everything bad, that they may depart and go away from Dadbeh
the son of 'Asmanduk and from Šarqoi (11) the daughter of
Dada, his wife and from Honiq and from Yasmin and from
Kufitai and from Mahduk[2] and from Abraham and from Pannoi
and from Šili, the children of Šarqoi, and from their house,
from (12) their possessions, and from all their dwelling in
which they dwell, from this day and forever. In the name of
YHWH of hosts. Amen. Amen. Selah. May YHWH guard you from
all evil, may He guard your life.[3]

Exterior

(13) For[4] the inner room of the hall.

NOTES ON TEXT TWENTY-THREE

[1] An unexplained word which could be read as an imperative of the root נושׂ and with the meaning "spare!" Note plural in respect for deity (?).

[2] "Daughter of the moon."

[3] Psalm 121:7.

[4] Lit., "of."

TEXT TWENTY-FOUR

אסותא מן שמיא לדדבה בר אסמנדוך (2) ולשרקוי בת דאדא
איתתיה ולחוניק וליסמין (3) ולכופיתי ולמהדוך ולפנוי
ולאברהם ולשילי בני שרקוי (4) ולביתיהון ולקינינהון
ודיהרן להון בנין ויחון ויתקימון ולא ינגע בהון (5) כל
מזיק דאית בעלמא ובישמיה רבה דיקרי אלהא קדישא דחרשי ליה
(6) דכביש השוכה תחות נהורא מחתא תחות אסותא סיתרא תחות
בינינא חבלתא (7) תחות שמתא רוגזא תחות ניזוא כבישין
כולהון בני חשוכה תחות כורסיה דאלהא דה ..... (8)
שמיה אסירין כבישין דיוי נקיטן כדנא רוחי בישתא וחומרי
זידניתא ושומהתא (9) ורברבי דחשוכה ורוח סרי ונאלי
ומבכלתא דליליה ודימתא ולוטתא ואנקתא וקיבלי ומללתא
ומומתא (10) וראישתקופתא ואשלמתא פגעא ופגעיתא ובת קלא[1]
דקריה ואסרה דמיסכינותא ושידי ודיוי וסטני (11) ופתכרי
ולילית<א> וחרשי בישי ועובדי תקיפי ושבע מבכלתא דליליה
ודימתא אסירן כבישן ומשכבן (12) מן דדבה בר אסמנדוך
ומן שרקוי בת דאדא איתתיה ומן חוניק ומן יסמין ומן
כופיתא ומן מהדוך ומן פנוי (13) ומן אברהם ומן שילי
בני שרקוי ומן ביתיהון כוליה ומן קיניהון ומן דירתיהון
כולי<ה> מן יומא דנן ולעולם אמן (14) אמן סלה ויאמר
יהוה אל הסטן יגער יהוה בך הסטן יגער יהוה בך הבוחיר
בירושלים הלא זה אוד מו[צ]ל מיאש

TRANSLATION OF TEXT TWENTY-FOUR

Salvation from the heavens for Dadbeh the son of
'Asmanduk (2) and for Šarqoi the daughter of Dada, his
wife and for Honiq and for Yasmin (3) and for Kufitai
and for Mahduk and for Pannoi and for Abraham and for
Šili, the children of Šarqoi, (4) and for their house
and for their possessions, that they may have sons, that
they may live and be established, and that no harmer (5)
in the world may touch them. And in His great name which
is called "The Holy God"--to which belong black-arts[2]--
(6) which suppresses darkness under light, plague under
healing, destruction under construction, injury (7) under

ban, anger under repose. All the sons of darkness are suppressed under the throne of God ..... (8) (by) His name devils are bound (and) suppressed. Gripped in the same way are evil spirits, impious amulet-spirits, (magical) names, (9) princes of darkness, the rebellious spirit, incubi, monsters of night and day, curses, necklace-charms, countercharms, words, adjurations, (10) knockings, rites, male plague, female plague, the voice from heaven which calls, the bond of poverty, demons, devils, satans, (11) idols, liliths, evil black-arts, powerful (magical) practices, and the seven monsters of night and day. Bound, suppressed, and forced to lie (12) away from Dadbeh the son of 'Asmanduk, and from Šarqoi the daughter of Dada, his wife, and from Ḥoniq and from Yasmin and from Kufitai and from Mahduk and from Pannoi (13) and from Abraham and from Šili the children of Šarqoi, and from all their household, and from their possessions, and from all their dwelling place, from this day and forever. Amen. (14) Amen. Selah. And YHWH said to Satan: May YHWH rebuke you, Satan, may YHWH who has chosen Jerusalem rebuke you. Is not this a fire-brand sna[tch]ed from the fire?[3]

NOTES ON TEXT TWENTY-FOUR

[1]Read בַּת קָלְא. In Jewish theology, בת קול is a mysterious voice or echo from heaven through which it was necessary for God to communicate after the death of "the last prophets, Haggai, Zechariah, and Malachi" and the concomitant withdrawal of the holy spirit (i.e., spirit of prophecy or revelation) from Israel. See G. F. Moore, *Judaism*, vol. I, pp. 421-422 and the references given there.

[2]Perhaps omitted after מריק but remembered and added here.

[3]Zechariah 3:2.

TEXT TWENTY-FIVE

סכ<י>רי פומיהון דכולל<י>הון עממיה תגממיה (2) ולישניה
מן קמה דבהמנדוך בֹת סמא{י} (3) ורחמיאל מלאכה וחביאל
מלאכה וח[נ]ניאל מלאכה (4) אינון מלאכין ירחמון,
ויחבבון ו[י]חנון] ויחבקון ית בהמנדוך (5) בת סמא באנפי
כל בני אדם [דא[ולד ית חוה ניעול לקדמיהון, (6)
מילבושהון, ילבשונה ומיכסותהון, [וכ[סונה מיעיל חיסדא
דאלהא, (7) עימה, יתבין, מיזיה מיזי, (מיזיי) חין,
כדשפיר בשום יהוה ביה אלאל רבה (8) דחילא ודמימריה כל
אסו, הדין רזא דריסת קים ושריר לעולם ועד קלק .....

Exterior

(9) קל קלא ברזי קלא קלא דב...כ...רוניתא קלא דאיתחא
בתולתא דימחבלא ולא ילדא חסי נחב[י] (10) נחבי וניחי
אפרה בר שברדוך לגוף, ביתיה ולגו{גו}פה דבהמנדוך בת
סמא (11) איתחיה כי אבליתי דימחבלא ולא ילדא כי אסה
חדתחא ליכלילי אמן ואמן (12) ושריר וקים אסותא מן שמיא
לבהמנדוך בת סמא (13) אפרפרט ..... חאמ[י]ץ אעיקיהי .....
אמן אמן סלה אסותא ושלמ[א מן] שמיה לעולם ו[לעד] ועד

TRANSLATION OF TEXT TWENTY-FIVE

Closed are the mouths of all of them--nations, legions, and (2) languages from Bahmanduk the daughter of Sama. (3) And may these angels--the angel Rahmiel, the a[ngel] Habbiel, and the angel [Ha]nniniel--(4) love, honor, be gracious (to), and embrace Bahmanduk (5) the daughter of Sama in the presence of all the sons of Adam [whom he f]athered by Eve. Let us enter before them. (6) They will clothe her with their clothing, [they will c]over her with their garments, the robe[2] of the kindness of God. (7) With her they are sitting all around (giving) grace[3] as it is appropriate in the name of YHWH who is Yah, El-El the Great, (8) the fearful, whose Word is full salvation. This mystery is certified, established, and confirmed forever and ever. ....

Exterior

Hark! The sound is against[4] mysteries. Hark! The voice of ..... the sound of the woman, the young woman[5] who travails but does not give birth. Quickly (let these sounds) be hidden,[6] (10) be hidden and let 'Epra the son of Šaborduk come to the inside of his house and to the body of Bahmanduk the daughter of Sama, (11) his wife. (She is) like a young woman who travails but does not give birth. (She will become) like fresh myrtle (used) for crowns. Amen and Amen. (12) Confirmed and established is salvation from the heavens for Bahmanduk the daughter of Sama. (13) 'PRPRT ..... leaven, press it ..... Amen. Amen. Selah. Salvation and peac[e from] the heavens forever and [ever] and ever.

NOTES ON TEXT TWENTY-FIVE

[1]Here and in several places throughout the text the scribe used word dividers. Cf. Rossell, *Handbook*, p. 15.

[2]Or, "cloak."

[3]Either the noun "grace" (חין), in which case the verb is to be supplied; or a verbal form of חנן as if from חון.

[4]For this use of ב, cf. *UT*, 93, 10.4[b].

[5]Cf. *UT*, 377-378: "There is no word in the Near Eastern languages that by itself means *virgo intacta*."

[6]The root of the word is חבי and not חבב, as Montgomery (p. 178) suggests. The unpleasant sounds are to be silenced when the husband comes so that he will be thinking only of his wife.

TEXT TWENTY-SIX

בישמך במימרך מרי כל אסותא אלהא דרחמי (2) אסותא דישמיא
תהוי לגי>ה לביתיה דהורמיז בר ממא [ול]דירתה דדודי בת
(3) מרתא ולברגלל בר דודי ולברשיבבי בר טשיהראזד [ל]ביתה
כול{י}ה ולדיר[תה] (4) כולה לאס מן סליק ו{ואטפי} ואטרפי
דאס מן מנא אינש לאס לא סליק ואטרפי דאס אינש (5) מנה
ביהיבדין ו{י}אינש לאס לאס לא סליק ואטרפי דאס אינש מנה
כינתי ומניתי עליכון רוחין ושיקין (6) ושובטין וירורין
ופגעין ושיבין וחרשין בישין ועובדין תקיפין ופתכרין
ולילית׳ה ביש[תה] (7) יתכרית ואסרית יתכון באיסור[י] נחשא
ופרזלא וחתמית יתכון בצורת עיזקתא דנורא דאל ... (8) ...
.. ופטרית יתכון מינהון מן הורמיז בר ממא ומן דודי בת
[מרת[א ומן ברגלל בר דודי ומן ברש[יבבי בר] טשיהראז[ד]
(9) ..... [ומן] מהוי בר דודי בשום [ר]ופיאל וסוריאל
וגבריאל ..... וריר ורחמיאל ורחטיאל נריניאל וחוריאל
וסרריאל ובחותם יהוה צבאות קים עלמין אמן אמן [אמן]

TRANSLATION OF TEXT TWENTY-SIX

In Your name and by Your Word, Lord of all salvation,
God of love. (2) May the salvation of the heavens belong
to the house of Hormiz the son of Mama [and to] the dwelling of Dodi the daughter of (3) Marta and to Bar-Gelal the
son of Dodi and to Bar-Šibebi the son of Teshiharazad.
[For] all her house and all [her] (4) dwelling. L'S MN
SYLQ W'TRPY D'S MN MN' 'YNŠ L'S L' SLYQ W'TRPY D'S 'YNŠ
(5) MNH BYHYBDYN W'YNŠ L'S L'S L' SLYQ W'TRPY D'S 'YNŠ MNH
I have prepared and I have arranged (charms) against you,
spirits, demons, (6) bands (of spirits), howlers, plagues,
circle-spirits, evil black-arts, powerful (magical) practices, idols, and the ev[il] lilith (7) ...... and I bind
you with bonds of bronze and iron and I seal you with the
figure of the signet-ring of fire ..... (8) ...... And I
separate you from them--from Hormiz the son of Mama and
from Dodi the daughter of Marta and from Bar-Gelal the
son of Dodi and from Bar-Š[ibebi the son] of Teshiharazad

..... (9) and from Mehoi the son of Dodi. In the name of
Rophiel and Suriel and Gabriel .... and Raḥmiel and
Raḥṭiel and Nariniel and Huriel and Serariel. And by the
seal of YHWH of Hosts it is established forever. Amen.
Amen. [Amen].

TEXT TWENTY-SEVEN

בשום[1]

טרדי בת אוני (2) הרמסדר טרדי אאאאאא[2] אסירי וחתימי (3)
שידא ודירא וסטאנא ולטאנא ולליאתא ב[י]שאתא (4) דמתחזא
באלליא ו{מתז} בימאמי ודמיחזי. טרדי בת ..... (5) [בש]ום
גבריאל מיכאל ורופיאל אמן אמן אמן אמן אמן סאלה הלליה כפי
אאאאאא.

TRANSLATION OF TEXT TWENTY-SEVEN

Tardi the daughter of 'Oni. (2) Hormisdar Tardi. In the name of ''''''. Bound and sealed are (3) the demon, the devil, the satan, the curse, and the e[vil] liliths (4) which appear during the night and during the day and which appear to Tardi the daughter of ['Oni] ..... (5) [In the n]ame of Gabriel, Michael, and Rophiel. Amen. Amen. Amen. Amen. Selah. Hallelujah! According to ''''''.

NOTES ON TEXT TWENTY-SEVEN

[1] The scribe apparently forgot at first to write בשום before the divine name and had to add it later above the line.

[2] Cf. note seven to Text Nineteen above.

TEXT TWENTY-EIGHT

חתים ומח[תם]ביתה ואיסקופתה דודי בתה מן כל פגעין בישי
מן כ]ל ר[וחין (2) בישין ומ]ן[מבכלתא ומן לליתא ומן כל
נזקין ומיזקין דלא תקרבון לה לביתה ולאיסקו[פתה] דודי (3)
בת אחת דיחתים ביתלתה עזקין ומחתם בשבעה חתמין ומן כל
פגעין בישין ומן כל רוחין (4) בישין ומן מבכלתא אמן ואמן
סלה

TRANSLATION OF TEXT TWENTY-EIGHT

Sealed and doubly-seal[ed] are the house and the threshold [of] Dodi the daughter of 'Ahat from all evil plagues, from al[l] evil (2) [sp]irits, fro[m] monsters, from liliths, and from all blast-demons and harmers, so that they will not come near to her, to her house, and to the thre[shold of] Dodi (3) the daughter of 'Ahat who is sealed with the three signet-rings and doubly-sealed with the seven seals--and from all evil plagues and from all evil (4) spirits, and from monsters. Amen and Amen. Selah.

NOTE ON TEXT TWENTY-EIGHT

The word נזיק in line two of this text occurs also in the parallel texts which follow (cf. 29.2, 29.4, 30.2, and 30.3) and is translated "blast-demon(s)" in each case. Another translation could be "damage," but, however it is translated, this word must be synonymous with זיק in text 31.2.

TEXT TWENTY-NINE

החים ומחחם ביתה{ה} ואיסקופתה דדידי בת אחת מן כל פגעין
בישין מן כל רוחין (2) בישין ומן מבכלתא ומן ליליתא ומן
כל נזקין דלא תקרבון לה לב[יתה ולאיס]קופתה (3) דודי בת
אחת דיחתים ביתלתה עיזקין ומ[נ]חתם ב[שבעה] חתמין מן כל מין
ליליתא ומן כל (4) [נז]קין דלא תקרבון לה לביתה ולאיסקופתה
דדודי ..... ופח ולעל[ם אמן א[מ]ן סלה

TRANSLATION OF TEXT TWENTY-NINE

Sealed and doubly-sealed are the house and threshold of Dodi the daughter of 'Ahat from all evil plagues, from all evil spirits, (2) from monsters, from liliths, and from all blast-demons, so that they will not come near to her, to her [house, and to the thres]hold (3) [of] Dodi the daughter of 'Ahat, who is sealed with the three signet-rings and dou[bly-sealed with] the seven seals from all species of lilith and from all (4) [blast]-demons, so that they will not come near to her, to her house, and to the threshold of Dodi .... and forev[er. Amen. A]men. Selah.

TEXT THIRTY

חתים ומחת{א}ם ביתה ואיסקופתה דודי בת אחת מן כל פגעין
בישין ומן כל רוחין (2) בישין ומן מבכלתא ומן ליליתא ומן
כל נזקא דלא תקרבון לה לביתה ולאיסקופתה (3) דודי בה אחת
דיחתימי ביתלתה עיזקין ומחתם בשבעה חתמין ‹מן› מבכלהא ומן
כל נזקין (4) ומנזקין דלא תקרבון לה לביתה ולאיסקופתה
דודי בת אחת אמן אמן סלה

TRANSLATION OF TEXT THIRTY

    Sealed and doubly-sealed are the house and threshold of Dodi the daughter of 'Ahat from all evil plagues, from all evil (2) spirits, from monsters, from liliths, and from every blast-demon and harmer so that they will not come near to her, to her house, and to the threshold (3) of Dodi the daughter of 'Ahat who is sealed with the three signet-rings and doubly-sealed with the seven seals ‹from› monsters, from all blast-demons (4) and harmers so that they will not come near to her, to her house, and to the threshold of Dodi the daughter of 'Ahat. Amen. Amen. Selah.

TEXT THIRTY-ONE

חתים ומחתם ביתיה {אי} ואיסקופתיה דאדק בר מחלפתה לממי
אינתל<י>ה מן כל (2) פגעין בישין ומן כל רוחין בישין ומן
מבכלתא ומן ליליתא ומן כל זיקין ומזיקין ודלא תקרבון לל<י>ה
(3) לבית<י>ה ולאיסקופת<י>ה דאדק בר מחלפתא דיחתים ביתלחת
שירין ומזותם בשבעה חתמין מן כל פגעין ביש<י>ן (4) מן כל
רוחין בישין מן מבכלתא ומן ליליתא ומן כל זיקין ומזיקין
דלא תקרבון ל<י>ה לבית<י>ה ולאיסקופת<י>ה (5) דאדק בר
מחלפתא ולממי אינת<י>ה מן יומא דנן ולעלם אמן אמן (6)
סלה

TRANSLATION OF TEXT THIRTY-ONE

Sealed and doubly-sealed are the house and threshold of 'Adaq the son of Maḥlapta, for Mami his wife,[1] from all (2) evil plagues, from all bad spirits, from monsters, from liliths, and from all blast-demons and harmers, so that you may not come near (3) the house and threshold of 'Adaq the son of Maḥlapta who is sealed with the three [signet]-rings and doubly-sealed with the seven seals from all evil plagues, (4) from all bad spirits, from monsters, from liliths, and from all blast-demons and harmers, so that you may not come near the house and threshold (5) of 'Adaq the son of Maḥlapta, for Mami his wife,[1] from this day and forever. Amen. Amen. (6) Selah.

NOTE ON TEXT THIRTY-ONE

[1] Did the husband order this incantation for his wife's peace of mind?

TEXT THIRTY-TWO

אסו[תא] מן שמיא תהי לה להנדו בת מחלפתא (2) דתיתסי ברחמי
שמיא מן אשותא ומן אזיתא מן אונא (3) ב ..... אמן סאלה
אסותא מן שמיא תהי לה לקאקי בת מחלפתא ..... (4) דיתבטל
מינה חלמי שגישי ורוחא בישא וסטאני בישי אמן אמן אמן סאלה
הללוי‹ה› אסותא (5) לזרנכש בת .. מחלפתא דתיתסי ברחמי שמיא
לזרנכש ולאחי ברה בסבע דרחמי אמן (6) אמן ס[אלה] ....
נהי אגרר אגרר יה ....

TRANSLATION OF TEXT THIRTY-TWO

Let there be salva[tion] from the heavens for Hindu the daughter of Mahlapta, (2) so that she may be saved by the love of the heavens from the fire, from the burning, from oppression. (3) ..... Amen. Selah. Let there be salvation from the heavens for Qaqi the daughter of Mahlapta ..... (4) so that confusing dreams may cease from her, and the evil spirit and the evil satans. Amen. Amen. Amen. Selah. Halleluja[h]! (Let there be) salvation (5) for Zarinkaš the daughter of Mahlapta, so that she may be saved by the love of the heavens, for Zarinkaš and for 'Ahi her son, by the satisfaction of love. Amen. (6) Amen. Se[lah]. ....

TEXT THIRTY-THREE

אפיכה אפיכה ארעה אפיכא ארעא דקאים[1] אפיכין כל נידרי ולוטתא
ואשלמתא וחרשי ולוטתא (2) וחרשי ושיקופתא בישתא דישרין
באנשי דנן באפילא בר מחלפתא ויבאיתחיה ובניה וכול דליה
בשום הפכיאיל מלאכא (3) דהפיך לוטתא ואשלמתא וחרשי בישין
דעבדן ליה ולא תישלטון ביתיה דאפילא בר מחלפתא ולא תישילטון
בה בהינדו בת (4) אחתא מין יומא דנן ושעתא דה וילעלם בשום
הפכיאיל ורחמיאיל ועקריאיל ויהזיאיל אתון אעברו דינא
ולוטתא ושיקופתא מין אפילה (5) בר מחלפתא והינדו בת אחתה
ב[שום ק]דוש קדוש קדוש יהוה צבאות מלא כל הארץ כבודו
אמין אמין סלה הלליה לישמך אני עושה

TRANSLATION OF TEXT THIRTY-THREE

Overturned, overturned is the earth. Overturned is the earth which is/was established.[1] Overturned are all vows, curses, spells, cursing black-arts, (2) and evil knocking black-arts which are dwelling among these people-- 'Apila the son of Mahlapta, his wife, his sons, and everything that he has. In the name of Hapki'el, the angel (3) that overturns the curses, spells, and evil black-arts which they have worked against him. Do not prevail against the household of 'Apila the son of Mahlapta--and do not prevail against Hindu[2] the daughter of (4) 'Ahata, from this day and this hour and forever. In the name of Hapki'el, Rahmi'el, ᶜAqri'el, and Yazi'el[3] shall you remove the judgment, the curse, and the knocking from 'Apila (5) the son of Mahlapta and Hindu the daughter of 'Ahata. In [the name of h]oly, holy, holy YHWH of Hosts. All the earth is filled with His glory.[4] Amen. Amen. Selah. Hallelujah! I am acting for Your name.

NOTES ON TEXT THIRTY-THREE

[1]Intending דקים, the scribe wrote דקא, tried to insert the י above the line between the ק and the א, then

changed his mind and finished the passive formation after the extraneous א. In the text appears דְקָאיִם, which Gordon suggests is "somehow corrupted from רקיעא"? (*Orientalia*, X, 1941, p. 118).

²This spelling is attested in Texts Thirty-One and Fifty-Eight. Gordon's reading of הינדוי requires one more letter than the space allowed.

³Or יחניאיל from the root חנן.

⁴Isaiah 6:3.

TEXT THIRTY-FOUR

[אס]ותא מן שמיה לגורוי בר טאטי ולאחת בת דודא איתתיה
דיזח מיניהון מ[ן] די[ה]רתהון שידי ודי[ו]י ברחמי דישמיה
מי בכין דמיתין להון דיחיי להון בכין ויק[רבון] (2)
ומיחי[ן] אישתכחון מן קודם אילי ניסתרתו (ואלי ניסתרתו]
בשום אחה ש.....מיס ומרכבתך על כל האפניס שלח להון
להדרבדו בר ..... (3) אל ריביהון דכל[הון] הא דיותמו
שים בפומי וכל דע .....רין הה בריך¹ אתה יהוה על דיבריח
שום בשום ..... (4) יופיאל שמך יחיאל קרי לך שסנגיאל
יהוה וכן יה[וה]..... שמחת .....[אר]מסה מיטטרון יה בשום
טיגין (5) טריגיס בלביס שבגס שדרפס אילה אינון מלאכיה
דיממטין לאסותא [לכל] בני אינשה אינון (6) יתרן ויפקון
באסותא דהדין בית[ח] וקינינה ודאיתחיה ודיב[נה] ודבנתה
ודכל אינשי ד[בי]חיה (7) להדין גורוי בר טאטי מן יומא
דין ולגליל עלם אמן אמן סלה הלליה

TRANSLATION OF TEXT THIRTY-FOUR

[Sal]vation from the heavens for Guroi the son of Tati and for 'Ahat the daughter of Doda, his wife, so that [demons and de]vils may fly away from them, from [their dwel]ling by the love of the heavens. Who, then, is of their dead ones? (Who) is of their living ones, then? They shall co[me near] (2) and dead ones shall be discovered. From these are you protected. In name has he come .... he has sent to them Hadarbadu the son of ..... (3) to the law-suits of all of [them]. Behold, Diwatmu has placed in my mouth ..... Hah! Blessed[1] art Thou, YHWH, because of the name of .... (4) Yophiel is your name. They call you Yehiel, Sasangiel, YHWH, and thus YHWH ..... names ..... Hermes, Metatron, Yah. In the name of Tigin, (5) Trigis, Balbis, Sabgas, Sadrapas. But these are the angels which bring salvation [to all] the sons of men. They (6) will come and go forth with the salvation of this household and possessions, and of his wife, and of [her] (sic) sons, of her daughters, and of all the people of his (sic) household. (7) [Salvation from the heavens] for this Guroi the son of Ṭaṭi, from this day and for the duration² of eternity. Amen. Amen. Selah. Hallelujah!

NOTES ON TEXT THIRTY-FOUR

¹The text may be transcribed ברוך (Hebrew) or בריך (Aramaic). The same word occurs in several texts which follow.

²Lit., "unfolding."

TEXT THIRTY-FIVE

שמע ישראל יייי אלהינו יייי אחד על פי יייי יחנו ועל פי
יייי יסעו (2) ואת משמרת אבר שמרו על פי יייי בל<י>ד משה
ויאמר יייי אל הסטן יגער יייי (3) בך הסטן יגער יייי בך
הבוחיר בירושלים הלא זה אוד מוצל מאש תוב אסירת ואחידת
אנתי (4) רוחא בישתא ולילית̇א תקיפתא דלא תיתחזן להון
לבריכיהביה בר מאמי והדא איצפנדרמיד בת הותדורא (5) לא
בימה ולא בלילה ולא בכל רמש וצפר ולא בכל שעתה ושעתה ולא
בכל אידיא אידיא אילהין זעי (6) מן קדמיהון ושקולי גיטכי
ופיטורכי וספר תירוככי ואן]יגר[יתכי כמא דכתבין שידין
גיטי[ן] לינשיהון ותוב לא חדרין [עליהון][1]

TRANSLATION OF TEXT THIRTY-FIVE

Hear, O Israel, YHWH is our God, YHWH is One.[2]
According to the command of YHWH they would encamp, and
according to the command of YHWH they would travel. (2)
The observance of the Mighty One they kept according to
the command of YHWH through Moses.[3] And YHWH said to
Satan: May YHWH rebuke (3) you, Satan, may YHWH who chose
Jerusalem rebuke you. Is not this a fire-brand snatched
from the fire?[4] Again, bound and seized are you, (4) evil
spirit and powerful lilith, so that you may not appear to
Brîk-Yah-b^e-Yah[5] the son of Mami and this 'Ispandarmed the
daughter of Hotdora (5) either during the day or during
the night, during any evening or morning, during any hour,
during any time. But depart (6) from their presence and
take your divorce and your separation and your letter of
dismissal. [I have written against] you as demons write
divorces for their wives and furthermore, they do not
return (to them).

NOTES ON TEXT THIRTY-FIVE

[1]Approximately two spirals of letter remain. Most of
the individual letters can be read (cf. Montgomery, p. 209)
but the meaning of them is unclear unless one accepts the

contention of Rossell that the letters form the text of Hosea 2:4-6 (*Handbook*, p. 87 and p. 3).

[2] This translation of Deuteronomy 6:4 is given by Cyrus H. Gordon in *JNES*, Vol. 29, No. 3, July, 1970, p. 198 in an article entitled HIS NAME IS "ONE."

[3] Numbers 9:23.

[4] Zechariah 3:2.

[5] Professor Gordon has given the following explanation of this phrase in a private note: "יהביה is a divine name with 'ב of predication or equivalence' - the literal meaning is 'Yah-is-Yah.'" However, a simpler explanation is possible. The ‍ב may be a reflection of "the traditional Ἰαβε of Theodoret and Epiphanius" (*BDB*, p. 218). If so, these consonants would be pronounced יַהְבֶּיה. Cf. the name Yahu-b^e-Yahu in Text 4.4.

TEXT THIRTY-SIX

בישמך מרי שמיא וארעה מזמן הדין כסא לישמיה דאנור ...ד
בר פרכוי דנישת{י}חן ונישתגר ונישתבב (2) בתר אחת בת נבאזך
אמין כיבשי עלמא לא איתכבישו אילה על ...ית... ישכב גלון
דבר אינשא בליביה דוך ד..קי (3) נסבין חרך ואחרוניאחא דקרי
ענני שימשא מטללן ונורייא כללה ..... ינהו[לן] ורזי רחמתא
ו.רסתנין על ב ..... (4) היא תיפרוסינון על הדאין א[נור..]
בר פרכוי עד דנישתיחן ונישתבב בתר אחת [בת נבאזך]........
רבי שוחאה וברזי רחמתא בדיל ד ..... (5)..... לא פסקין מין
ליביה וקיטרא ..... דוכרניה בשמיה דרחמיאל מלאכה ובשמה
דדליבת עזיזחא מ{ל}אכה ..... אילהי מרתיהון דרזי כולהון
אמין אמ[ין].....

TRANSLATION OF TEXT THIRTY-SIX

In Your name, Lord of heaven and earth, designated is this bowl for the name of 'Anur the son of Parkoi, so that he may become inflamed, heated, and long (2) after 'Ahat the daughter of Nebazak. Amen. Presses of eternity have not been pressed. To her upon ..... let him lie down, let him spend the night. The man has spoken in his heart ..... (3) They are carrying *hrk*, hot spices which they call herbs of the sun, *mtlln*, and pepper .... them and the secrets of love .... (4) She shall sprinkle them on this 'A[nur] the son of Parkoi, until he becomes inflamed and longs after 'Ahat [the daughter of Nebazak] ..... and in lust and in the secrets of love in order that ..... (5) ..... they are not severing from his heart. And the charm ..... in the name of the angel Rahmiel and in the name of Dlibat the powerful[1] angel .... the gods, the ladies[2] of all secrets. Amen. Am[en].

NOTES ON TEXT THIRTY-SIX

[1]Montgomery: "passionate."

[2]מריהון not מרתיהון.

TEXT THIRTY-SEVEN

.... (2) יהוה צבאות לאסותה] ....
מתאניש [(3) בת ראשן דפרק הוית היה (4) פשר מצזן נשני]ן
קציצי אב. רקיעי ..... וחתים (5) למתאניש בת ר]אשן[קמיעה
בשמיה דיהוה צבאות למתאניש בת [רא]שן וצירין (6) מינה מן
בנה מן ביתה מן דירתה כולה פגעין בישין ושידין בישין
ולילייתא בי]ש[תא (7) וכשירה וענק]תה[..... כיפתא ומבכלתא
ובנתא דברא וטומי ובר ניפלא משבענא [עליכון] (8) מידעם
ביש דשרי בביתי[ה] ובדרתיה דחליפאי בר שישין שידא ודרשי
בראי ואסטרובא הני .... (9) ....
קיתא חרסוס אינגע פגע לילי סדרא וטבא ושידי בני טילי וכל
זיקין ומזיקין בישין דדכרנא שמיה]ון ודלא (10) ד[כרנא
שמיהון מומינא ומשבענא ומקימנא וגידנא ומקימנא עליכון
בשמיה מו דקץ שץ מץ בץ קץ קץ קץ בץ ....ין (11) אהיה
אשר אהיה אלהא רבא מיצואה שמו הוא אלהא מרי כל אסותא
דכורסיה מחקן בי שחקי {לשחקים} ועלמיה מחקן ל ....
(12) ביהוה ולתושבחיה ולהימנותיה ולעבדיה הוא אלהא רבא
גיברא ....

TRANSLATION OF TEXT THIRTY-SEVEN

.... (2) YHWH of Hosts for salvation .... [of Metaniš] (3) the daughter of Rešan whom I have delivered .... (4) .... and sealed (5) for Metaniš the daughter of Re[šan]. This amulet is in the name of YHWH of Hosts for Metaniš the daughter of [Re]šan. And bound (6) from her, from her sons, from her house, from all of her dwelling, are evil plagues, evil demons, liliths --evil (7) and KŠYR--and necklace-[charms] .... menstruation, monsters, daughters of the wild, impurities, and miscarriage.[1] I adjure [you], (8) whatever evil that is dwelling in [the] house and the dwelling of Halipai the son of Šiššin, demon, Darši the foreigner, and 'Astroba .... (9) .... leprosy, plague, stroke, orderly and good lilith, demons, ghostly shades,[2] and all evil goblins and injurers [whose] names I am mentioning (10) [and] whose names I am [not] mentioning. I exorcise, adjure, make firm, bind up, and make firm against you in the name of MW, of QS, ŠS, Yah, BS, QS, QS, BS, ... (11) I-am-who-I-am, the great God whose name is Mesoah.³ He is God, the Lord of all salvation, whose throne is established in the heavens.⁴ His universe is established for .... (12) by YHWH and for His praise, for His faithfulness, and for His service. He is the great, the mighty God ....

NOTES ON TEXT THIRTY-SEVEN

¹"Spirit of the still-born child that causes distress and trouble" (Cyrus H. Gordon in class lecture).

²בני טילי equals Hebrew בני צל. For this צ - ט interchange, cf. also קיץ and קיט. This is Arabic ظ as in قَيْظ. Hebrew has two separate roots here: צלל (shade) and טלל (dew).

³Equals מצוה "(sacred) Commandment"?

⁴שַׁחְקָא, pl. שְׁחָקֵי, means "clouds [of heaven]."

TEXT THIRTY-EIGHT

אס⟨י⟩ר וזתים ומחאתם ביתיה וחיי דנא אישפיזא בר ארהא
וינדונדישנט בר (2) איספנדרמיד ותר...[ב]ת סימכוי מן
שאמיש וכימא מן דירא מן סאטנא מן שדא דכירא (3) מן ליליתא
נקיבתא מן רוחין בישין מן חומרא ז⟨י⟩דניתא מן רוח ליליתא
דיכרא ו}א{נקבתא עינאנא דיכרא (4) נקבתא עינא חאסמיתא
עינא דחזי אף בית ליבא רזא דאוד ידיה {חיל בישין} הוא
מרא זא⟨ד⟩נותא מן חיל ביש (5) סניא מן חזינא ט[רו]דא מן
רוחין בישין מן הוא מרא זאדנותה בשם אתאחשת לא ש⟨י⟩די
דיוי חל⟨ו⟩מרא [זידניתא] לא חרמא ..... בישתא ואיתאתיה

TRANSLATION OF TEXT THIRTY-EIGHT

Bound, sealed, and doubly-sealed are the house and
life of this 'Ispiza the son of 'Arha, Yandundišnat the
son of (2) 'Ispandarmed, and ..... the daughter of Simkoi--
from the sun and summer (heat), from the devil, from the
satan, from the male demon, (3) from the female lilith,
from evil spirits, from the impious amulet-spirit, from
the lilith spirit--male or female--the eye of a male (4)
(or) a female, the envious[1] eye, the eye of those who see
even inside the heart, the secret of the fire-brand of his
hand--that impious lord--from the evil, hated army, (5)
from trou[ble]some seer, from evil spirits, from that impious lord. In the name of 'T'HŠT, not demons, devils, [im-
pious] amulet-spirits, or destruction ..... evil and his
wives.

NOTE ON TEXT THIRTY-EIGHT

[1] Or, "begrudging." Cf. also Text 42.9.

TEXT THIRTY-NINE

לישמך אני עושה אסותא מן שמיא תיהוה ליהון לדדאי בת שירין
ולבורזין (2) בת דדאי ותיהסי ברחמי שמיא מן רוחי זידניתא
ומן שידין ומן שובטין ומן פגעין ומן (3) לטבין ומן חיזונין
סניין ומן שידין ומן פגעין ומן בל חיזונין סניין ומן כל
מינין בישין בשום (4) יהוש יהוש יהוש יהוש יהוש יהוש
יהוש יהוש יהוש יהוש יה ותיזיחין .... (5) ותיפקון מן
ביתה ומן דירתה ומן בית מישכבה ומן כל חילמין בישין ומן
חיזונין [סניין ומן מאחין ארבעין] ‹תמנ›יא (6) הדמי קומתא
אומיתי ואשבעיתי עליכון רוחין ושידין וחר[שי בישין ו]מינין
בישין .... (7) ....
יהוה על ימה דסוף בזאתה רופין וחולין לבדך ודברך אעֹבר
.... (8) ..... ין כל מינין בישין וכל
חיזונין סניין ביהוש יה יהוש יה ומ ....

TRANSLATION OF TEXT THIRTY-NINE

I am acting for Your name. Let there be[1] salvation from the heavens for them, for Dadai the daughter of Širin and for Burzin (2) the daughter of Dadai. She will be saved by the mercies of the heavens from impious spirits, from demons, from bands (of spirits), from plagues, from (3) no-good ones, from hated apparitions, from bands (of spirits), from plagues, from all hated apparitions, and from all types of evil. In the name of (4) YHWŠ, YHWŠ, YHWŠ, YHWŠ, YHWŠ, YHWŠ, YHWŠ, YHWŠ, YHWŠ, YHWŠ, YH. And you will go away ..... (5) and depart from her house, from her dwelling, from her bedroom, from all bad dreams, from [hated] apparitions, [and from the two-hundred forty-] ‹eight› (6) members of the body. I make you promise and swear, spirits, demons, [evil black-a]rts, and (all) types of evil .... (7) ....
YHWH. By the Red Sea you have split. Healers and sick ones by yourself. And your word removes ..... (8) .....
.... all types of evil and all hated apparitions. By YHWŠ, YH, YHWŠ, YH.

NOTE ON TEXT THIRTY-NINE

[1]תיהוה or תִּהְיִי‎ (Phonetic spelling for תִּהְיֶה).

TEXT FORTY

באהיא מילי חריא דינדרו ואשלימו ית אבן בר עוי>רתי וית
מחישי בת ..... [וית] רורזיל בת מ<מ>איי (2) מחלפתא
בת ורזין שישין בת טאטי אימי בת עוירתי טאטי בת עוי>רתי
נוכרייתא בת (3) פרסא {די} נדרו ואשלימו לאלהי דישמיא
ולאלה<י> דארעה נדרו ואשלימו (4) לאלהי דיכרי ולאיסתרתא
ניקבתא נדרו ואשלימו לפתכרי (5) ולאיסתרתא נדרו ואשלימו
לבדט בת בדט ברתיה דאדקוי

TRANSLATION OF TEXT FORTY

By 'HY'. The angry words[1] which they have vowed and performed against 'Abn the son of ᶜAwirti, against Mehiši the daughter of ...., against Rurzil the daughter of Ma⟨m⟩ai, (2) Mahlapta the daughter of Warzin, Šisin the daughter of Tati, 'Immi the daughter of ᶜAwirti, Tati the daughter of ᶜAwirti, Nukrayta the daughter of (3) Parsa. They have vowed and performed by[2] the gods of the heavens and the god⟨s⟩ of the earth. They have vowed and performed (4) by[2] the male gods and the female 'Istars. They have vowed and performed by[2] the idols (5) and by[2] the 'Istars. They have vowed and performed by[2] Badat the daughter of Badat, the daughter of 'Adqoi.

NOTES ON TEXT FORTY

[1] Lit., "words of burning." Cf. Proverbs 26:21 for another example of חרר used in the sense of engendering controversy (לְהַרְחַר רִיב).

[2] Or, "for," in the sense of "on behalf of."

TEXT FORTY-ONE

שדין ומישכימין על ד..ר (2) אסירין[1] על זרחיציא לפי כבז
כבי (3) ניא סרגושה[2] ליתזריבן וזדנבן ונתהפכון (4) כל
חרשי בישי וכל מעבד⟨י⟩ תקיפי דעבידין בה (5) ודמיתעבדין
בה באיסקובתיה דברי⟨ך⟩ מריא בר (6) רישינדוך ונתהפכון
על עבדיהון ועל משדרניהון בשוט אל מהמין (7) עוזיאל ועשר
ועזריאל אמן אמן אמן סלה אסותא מן שמיה לאיסקופתיה (8) דבריך
מריא בר רישינדוך דניתבטלון מינ⟨י⟩ה כל סטני בישי וחרשי
בישי ומעבדי תקיפי (9) ושידי ודיוי {ו} ופתכרי לטבי ובני
איגרי מן ביתיה דבריך מריא בר רישינדוך בשום יהיהיהיהיה-
יהיה (10) יהיהיהיהיהיה יהיהיהיהיהיהיה אשבעת עליכון
את בר איגרי[3] קלילא איסרה טבא דאישתמש בביתיה (11) די
בריך מריא בר רישינדוך דניתבטל מן ביתיה די בריך מריא בר
רישינדוך בש[ום א]דניאל ורוח. מן כורמין (12) מן בור
אדסבוך ובר יומין ותיקא {ותיקא} בטילי כל סני ופתכרי
ושידי ודיוי כל מעבדי ביש[י מן א]יסקופתיה (13) דבריך
מריא בר רישינדוך בשום אדניאל חד מן כורמין אמן אמן אמן
סלה

TRANSLATION OF TEXT FORTY-ONE

Cast out and thrust upon D..R, (2) bound upon Zar-
ḥisiya' according to ... ... (3) ... .
...... and let be overturned (4) all evil black-arts and
all powerful (magical) practices which have been worked
(5) and which are now being worked against the threshold
of Brî⟨k⟩-Marya the son of (6) Rišinduk. Let them be
overturned upon the ones who are working them and upon the
ones who are sending them, in the name of 'El the Trust-
worthy, (7) ᶜUzzi'el, ᶜŠR, and ᶜAzri'el. Amen. Amen.
Selah. Salvation from the heavens for the threshold (8)
of Brîk-Marya the son of Rišinduk, so that all bad satans,
evil black-arts, powerful (magical) practices, (9) demons,
devils, idols, no-good ones, and roof-spirits may be abolished from him, from the house of Brîk-Marya the son of
Rišinduk, in the name of YHYHYHYHYHYH (10) YHYHYHYHYHYH-
YH YHYHYHYHYHYH. I have adjured you (pl.), you (sg.)

fleet[4] son of roofs, the good prince who has officiated[5] in the house (11) of Brîk-Marya the son of Rišinduk, so that he may be abolished from the house of Brîk-Marya the son of Rišinduk. In the nam[e of 'A]dani'el and the one[6] from Kurmin, (12) from BWR 'DSBWK and the son of days[7] and safety. Abolished are all haters, idols, demons, devils, (and) all ba[d] practices [from the th]reshold (13) of Brîk-Marya the son of Rišinduk, in the name of 'Adani'el, one from Kurmin. Amen. Amen. Amen. Selah.

NOTES ON TEXT FORTY-ONE

[1] Or, אטירין, i.e., "bent."

[2] "Prince of the Soil"?

[3] The "lunatic" of the Syriac New Testament is one "possessed by a roof spirit." Cf. Matthew 17:15. The same expression is found also in Matthew 4:24.

[4] Or, "cursed."

[5] Or, "made use of."

[6] דה for הד.

[7] Euphemism for עתיק יומין?

TEXT FORTY-TWO

מזמן הודי⟨י⟩ן[1] קמי⟨ע⟩א {י} לאסותא לאיסקופתיה ול[ביתיה
ד]בריך מרי{י}א בר (2) רישינדוך ולדוסתאי בת דודאי{י}
{לנט} ולנטרתא להון ולבניהון לבנתהון דניחסון בעגלא (3)
ב[2]רחמי שמיה פגפג מיאיס שהוא מבריח את כל הוררווות[1] {וכל
הורוח[1]} בין זכר רבין נקיבא ששינא אח (4) מקומר ויבא
למקום שאל⟨י⟩נו מקומו דימי בראשית ות.והובעיירכיאיס וגעיאיס
והטי.אים וניקבה (5) באיסקופתיה דבריך מריא בר רישינדוך
יהי גוער ויהי אסור ויהי מנודא ויהי נזוף אותו הורוח[1]
מיפני ביד ייי (6) בדבר אילוה ובמאמר קודוש אמן אמן סלה
משבענא לכון מלאכין קדישין טבין ומהימנין צלל דלל קלל[3]
אמללאלל אמליל אמליאל אמללאל (7) דתינטטרון יח בריך
מריה (sic) בר {דוסתאי} רישינדוך רית דרשתאל⟨י⟩ בר (sic)
דודאי איח{י}היה רית בניהון רית בנתהון רית בעיררהון רית
קיניונהון רית (8) כל איסקופת ביתיהון [מ]יד סמאל וקפפיאל
מלאכי חבלתא ומיד כל חרשין בישין ומעבדין תקיפין ומיד כל
זיקין ומזיקין בישין ומיד כל רוחין ושידין ודל⟨י⟩וין (9)
ולילין ומיד כל פתכרין וטעין ומיד לוטחא וקריתא ונידרא
ואשלמתא ומיד עינ⟨נ⟩א בישתא וחסמתא ומיד כל [מ]ידעם ביש
בשו[ם] אדמדמי אופיח (10) אמיא דווד יאהודא וירוח אמן אמן
סלה {אא.}. אסותא מן שמיה ויאמר {ויאמר} יהוה אל הסטן
יגער {יהסט} יהוה בך הסטן יגער יהו{ו}ה בך {הב} הבוהיר
בירושולים הלא (11) זא (sic)[א]וד {א}וד} מוצל [מאש]
..... דבריך מריה(sic) בר רישינדוך ודדוסתאי בת דודא
איתחיה ומן בניהון ומן בנתהון מן בע⟨י⟩רהון ומן קינינהון
דלא יקרבו לאיסקופתא כל מידעם ביש (12) אמן [אמ]ן סלה
הלוליה (sic) ברוך אתה יהוה רפא חולי כל בשר ומיפלא⟨ה⟩
לעשות אמן אמן סלה

TRANSLATION OF TEXT FORTY-TWO

   This amu⟨le⟩t is designated as salvation for the threshold and for [the house of] Brîk-Marya the son of (2) Rišinduk, and for Dustai the daughter of Dodai, and as protection for them, for their sons (and) for their daughters, so that they may be saved speedily (3) by the mercies of the heavens. PGPG MY'YS is he who puts to

flight every spirit, whether male or female, which has
changed (4) its place and has come to a place which is not
its own from the days of creation. WT.WHWB^{c}YRKY'YS WG^{c}Y'YS
WHṬY.'YM and female (5) in the threshold of Brîk-Marya the
son of Rišinduk. Let that spirit be rebuked, bound, excom-
municated, and banned from my presence by the authority of
YYYY, (6) by the Word of God and by a holy commandment. Amen.
Amen. Selah. I adjure you, holy, good, and faithful angels
ṢLL, DLL, QLL, 'MLL'LLL, 'MLYLL, 'MLY'L, 'MLL'L, (7) that you
guard Brîk-Marya the son of Rišinduk and Dustai the son (sic)
of Dodai, his wife, their sons, their daughters, their cattle,
their possessions, and (8) the entire threshold of their
house from the hand of Sama'el and Qaṣpi'el, the angels of
destruction, from the hand of all evil black-arts and powerful (magical) practices, from the hand of all evil blast-
demons and harmers, from the hand of all spirits, demons,
devils, (9) and lilis, from the hand of all idols and errors
(?), from the hand of the curse, the invocation, the vow,
and the spell, from the hand of the evil and envious eye, and
from everything bad. In the name of 'DMDMY, 'WPYT, (10) 'MY',
DWWD, Y'TWD', WYRWḤ, Amen. Amen. Selah. Salvation from the
heavens. And YHWH said to Satan: May YHWH rebuke you,
Satan, may YHWH who chose Jerusalem rebuke you. Is not (11)
this a [fir]e-brand snatched [from the fire]?[4] ..... of Brîk-
Marya the son of Rišinduk and of Dustai the daughter of Dodai,
his wife, from their sons, from their daughters, from their
cattle, and from their possessions, so that nothing bad may
come near to the threshold. (12) Amen. [Am]en. Selah.
Hallelujah! Blessed art Thou, YHWH, Healer of the sick of
all people, Performer of miracles. Amen. Amen. Selah.

NOTES ON TEXT FORTY-TWO

[1] The Hebrew definite article, to be read הן before the
ה. Cf. also Gordon's notes in *Orientalia*, X, 1941, p. 129.

[2] Or, כ.

[3] The first letters of these three words form the word
צדק.

[4] Zechariah 3:2.

TEXT FORTY-THREE

תוב ועורין כולהון פתיכרי דיכרי וניקבתא וחרשי ונידרי
ולוטתא ורוחה בישתא אסירין ופכירין וחיתימין סכירין פומהון
{ומטרשן} ועורין עיניהון ומטרשן אודניהון דלא לישמעון
עלוה על אמטור בת שלתא ועל זרעוה ועל ביתוה פקיניני֯ה (2)
אסירין מן ידהון דלא יהלכון ופכירין מן רינלהון דלא ישפון
{כבישין דישין ודריכין בשום} כבישין דישין ודריכין כל
פתיכרי ואיסתרתא כל ביידני קשיי וחרשי ומעבדי ונידרי
ולוטתא ושדא דשדרתא ורוחי בישתא דלא (3) ניחטון בה באמטור
בת שלתא ובזרעוה ובביתוה ובקיניג<ו>ה הא אסירין וחיתימין
כולהון בשום אהאהאה אמן אמן סלה יהוה יהוה יהוה אל שדי
אל שדי אל שדי בשום אאה אאה אאה בשום שמא רבא אסירין
שמיה (4) וארעא ורתיחנין כולהון דלא ישתרון נשקין יהיהיה
והון ובישדריה דמלכה רבא בשושילחא דפרזלא ועברא בשום אזא
מפא לכף בכבשיאל מלאכה בצוריאל מלאכה בגבריאל מלאכה בארי אל
מלאכה בדניאל (5) מלאכה {בצוריאל מלאכה} ברדטיייאל מלאכה
בברקיאל מלאכה ברחמיאל באדאניאל אחרן כולכון מלאכין קדישין
בחירין דכין וקדישין ניצחנין וידתינין מומינא עליכון (6)
מומא רבא ומשבענא עליכון שבועתא רבתא דחיזיהון ות<לע<ברון
ותבטלון כל חרשי וכל פתכרי ואיסתרתא ונידרי ולוטתא ושדא
דשדרתא וכל (7) רוח פריח ושכין בן דמישתדרין ובן ו דלא
מישתדרין דיכלון מן אמטור בת שלתא ומן זרעוה ומן ביתוה
פקינינוה ויזלון (8) ויתהפכון על עבדיהון ועל משדרניהון
מן יומא דנן ולעלם אמן אמן סלה

TRANSLATION OF TEXT FORTY-THREE

Again, blinded are all idols, male and female, black-arts, vows, curses, and the evil spirit. They are bound, tied, and sealed. Their mouths are shut, their eyes are blinded, and their ears are deafened so that they will not hear (anything) against 'Amṭur the daughter of Šilta, against her offspring, against her house, and her possessions. (2) They are bound by their hand so that they may not walk (sic) and they are tied by their foot so that they may not move.[1] Conquered, thrashed, and down-trodden are

all idols and Istars, all hard ...... black-arts, (magical)
practices, vows, curses, the column of the spine, and evil
spirits, so that they may not (3) sin against 'Amtur the
daughter of Šilṭa; against her offspring, against her household, and against her possessions. Lo, all of them are
bound and sealed in the name of 'H'H'H. Amen. Amen. Selah.
YHWH. YHWH. YHWH. 'El Šaddai. 'El Šaddai. 'El Šaddai.
In the name of ''H. ''H. ''H. In the name of the Great
Name are bound the heavens (4) and the earth. All of them
are terrified so that weapons may not be released. YHYHYH.
WHWH. And by the rope of the great king, by the chain of
iron and lead. In the name of 'Z', MP', for a sole/palm.
By Kabši'el the angel, by Suri'el the angel, by Gabri'el the
angel, by 'Ari'el the angel, by Dani'el (5) the angel, by
Suri'el the angel, by RDTYWI'el the angel, by Barqi'el the
angel, by Raḥmi'el, by 'Adani'el. You, all of you angels--
holy, chosen, pure, holy, glorious, and religious--I adjure
you (6) with the great oath and I make you swear the great
promise that you will turn away, remove, and abolish all
black-arts, all idols, 'Istars, vows, curses, the column of
the spine, and every (7) flying and resting spirit, whether
they are sent or not sent, so that they may cease from 'Amtur
the daughter of Šilṭa, from her offspring, from her household, and her possessions, and go (8) and be overturned upon
the ones who are working them and upon the ones who are sending them from this day and forever. Amen. Amen. Selah.

NOTE ON TEXT FORTY-THREE

[1]Lit., "skip."

TEXT FORTY-FOUR

בישמוך מרי אסותא ברי<א> [1] ואסותא מרל<י> ש[נ]תא ולמאמא (2)
בת דודי מן איסור[א] [2] דילהו [3] מן קולי וש.. והת[ל]ו[מ]ל<י<ן
עו... דילהו [3] מן (3) שוש<י<לחא דפרזלא מן כוכבתא מנורתא
דנפלת וכבישא מן ל<ו<טחא (4) ואנקתא קריחא ושקופתא מן
בגיתא [4] וסטנא ומן מרכבתא בישתא אסירין והתימ<י<ן (5) מן
{מ}מכתא וחשוכה מן שמתא ואיסורא ומן אול<י [5] בזמנא מלכא
רע (sic) וחתמתא דארעה (6) מן חתמתא דירקיעה ומן ש<י<די
ודיוי מן {לוט} ל<ו<טחא ואע<נ<קתא וקריתא ושיקופתא מן
{מן} כל מידעם (7) ביש{י} אסיר וחתים בחתמא ויחירומא
ארעה ושמיה קדם שמיה יחיב עליהון וב . . זרף .... רבא
אבחמש<י<ן [6] (8) רגופא רבא אהדר {ר} מידעם ביש< ית אסותא מן
שמיה לדודי בת ממא (sic) {מן} מ<א<חת<ל<י<ן ארבל<ע<י<ן ותמניא
הדמין דית (9) בה ברי<א< אסותא ..... לד<ו<די בת מאמא
ברי<א< אסותא ופשרתא אחדר לוטחא ואקנתא {מן לוטחא} והתים
ומן (10) לוטחא דנתחת[ום כל א[ו]רעא ..... ברי<י<ה ..... א׳
אלכ...אל בישמיה דא ... כ ... באר ..... ביש מן גבריאל<ל<
ומכל מרעאיל אמן אמן סלה

TRANSLATION OF TEXT FORTY-FOUR

In Your name, Lord of salvation. (Let there be)
health and salvation, Lord of ye[ar]s, even for Mama (2)
the daughter of Dodai from her bond; from sounds[7] and ...
..... of her; from (3) the chain of iron; from the shining
star which has fallen and is conquered; from the curse,
(4) the necklace-charm, the invocation, and the knocking;
from the rebellion and the satan; and from the evil chariot.
Bound and sealed (5) from the wound and darkness, from the
ban and the bond, from ..... the evil king and the seal of
the earth, (6) from the seal of the firmament, from de-
[m]ons and devils, from the curse, the necklace-charm, the
invocation, and the knocking, from everything (7) bad.
Bound and sealed with the seal, the ban, the earth, and the
heavens. Before the heavens, sitting upon them. ....
the great 'BHMSYN[8] (8) RGWP' the great has turned back
everything evil. ..... Salvation from the heaven: for Dodai

the daughter of Mama, two-hundred forty-eight members which
are (9) in her. Health (and) salvation .... for
Dodai the daughter of Mama. Health, salvation, and release.
He has turned back the curse and the necklace-charm. From
the curse. And sealed even from (10) the curse with which
[the whole ea]rth is sealed .... her son ....
in the name of .... evil. From Gabri'e[l]
and Micha'el. MR^c'YL. Amen. Amen. Selah.

NOTES ON TEXT FORTY-FOUR

[1] Cf. Line five.

[2] Cf. Line nine.

[3] Lit., "which is to her" or "of her."

[4] בניתא for בנידא "rebellion, faithlessness."

[5] Or, קטלי "chains"?

[6] Gordon reads אפחם..י֯ (*Orientalia*, X, 1941, p. 129).

[7] Or, "voices."

[8] "Father of the Fifty"?

TEXT FORTY-FIVE

קפרגיה פרגיה רגיה גיה יה ה (2) רחואהמית יהוה צבאות
דנת[הפכ]ון (3) רחשיה דאכרכוי בר מאמא לעבדיהון [.......
ולמ[שדרניהון (4) בשום יה יהו אהיה יהוה אמן א[מן סלה]

TRANSLATION OF TEXT FORTY-FIVE

QPRGYH, PRGYH, RGYH, GYH, YH, H. (2) RHW'HMYT YHWH of Hosts, that there may be ove[rturn]ed (3) the black-arts of 'Akarkoi the son of Mama upon the ones who are practicing them .... and upon the ones who are sending them. (4) In the name of YH, YHW, 'HYH, YHWH. Amen. A[men. Selah].

TEXT FORTY-SIX

אסותא וחולמנא תיהוי לה לאיסקופתיה (2) דהורמזדד בר דודי
דיזיעון מינה חרשי ומעבדי סניי ורשיפי חרשי (3) דמערבה
ומדנחא חרשי ציפונא ודרומא חרשי דמאה עסרין ושבע מדינתא
חרשי (4) דריעיא .... זוער ואיתבהילו ואישתממתו
מן קיטריכון ומן עובדי דאיתעבדתון (5) ויתנטר הדין הורמזדד
מן כל מדעט ביש ראסותא¹ חתימא ומחתמא קומתיה דיתעיתריך
ארבעין וחמנא הדמי [קומתיה]............. (6) ....
הורמזדד ..... ניתבחנה יתח....ית

TRANSLATION OF TEXT FORTY-SIX

Let there be salvation and soundness for the threshold (2) of Hormizdad the son of Dodai. Let black-arts and hated practices depart from him and ..... black-arts (3) of the west and east, black-arts of the north and south, black-arts of the one-hundred twenty-seven provinces, black-arts (4) of the pasture .... Depart! Hurry off! Be banished from your (magical) knots, from the practices by which you have been bewitched, (5) and let this Hormizdad be preserved from everything bad. And salvation. Sealed and doubly-sealed is his body .... of the two-hundred forty-eight members of [his body] .... (6) .... Hormizdad ....

NOTE ON TEXT FORTY-SIX

[1]This and two following phrases are enclosed by lines apparently drawn by the scribe in an attempt to draw attention to them for reasons not known.

TEXT FORTY-SEVEN

Case

אודון בבליס
אלוה יייי
ממרור
איסתרין במובא

מזמן הדין קמיעה לאסותא לנטרתא ולחתמתא דביתיה
דפרוך בר ארזניש דיר{י}תיה כולה הדא היא עיזקתא דשלמה מלכה בר
(2) דויד דאניש לא מצי מזולא לאחס ואינש קדמה לא קאים לכל
שידא ולבו ולנבו לשידי ולבר אינרי ולכל ירורי ליליין
ומבכלין ולכל סטני ופתכרי ולוטתא ושיפורי ושמתחא (3)
וחומרי ורוחי וירורי ונאלי ולטבי ובאלבי ובני איגרי ורוחי
טומאה וללילין דיכרי וניקבתא כולהון אסירין וחתימין להון
לפרוך בר ארזניש לאחתא בת קאקאי למירים בת אזוחא לארזניש
בת אחתא (4) גריגני ומרבה בני אחתא ולבחדשבה בת אחתא
ולביחלי>ה כוליה ולדירתיה כולה מן יומא דין ולעולום (sic)
אמן אמן סלה

TRANSLATION OF TEXT FORTY-SEVEN

Case

'WDWN BBLYS
God the Lord
MMRWR
Istars BMWB'

This amulet is designated for the salvation, for the guarding, and for the sealing of the house of Parruk the son of 'Araznis̆ (and) all of his dwelling. This is the signet-ring of King Solomon the son of (2) David, the luck of which no one has mastered[1]--By 'HS[2]--and before which no one is standing. Every demon, Bo, Nebo, demons, roof-spirits, all howlers, lilis, monsters, all satans, idols, curses, excommunications, bans, (3) pebble-charms, spirits, howlers, incubi, no-good ones, bâlbê, roof-spirits, spirits of uncleanliness, and lilis male and female--all of them are bound and sealed for Parruk the son of 'Arazniš, for 'Ahata the daughter of Qaqai, for Miriam the daughter of 'Ahata, for 'Arazniš the daughter of 'Ahata, (4) GRYGNY and Marabba the sons of 'Ahata, for BTHDŠBH the daughter of 'Ahata, and for all his[3] house and all his dwelling, from this day and forever. Amen. Amen. Selah.

NOTES ON TEXT FORTY-SEVEN

[1]Gordon (*AOR*, VI, 1934, p. 322) has translated this phrase "to which no one can go," and has read לאחם rather than לאחס.

[2]Perhaps the magician wanted to clue in the reader concerning the mysterious words written in the case. The first line becomes חפף מט ש שכמח by *Athbash*, a principle the magician assumes anyone would know. These letters are in turn to be deciphered according to the rule of אחס and thus become חיל רע נ נדרא: "An evil army is the curse." For רע instead of ביש in these texts, cf. Text 44.5.

Case Line three becomes יינפנ by *Athbash* and יייי by 'Aḥas.

Case Line four becomes איסתרי טשיפשת by *Athbash* and איסתרי בנגינא: "the Istars are in defeat" = "defeated" by 'Aḥas.

On this case, cf. my article, "Some Cryptograms In the Aramaic Incantation Bowls" (*JNES*, 33, 1974), pp. 405-407.

[3]Referring to Parruk.

TEXT FORTY-EIGHT

שידא נטיא טטיא קליא בתיא נוריאל צור קדיש (2) חתימין ומחתמין
ומסגן אחת בת אימא רבי ומלכי ודיפשי בני אחת ויניי (3) בת
אחת ואח[ת] בת אימא ואטיונא בר קרקוי וקרקוי. בת שילתא
ושילתא בת אימי (4) אינון וביתיהון ובניהון וקינינהון
חתיהין בעיזקתא דאל שדי בריך הוא ובעיזקתא דשלמוה (5)
מלכא בר דויד דעבד עיבידתא בשידי דיכרי ובליליתא ניקבתא
חתימין ומחתמין ומסגן מן שידא דיכרא (6) ומן ליליתא ניקבתא
ומן [עב]דא ומן לוטתא ומן קריתא ומן אישתקופתא ומן עינא
בישתא ומן חרשין בישין מן חרשי אימא (7) וברתא ומן חרשי
כלתא וחמתא ומן חרשי איתתא זידניתא מחשכא עינין ומפחא
נפש ומן חרשי בישי דעל ידי אינשא (8) מיתעבדין ומן כל
מידעם ביש בשום יהוה יהוה צבאות שמו אמן אמן סלה הדין
קמיעה לבטלא שידא טיטינוס ח{י}תימין פגרי דעש (9) ופגרי
קל פגרי דעש קל מילי מילי אתינלא

TRANSLATION OF TEXT FORTY-EIGHT

The demon NTY', TTY', QLY', BTY', Nuri'el, Holy Rock.
(2) Sealed, doubly-sealed, and fortified are 'Ahat the daughter of 'Imma; Rabbi, Malki, and Dipši the sons of 'Ahat; Yanai
(3) the daughter of 'Ahat, 'Aha[t] the daughter of 'Imma,
'Atyona the son of Qarqoi, Qarqoi the daughter of Šilta, and
Šilta the daughter of 'Imma—(4) they, their houses, their
children, and their possessions are sealed with the signet-
ring of 'El Šaddai, blessed be He, and with the signet-ring of
King (5) Solomon the son of David, who worked spells on male
demons and female liliths. (They are) sealed, doubly-sealed,
and fortified against the male demon, (6) the female lilith,
the [sp]ell, the curse, the invocation, the knocking, the evil
eye, and evil black-arts—against the black-arts of mother (7)
and daughter, against the black-arts of daughter-in-law and
mother-in-law, against the black-arts of the impious woman who
darkens the eyes and blows away the life, against the evil
black-arts which are practiced by (8) men, and against everything bad. In the name of YHWH, YHWH of Hosts is His name.
Amen. Amen. Selah. This amulet is to abolish the demon

Titinos. Sealed are the bodies of ᶜṢ (9) and the bodies of
ᶜṢ QL, the bodies of ᶜṢ QL. MYLY, MYLY, 'TYGL'.

TEXT FORTY-NINE

(2) .... אסותא מן שמיא ....
(3) וחתמתה ונטרתא לדירתיה ולאיסקופתיה (4) ולמותביה
[ול]ביתיה ודאיסקופתיה דחדין פרוכדד בר זבינתא (5) וד-
קאמוי בת זארק וכל שום דאית להון דיתנטרון פרוכדד דנן
בר (6) זבינתא וקאמוי דא בת זארק אינון ובניהון ותנתחון
ותוריהון וחימאריהון ועבדיהון (7) ואמחתהון וכל בעירד
דרבא וזעירא דאית בהדא דירתא ואיסקופתא דאית בה ודהוי
בה [מיכען] (8) ועד עלם ויבטלון מינה דהדא דירתא ואיס-
קופתא דחדין פרוכדד בר זבינתא ודקאמוי בת זארק חרשין
(9) ארמאין חרשין יהודאין חרשין טיאעין חרשין פרסאין
חרשין הינדאין חרשין יונאין חרשין די כיתין חרשין (10)
דמיתעבדין בשבעין לישנין בין דאיתתא ובין דגברא כולהון
שביתין ובטילין מן מימריה דאל קנא ונוקים הוא דשלח (11)
עזא ועזאל ומיטטרון איסרא רבא דכורסיה אינון ייתון
וינטרון דירתיה ואיסקופתיה דפרוכדד בר זבינתא ויקאמוי
בת זארק (12) וניתקימון בה בהדא איסקופתא בנין ובנן
ותורין וחימארין ופר<ו>כדד דנן בר זבינתא וקאמוי דא בת
זארק ובניהון ובנתהון ועבדיהון ואמחתהון (13) בין דיכרי
ובין ניקבאתא וגמלי ורכשי ותורי וחימארי וכל בעירא רברבא
וזעירא וכל מידועם דאית בה ודחאוי בה בהדא (א>יסקופתא
ויתפתחון להון לחדין פרוכדד דנן בר זבינתא ולקאמוי דא
אינתתיה בת זארק תרעי דימזונה מארבע כנפי ארעה מילעילא
ומילרע בישמיה דכבשיאל מלאכה דהוא כביש כל (15) מידועם
ביש מן איסקופתיה דחדין פרוכדד בר זבינתא ודקאמוי דא
בת זארק (א) יהוה שמו אמן אמן סלה

TRANSLATION OF TEXT FORTY-NINE

.... (2) .... Salvation from the heavens, (3) and sealing and protection for the dwelling, for the threshold, (4) for the residence, [for] the house, and for the threshold of this Parrukdad the son of Zebinta (5) and for[1] Qamoi the daughter of Zaraq, and everything which they have, that they may be guarded--this Parrukdad the son of (6) Zebinta and this

Qamoi the daughter of Zaraq, they, their sons, their daughters, their oxen, their donkeys, their slaves, (7) their handmaidens, and all large or small cattle which is in this dwelling and threshold--which is in it and which is going to be in it--[from now] (8) and forever. And there will cease from this dwelling and threshold of this Parrukdad the son of Zebinta and of Qamoi the daughter of Zaraq, Aramean (9) black-arts, Jewish black-arts, Arabic black-arts, Persian black-arts, Indian black-arts, Greek black-arts, black-arts of the Romans, black-arts (10) which are practiced in the seventy languages, either by woman or by man. All of them are brought to an end and annulled by the command of the jealous and avenging God, the One who sent (11) ᶜAzza, ᶜAzzael, and Meṭaṭron, the Great Prince of His throne. They will come and guard the dwelling and threshold of Parrukdad the son of Zebinta and of Qamoi the daughter of Zaraq. (12) And let there be preserved on this threshold sons, daughters, oxen, donkeys, and this Parrukdad the son of Zebinta and this Qamoi the daughter of Zaraq, and their sons, their daughters, their slaves, their handmaidens--(13) both male and female-- and camels, steeds, oxen, donkeys, all large or small cattle, and everything there is or is going to be on this threshold. And there will be opened for this (14) Parrukdad the son of Zebinta and for this Qamoi his wife, the daughter of Zaraq, the gates of sustenance from the four corners of the earth, from above and below. In the name of the angel Kabši'el, who conquers everything (15) bad from the threshold of this Parrukdad the son of Zebinta and of this Qamoi the daughter of Zaraq. YHWH is His name. Amen. Amen. Selah.

NOTE ON TEXT FORTY-NINE

[1]Lit., "of."

TEXT FIFTY

חתים ומ[חת]ם ביתיה דזידין שבור בר איליׄשבא בשבעין קיטרין
{בשם} (2) בשבעין איסרין בשבעין חתמין בש[ו]שירא בזוזמרי
בעיזקתיה דיוכברזיוא בר רבי ובעיזקתיה (3) דכסדיאל גברא
מלאכא איסרא דכסדאי ובעיזקתיה דמיכאל גברא מלאכה איסרא
דאוריתא ובעיזקתיה דגבריאל (4) גברא מלאכה איסרא דנורא
ובעיזקתיה דאספנדס דיוא גינאה דישלומה מלכה בר דאויד
ובעיזקתיה דישלומה מלכה בר דאויד} {ובעיזקחה (5) ובעיזקתיה
דישלומה מלכה בר דאויד} ובחתמא ר[ב]א דמרי עלמא דלא
קיטריה מישתרי ולא חתמיה מיתבר ברוך אתא יהוה אלהי ישראל
אמן אמן סלח (6) תוב חתים ומחתם ביתיה דזידין שבור בר
איליׄשבה בשבעין ריטרין בשבעין איסרין בשבעין חתמין בשושירא
בזוזמרי בעיזקתיה דיוכברזיוא בר רבי (7) ובעיזקתיה [ד]-
כסד[יא]ל [גברא מלאכה איסר]א דכסד(י>אל ובעיז[ק]תיה ד-
מיכאל גבר[א] מלאכא איסרא דאוריתא ובעיזקתיה דגבריאל
גברא מלאכה איסרא דנורא ובעיזקתיה (8) דאספנדס דיוא גינאה
דשלומה מל[כ]א ב[ר ד]אויד ובעיז[קתיה] דישלומה מלכה בר
דאויד ובחתמא רבא [ד]מרי עלמא דלא ריטרי משתרי ולא חתמיה
מיתבר ברוך אתא יהוה אלהי ישראל אמן אמן סלח

TRANSLATION OF TEXT FIFTY

Sealed and dou[bly-se]aled is the house of Zidin Šabor the son of 'Elišeba, with seventy knots, (2) with seventy bonds, with seventy seals, with the twisted chain, with ZWZMRY,[1] with the signet-ring of Yokabarziwa the son of Rabbe, with the signet-ring (3) of Kasdi'el the mighty[2] angel, the Prince of the Chaldeans, with the signet-ring of Michael the mighty angel, the Prince of the Law, with the signet-ring of Gabriel (4) the mighty angel, the Prince of Fire, with the signet-ring of 'Aspanadas-Diwa, the jinnee of King Solomon the son of David, and with the signet-ring of King Solomon the son of David, (5) {and with the signet-ring of King Solomon the son of David}, with the g[re]at seal of the Lord of the Universe whose knot cannot be untied and whose seal cannot be broken. Blessed art Thou, YHWH, God of Israel. Amen. Amen. Selah. (6) Again, sealed

and doubly-sealed is the house of Zidin Šabor the son of
'Elišeba, with seventy knots, with seventy bonds, with
seventy seals, with the twisted chain, with ZWZMRY, with the
signet-ring of Yokabarziwa the son of Rabbe, (7) with the
signet-ring [of] Kasdi['e]l [the mighty angel, the Prin]ce
of the Chaldeans, with the sig[net]-ring of Michael the
mighty angel, the Prince of the Law, with the signet-ring of
Gabriel the mighty angel, the Prince of Fire, with the
signet-ring (8) of 'Aspanadas-Diwa, the jinnee of King
Solomon the so[n of D]avid, with the sig[net-ring] of King
Solomon the son of David, and with the great seal [of] the
Lord of the Universe whose knot cannot be untied and whose
seal cannot be broken. Blessed art Thou, YHWH, God of
Israel. Amen. Amen. Selah.

NOTES ON TEXT FIFTY

[1] Two fellow students have suggested possible readings
for this phrase. John Lawrenz suggested "coin of my Lord."
Bill Bixler suggested "Zeus my Lord."

[2] Reading גַבְרָא not גַּבְרָא throughout the text.

TEXT FIFTY-ONE

חתים ומחתם ביתיה ובוסתניה {דא} דזידין שבור בר אילישבה
בשבעין {קיט} קיטרין בשבעין איסרין בשבעין חתמין בשרשירא
בזוזמרי באיזקתיה דלי<וכברזיוא בר רבי ובעיזקתיה דכסדיאל
גברא מלאכה איסרא דכסדאי ובעיזקתיה דגבריאל גברא מלאכה
איסרא דנורא ובעיזקתיה דאספנדדירא גינאה דישלומה מלכה בר
דאו<י>ד ובעיזקתיה דישלומה מלכה בר דא̇יד ובחתמא רבא דמרי
עלמא [ד]לא ריטריה מישתרי ולא חתמיה מיתבר ברוך אתא יהוה
אלהי ישראל אמן אמן סלה חתים ומחתם ביתיה ובוסתניה דזידין
שבור בר אילישבא בשבעין ריטרין בשבעין איסרין בשבעין חתמין
בשרשירא בזוזמרי בעי[ז]קתיה דיוכברזיוא בר רבי ובעיזקתיה
דכסדיאל גברא מלאכה איסרא דכסדאי ובעיזקתיה דמיכאל גברא
מלאכה איסרא דאורי[ת]א ובעיזקתיה דגבריאל גברא מלאכה
איסרא דנורא ובעיזקתיה דאספנדס דירא גינאה דישלומה מלכה
בר דאויד ובחתמא רבא דמרי עלמא דלא קיטריה[]מי שתרי ו[לא
חתמיה מיתבר ברוך אתא יהוה אלהי ישראל אמן אמן סלה

TRANSLATION OF TEXT FIFTY-ONE

Sealed and doubly-sealed are the house and garden of Zidin Šabor the son of 'Elišeba, with seventy knots, with seventy bonds, with seventy seals, with the twisted chain, with ZWZMRY,[1] with the signet-ring of Yokabarziwa the son of Rabbe, with the signet-ring of Kasdi'el the mighty angel, the Prince of the Chaldeans, with the signet-ri[ng] of Gabriel the mighty angel, the Prince of Fire, with the signet-ring of 'Aspanadas-Diwa the jinnee of King Solomon the son of David, and with the signet-ring of King Solomon the son of David, with the great seal of the Lord of the Universe [whose] knot cannot be untied and whose seal cannot be broken. Blessed art Thou, YHWH, God of Israel. Amen. Amen. Selah. Sealed and doubly-sealed are the house and garden of Zidin Šabor the son of 'Elišeba, with seventy knots, with seventy bonds, with seventy seals, with the twisted chain, with ZWZMRY,[1] with the sig[net]-ring of Yokabarziwa the son of Rabbe, with the signet-ring

of Kasdi'el the mighty angel, the Prince of the Chaldeans,
with the signet-ring of Michael the mighty angel, the Prince
of the La[w], with the signet-ring of Gabriel the mighty
angel, the Prince of Fire, with the signet-ring of 'Aspanadas-
Diwa the jinnee of King Solomon the son of David, and with
the great seal of the Lord of the Universe whose knot cannot
b[e untied and] whose seal cannot be broken. Blessed art
Thou, YHWH, God of Israel. Amen. Amen. Selah.

NOTE ON TEXT FIFTY-ONE

[1]Cf. Note one to Text Fifty.

TEXT FIFTY-TWO

אסירין[1] ומסירין כל זיקין ומזיקין בישין .... י יבטלון
(2) חרשי יתבדרון עובדי יתחפכון חרשי לעבדיהון אתרוס פ
בתרוס (3) פתרוס מתרוס יאוסס אפסוס ביסס ביתוס ואדמסס
חרי בדיקולא (4) בזייא לפומיכי חרשתא נשי מיביד בירתי
מישמי קדורתי תלתאהון מלאכא (5) דחד אקוק וחד מקוק וחד
פכיר תלי בסיכתא דמישפלי דמידלי דמיטוטיניזופי גרמי (6)
שתרפי איסירי ידי וריגלי דגברי ודנשי דעבדו דביש לבריכ-
יהביה דנן ודעבדין דביש לבריכיהביה דנן (7) בר מרת
ויתעקרון כל חרשין בישין מן הדין בריכיהביה בר מרת ומין
מזליה ומין כוכביה ומין ביתיה כוליה (8) ומין דירתי<הון
כולה ויתהפכון לאחוריהון ויחדרון ויאזלון על עבדניהון
ועל משדרניהון מין יומא דין ולעלם בשום יהיהיה אלהים
(9) צבאות אמן אמן אמן סלה הלל ויה וכתוב[2] יפול מצדך אלף
ורבבה מימינך אליך לא יגשו[3] לא תאונה אליך רעה ונגע לא
יקרב [באהלך]

TRANSLATION OF TEXT FIFTY-TWO

Bound and turned aside[4] are all blast-demons and
evil harmers .... the black-arts (2) will
cease, the (magical) practices will be scattered, the
black-arts will be overturned on the ones who worked them.
'Atros and Batros, (3) Petrus, Mithras, Jesus, 'Abyssos,
Byssos, Bythos, and Hermes.[5] Excrement in torn (4) bas-
kets for your mouths, O witches! Women ....
.... the three angels--(5) one is 'Aqoq, one is Maqoq,
and one is Pekir. Hung on a peg which is lowered and
raised DMYTYTYNYZWPY the bones (6) ŠTRPY. Bound are the
hands and feet of men and women who have worked evil on
this Brîk-Yah-be-Yah[6] and who are working evil on this
Brîk-Yah-be-Yah[6] (7) the son of Marat. All the evil
black-arts will be uprooted from this Brîk-Yah-be-Yah[6]
the son of Marat, from his constellation, from his star,
from all his household, (8) and from all his dwelling.
They will be overturned backwards. They will return and
go upon the ones who worked them and upon the ones who
sent them, from this day and forever. In the name of

YHYHYH Elohim (9) (of) Hosts. Amen. Amen. Selah. Hallelujah! It is written: "One thousand may fall at your side, even ten thousand at your right hand. But to you it will not come near. No disaster will befall you, yea calamity will not come near [your tent]."[7]

NOTES ON TEXT FIFTY-TWO

[1] Or, אסותא.

[2] Or, כתיב.

[3] The scribe has written third person plural instead of the *Massoretic Text* third person singular.

[4] Or, as Professor Gordon has suggested in a private note, "handed over," from מסר, "to transmit."

[5] Cf. Gordon's notes on this list of names in *AOR*, VI, 1934, p. 327.

[6] On this name, see note five to Text thirty-five above.

[7] Psalm 91:7, 10.

TEXT FIFTY-THREE

מזמן הדין קמיעה לדובר בה שיותר ויתסי ברחמי בשמיה מן
רוח חרשי ומן רוח מעבדי ומן דינא דאיתא ומן דינא דגברא
ומן לוטתא דאבא ומן לוטתא דאימא ומן לוטתא דגברא ומן
לוטתא דאיתא ומן ל{ו}ט{תא}. דאחי וקרבי (2) ומומינא לכון
ומשבענא לכון כל רוחין בישותא דיכרא וניקבתא ושידין
ושרבטין ירודין ופגעין דיכרי ופתיכרי ולילין וחלחולין
וליחנין ופרגוס ושבעה בני אי{ק}נורי וקיריא והפטוס
וניגזכורית וטונית וצוהרית וקמקאית (3) ונדריא ברכלטוס
דהוא איריס קומתיה מאה ושבעין אמין ויתיב תחות נרזבי
וקטיל ולה{י}א וימורתיתיאל שידא דמזע ומרתית {י} ית
כל הדמי קומתים (sic) דיבני אינושה ותומה בר קורקין
דמרתית (4) ית גיסא דשמולא ותבבסים שידא דימשגיש ית
גיסא דימינא ובנק רוחא טוחא דימנשקא ית רעיוני ליבא
ורתחנא שידא ברבורי ומרי כוח ואברסנס שידא מהבלנא והרקסין
שידא מהכזנא (5) וכלבי שידא מחריבא וריבני היצבי ובני
טולניתא ושבעה זרעין תקי{ט}פין דלורין של{י}דא ברבורי דמית-
קרי קרסקס תרמרס ויקבלון גיטיהון סרבלץ גרדנץ דתימנה תשמץ
דמידמין (6) לגברא באיתא ולאיתא בגברא ומרשען ומשנקן
ומסלעמן ומרתחן ית כל הדמי קומח{י}ה דיבני אינושה ועלפה
בת צילה ופרגוס לילית דאישתדרת על שאול בר קיש (7)
ושגישת ית רעיונוהי וחלחולא וסמכיא בת מצע ולוזיה וקיתיא
ופגעה וסטנא ונאלא וכל פתיכרין כולהון ופיקדין ואיכרין
וחומרין וזידנין ופלנא ופנאי (sic) מהץ ומחצא (8)
וריפסא ופגיחא וארגז בת קסס ורוחא בישתא דיתבא על מנחא
ומדמעא עינין ורחבא ודיבא וציר עינין והרהורין וצב עינין
וניתעא וגישמא בישא ורפסין (9) ורוחא בישתא דימזהבלא ית
בני אינושה וא{הדון ברינון שידא דימרתית ית איברא דסמולא
ותרסין שידא דימרתית ית ריגלא דימינא ורטבי רוחא (10)
בישתא דיתבא על טקין טורין ומרתחא ית איברא דימינא ומחוגת
בת ציל דימרתחא ית כל שדרא דאינשה ורזזום רוחא בישתא
דשתקא ולא (11) ממללא ונפלא על בני אינושה סטינא וכיאבורא
וציחרת רוחא בישתא דימפללא בלישנא תקיפא ובני עורי דמית-
קרי סרגז ואנינרי ויכל (12) דמיחזי כמויי וריבני נפלי
ואשרת מלכ{ת}א דשידי וצילחתא ותמועש בנה ומוזתרסין תריסין
רבס סתני שתסיס וצילבדר (13) קק תסיף חרסין ורוכן וכל
זיקין ומזיקין בישין דימעיקין ליה לדובר שיותר מומינא
לכון ומשבענא לכון דתתז{ע}ון (14) ויתפקון מיניה מאתך

ארבעין. ותמורי הדמר קומתיה לא תקומון במיקמיה ולא תשכבון
בבית (15) מישכביה מן יומא דנך ולעלם בשום הגמג הפגפג
המגמג המגמג סיכין טורס בהטיג (16) לקו ייאי חבוז לנד-
גמפג בחלחל טהין והייחיהא רדסטריביות קקק חיה באדוניא
(17) וכסא ר\ב\רבא למריה יההואה שם מפורש דאיתגלי למשה
באסנה בהדין (18) סמארר חפדטא ית פמיה ויעחנא בייתסי
ית כ בר שי (19) חירא

TRANSLATION OF TEXT FIFTY-THREE

This amulet is designated for DWBR the son[1] of
SYWTW, and he will be saved by the mercies in the heavens
from the spirit of magicians, from the spirit of "prac-
titioners," from the spell of woman, from the spell of
man, from the curse of father, from the curse of mother;
from the curse of man, from the curse of woman, and from
the cur⟨se⟩ of brothers and relatives. (2) I adjure you
and make you swear, all you evil spirits--male and female--
demons, bands (of spirits), howlers, male plagues; idols,
lilis, poisonings, bowls, PRGWS, the seven sons of roofs
and towns,[2] HPTWS, NYGZKWRYT, TWNYT, SWHRYT, QMQ'YT, (3)
and vows by RKLTWS who is 'YRYS. His height is one-
hundred seventy cubits and he sits under roof-spouts kill-
ing and annoying.[3] And Mratt^{e}ti'el, the demon that
terrifies and shakes all the members of the bodies of the
sons of man. And TWMH the son of QWRQYN who shakes (4)
the left side. And TBBSYM, the demon who confuses the
right side. And BNQ the TWT' spirit, who confounds the
thoughts of the heart. And RTTN' the BRBWRY demon. And
the Lord of Power. And 'Abrasgas the destroying demon.
And HRQSYN the ..... demon. (5) And KLBY the destroying
demon. And the sons of HYSBY. And the sons of TWLNYT'
and the seven powerful descendants of LWDYN the BRBWRY
demon who is called QRSQS, TRMRS. And they will take
their divorces. SRBLS, GRDGS of TYMNY, TSMS that appear
(6) to man as[4] woman and to woman as[4] man, and harm and
strangle and swallow and shake all the members of the
body of the sons of man. And ^{c}LPT the daughter of SYLH.
And PRGWS, the lilith that was sent against Saul the son
of Kish (7) to confuse[5] his thoughts. And poisoning and

SMKY' the daughter of MSS and LWZYH, QYTY', plague, satan, incubus, all the idols--all of them--pledges, farmers, pebble-charms, impious-ones, dissension, plagues of male and female smiter, (8) stamping, plague,[6] 'Argaz the daughter of QAA, the evil spirit that sits on the brain and makes the eyes weep, greed, gonorrhoea, fluid of the eyes, imaginations, swelling of the eyes, NYT^c', bad breath, stampings, (9) and the evil spirit which destroys the sons of man. And Lord BRYNWN the demon that shakes the left arm. And TRSYN the demon that shakes the right foot. And RTBY the evil spirit that sits on TQYN mountains and shakes the right arm. And MHGT the daughter of SYL who shakes the whole backbone of man. And RZZWM the evil spirit that is silent and does not (11) speak, and falls upon the sons of man. STYN', KY'BWR', and SYHRT the evil spirit that speaks with a powerful tongue. And the sons of ^{c}WRY who are called SRGZ, 'NYGRY, and YKL, (12) who appear as water. And sons of epilepsy. And 'ŠRT, the Queen of the demons. And headache. And TMW^{c}Š her son. And MZTRSYN, TRYSYN, RGS, STNY, ŠTSYS, and SYLBDR (13) QQ, TYSP, TRSYN, and RWKN and all blast-demons and evil harmers that oppress DWBR (the son of) ŠYWTW. I adjure you and I make you swear that you depart (14) and go forth from him, from the two-hundred forty-eight members of his body. You will not stand in his standing-place nor lie in his (15) bedroom, from this day and forever. In the name of HGMG, HPGPG, HMGMG, HMGMG, pegs, peacock, BHTYG, (16) LQW, YY'Y HBWZ LGDGMPG, BHLHL, THYN, WHYYHYH', RDSTRYBYWT, QQQ, HYH. By the Lord (17) and the great throne of the Master and YHHW'H, the Ineffable Name that was revealed to Moses at the bush. In this (18) .... his mouth ... . (19) ....

NOTES ON TEXT FIFTY-THREE

[1]The text has "daughter" here, but line thirteen uses masculine pronouns to refer to the same person.

[2]Normal plurals would be קְרָוָיָא, קְרָוִין.

³For this meaning of the root לחי cf. Jastrow, *Dictionary*, p. 693.

⁴For this exact use of ב cf. Exodus 6:3: וארא .... באל שדי.

⁵Lit., "and confused."

⁶פניחא for פגיעא.

TEXT FIFTY-FOUR

אדין צילמה דלוטתא ודליליתא ודי<מ>כוא ודמחותא (2) בישתא
ודעינא בישתא דיזחרון ויתבטלון ויתרחקון מן הדין (3) אדון
ומן בוזמנדד בני אחת ולא יחטון בהון {בשום} בשום טיטינוס
(4) חליה מץ פגרי רעש ופגרי רגש קל פגרי רעש קל פגרי רגש
(5) קל מילי ומילי אתיגל[א] סלד יאה קיצחס יצמציס כיבא
סין אקר קפי (6) דני וארא שה דבינ [יניתא חת]ס חניתיה לבד
שתי שתי פנד סקסין סקנירן (7) קץ שמיה הוקרון ק.[...].הדין
הו[א שמה [ר]בה דמלאך מותא דחיל ועריק [מן קדמוהי] אמן
אמן סל[ה הללוי]ה ושריר

TRANSLATION OF TEXT FIFTY-FOUR

This is the figure of the curse, of the lilith, of the blow, of the evil (2) strike, and of the evil eye, that they may depart, that they may be annulled, and that they may go far away from this (3) 'Adon and from Buzmandad, the sons of 'Ahat. And they will not sin against them. In the name of TYTYNWS (4) the hangman. Yah.[1] My body trembled. My body shook. Hark! My body trembled. Hark! My body shook. (5) Hark! The words and the words. 'TYGL', SLD, Yah! QYSTS, YSMSYS, KYB', SYN, 'QR, QPY, (6) DNY and 'R', ŠH, DBYN[YNYT', HT]M HNYTYH alone. ŠTY, ŠTY, PND, SQSYN, SQNYWN, (7) QS is his name. HWQRWN, Q[....... this i]s the [g]reat name before which the Angel of Death is fearful and flees. Amen. Amen. Sel[ah. Halleluja]h! and reliable.

NOTE ON TEXT FIFTY-FOUR

[1] By *Athbash* מץ becomes יה.

TEXT FIFTY-FIVE[1]

הדין (2) צילמה דר.א (3) לוטחא ודמחוחא בישחא ודעינא
בישחא וד.כיה (4) ודחנקניתא דרידקין[2] ויפקון ויתרחקון
מן חמריה ומן תור{י}יה (5) ומן חטביה דאיבאי בר מאמאי
בשום טיטינוס ת[ל]יה מץ פנרי (6) [רעש ופ]נרי רגש קל
פגרי רעש קל פגרי רגש קל מילי ומילי אחינלא סלד [ויאה
(7) קי]צחס מצמציס כיבא סין אקר קפי [דני ואר]א שה
דביניתא חתם [חניחיה] לבד (8) שתי שתי פנד סקסין סקנירן
שמיה [היק]רון ......[הדין הוא] שמא רבה (9) דמלאך מותא
דחיל וּעריק מן קד[מוחי]............[על פי (10) יהוה]
יחנו ועל פי יהוה יסעו את משמרת יהוה שמרו [על פי יהוה
ביד משה].

TRANSLATION OF TEXT FIFTY-FIVE

This is (2) the figure of the ...., (3) the curse, of the evil strike, of the evil eye, of the ...... (4) and of the strangler [of] children. They will get out and go far away from the donkeys, from the oxen, (5) and from the lover[3] of 'Ibai the son of Mamai. In the name of TYTYNWS the hangman. Yah.[4] My body (6) [trembled. My b]ody shook. Hark! My body trembled. Hark! My body shook. Hark! The words and the words. ...... SLD. [Yah! (7) QY]STS, MSMSYS, KYB', SYN, 'QR, QPY, [DNY, and 'R]', ŠH of the BYNYT', HTM, [HNYTYH] alone. (8) ŠTY, ŠTY, PND, SQSYN, SQNYWN is his name. [HWQ]RWN ...... [This is] the great name (9) before which the Angel of Death is fearful and flees .... [According to the command of (10) YHWH] they would encamp, and according to the command of YHWH they would travel. The observance of YHWH they kept [according to the command of YHWH through Moses].[5]

NOTES ON TEXT FIFTY-FIVE

[1] The photograph of this text which was published by Cyrus H. Gordon in *AOR*, IX, 1937 (Plate VI following page 95) is not clear enough to emend fully.

[2] For דירדקין?

[3] For this meaning of the root חטב in Aramaic, cf. Jastrow, *Dictionary*, p. 447, who notes that the word may also mean "to select, betroth oneself to." The Arabic cognate, ḫataba, means "demander (une femme) en mariage" or "se fiancer" (J. B. Belot, *Vocabulaire Arabe-Francais*, p. 168).

[4] By *Athbash*, מץ becomes יה.

[5] Numbers 9:23.

TEXT FIFTY-SIX

...... תלתין ויתר...א ותלתין א תלת ותלתין (2) בני מותין
{ין} טליץ ואכליץ דההיא {לוין} לוטתא וההוא (3) נידרא
והנהון חרשי והנהון מבדרי וההיא שיקופתא (4) וההוא עררתא
עררתא ואגרתא דלטני ונדרני ושתקיף עלי על ארגושנסף (5)
בר סמתנידך ההוא נידרא וההיא לוטתא וההיא שיקופתא והנהון
חרשי (6) וחנון מבדרי וההיא עררתא עררתא ואגרתא ניחדרון
חנון חרשי והנון מבדרי (7) וההיא לוטתא וההיא שיקופתא
וההיא עררתא עררתא ואגרתא דלטני ונדרני ואשלמני (8)
לאחלה ולאיסתר איסתר ניחדר החוא ‹נידרא› והדא (sic)
לוטתא והנהון חרשי והנהון מבדרי וההיא שיקופתא (9) וההיא
עררתא ואגרתא פיתר[1] ההוא נידרא וההיא לוטתא והנהון
חרשי והנהון מבדרי בלי‹שי ותקיפי (10) וההיא שיקופתא {ו-}
וההיא ער‹ר›תא עררתא ואגרתא ניחדר מיניה מן ארגושנסף בר
סמת ומן הורמסדוך (11) בת אימ‹יי› מינה{י}ון ומן ירתיה{נ}ון
ומן יר{י}ת ירתיהון ניחדר מינהון וניתבדר מינהון {עלה .
עלה} עליהון וניחדר כל (12) ליליתא מבכלתא דלויא ליה
לארגושנסף בר סמת מיניה ומן הורמסדוך בת אימי בשמיה בשמיה
קדישין (sic) ובשמיה דמיטטרון (13) איסרא רבה דכליה עלמא
ובשמיה דרפ‹י›אל איסרא דאסותא כולהין אמן אמן א סוברך[2]

TRANSLATION OF TEXT FIFTY-SIX

...... thirty .... The Lord.[3] Thirty. The Lord. Thirty-three. (2) The sons of death are walking about and devouring.[4] Of that curse, that (3) vow, those black-arts, those scatterings, that knocking, (4) that deadly enmity, and the 'Igarta[5] with which he has cursed me, vowed against me, and afflicted me, namely 'Argušnasp (5) the son of SMTNYDK. That vow, that curse, that knocking, those black-arts, (6) those scatterings, that deadly enmity, and the 'Igarta will return--those black-arts, those scatterings, (7) that curse, that knocking, that deadly enmity, and the 'Igarta with which he has cursed me, vowed against me, and performed against me--(8) to 'YLH and 'Istar, 'Istar. Let return that ‹vow›, that curse, those black-arts, those

scatterings, that knocking, (9) that deadly enmity, and the
'Igarta. Undone are that vow, that curse, those black-arts,
those evil and powerful scatterings, (10) that knocking, that
deadly enmity, and the 'Igarta. They will return from him,
from 'Argusnasp the son of SMT and from Hormisduk (11) the
daughter of 'Immi--from them, from their heirs, and from the
heir(s) of their heirs. They will return from them and they
will be scattered from them onto them (who sent them). And
let return every (12) lilith (and) monster that is clinging
to him, to 'Argusnasp the son of SMT. (Let them return) from
him and from Hormisduk the daughter of 'Immi. In His name.
In the holy heavens. And in the name of Metatron, (13) the
Great Prince of the entire universe. And in the name of
Raph⟨i⟩'el the prince of all healings. Amen. Amen. The Lord
is blessed.

NOTES ON TEXT FIFTY-SIX

[1] For פתיר?

[2] For מבורך?

[3] Cf. this name of God in Text 19.2 and throughout this text. Cf. also note seven to Text Nineteen.

[4] Cf. I Peter 5:8: ὁ ἀντίδικος ὑμῶν διάβολος ὡς λέων ὠρυόμενος περιπατεῖ ζητῶν τινα καταπιεῖν.

[5] In a private note, Professor Gordon has suggested that this word perhaps means "(personified) letter."

TEXT FIFTY-SEVEN

אסלי⟨ריתון וחתימיתון כולכון שידין ודיירין ולילִיתא בההוא
איסורא קשיא (2) עזיזא ותקיפא ומרירא דאסירא ביה סוסין
וסוסין אריר⟨ין⟩ דאמא פריך פרק ביסף (3) בן גואל לילִיתא
בישתא דמטעיא ליבא דבני אינשא ומִיתחזיא בחילמא דלילִיא
ומִיתחזיא בחי[זו]נא (4) דימִמא קליא רמיא בנאלא נפלא קטלא
דרדקי ודרדקאתא מרמוצי ומרמוציאתא כבישה וחתִימא מן ביתיה
ומן (5) איסקופתיה דבהרם גושנסף בר אשתר אנהיד בחומרתיה
דמיטטרון סרא רבא דמיתקרי אסיה רבא דרחמי כבר ביאשתא (6)
דההוא כביש שידין ודיירין וחרשין בישין ועובדין תקיפין מן
ביתיה ומן איסקופתיה דבהרם גושנסף בר אשתר אנהיד אמן אמן
סלה כבישין (7) חרשין בישין ועובדין תקיפין כבישין נשי
חרשאתא איניִן חרשיהון ועודיהון ולוטחיהון ואקריתהון מן
ארבעה מיצרי ביתיה דבהרם (8) גושנסף בר אשתר אנהיד כבישין
ודישין נשי חרשאתא כבישין בארעה וכבישין בשמיא כבישין
מזליהון וכוכביהון אסירין עובדי [י]דיהון אמן אמן סלה

TRANSLATION OF TEXT FIFTY-SEVEN

All of you are bound and sealed--demons, devils, and liliths--with that hard, (2) strong, powerful, and mighty bond with which horses are bound, even the accursed horses of 'Imma Prîk. PRQ. BYSP (3) the son of Gô'el.[1] The evil lilith which leads astray the heart of the sons of men, appearing in the dream of the night and appearing in the vi[si]on (4) of the day, burning, casting down with the incubus--they fell upon, they killed boys and girls, lads and lassies--is conquered and sealed from the house and from (5) the threshold of Bahram-Gušnasp the son of Išt(a)r-'Anahîd,[2] by the pebble-charm of Metatron, the Great Prince who is called the Great Savior of Mercies. He has prevailed by the fire (6) with which demons, devils, evil black-arts, and powerful (magical) practices are conquered from the house and from the threshold of Bahram-Gušnasp the son of Išt(a)r-'Anahîd. Amen. Amen. Selah. Conquered are (7) evil black-arts and powerful (magical) practices. Conquered are the women of black-artistry--

they, their black-arts, their (magical) practices, their curses, and their invocations, from the four borders of the house of Bahram- (8) Gušnasp the son of Išt(a)r-'Anahîd. Conquered and trampled down are the women of black-artistry. Conquered on earth and conquered in the heavens. Conquered are their constellations and their stars. Bound are the (magi (magical) practices of their [h]ands. Amen. Amen. Selah.

NOTES ON TEXT FIFTY-SEVEN

[1]"Joseph son of Redeemer." Professor Gordon has pointed out in a personal note the fact that rabbinic literature has the Messiah son of David and the Messiah son of Joseph (Jastrow, *Dictionary*, p. 852, gives references to such phrases). He also added the following observation: "It has occurred to me that Jesus is both the descendant of David and the son of Joseph - to fulfill both messiahships."

[2]"Venus."

TEXT FIFTY-EIGHT

רזהון דיפתכרי ויפ(ק)ון סטני ופתיכרי ול(ו)טתא אס(י)רן
(2) כולהין מן מהפ(י)רוז בר הינדו נ(י)דל(ר)י ולוטתא כל
פתיכרי דיכרי (3) ואיררתא ניקבתא (ב)שום כל בני אינשא
אס(י)רן כלהין מן מ(ה)פירוז בר הינדו (4) ויתה(פ)כ(ו)ן
(פון) ויזל(ו) על עובדי(הו) ועל מש(ד)ר(י)ניהון בשום הפכה
הפיכה סורה[1] שמיה (5) הפיכי כוכבי הפ(י)כי מזלי הפיכה
שע(ות)הון דכל בני אי(נ)שא חרשין (sic) ולוטתא דאבא וד-
(א)ימא ודברתא דכלתא (6) ודחמתא שדיא דרחקה ודקרבה דקמה
בדברא ודקמה במתא דקמא בדברא שדיה (ו) דלט(א) במתא (7)
שדיה דעל אפה נפלא ובבירכה רכנא ובפומה לטא וארעא אתקיפה
דאיסרא נכא לחתמע (sic) לוטתא (8). דחדאתתא (sic) ודעתקא
מן מהפירוז בר הינדו בשמריתכא מלאכה דאית ליה חד עשר
שמהן סטבבא סריה ככבא בפבבא (9) סידריה הידריה עזזיה
בתקפא ארקפא אלספא בממרריריא ולכל דעבד על (הילין) (שמ)התא
אילין אס(י)רן (10) וחתימן כל נידרי ולוטתא ופתיכרי
איסתרתא וכל רוחי בישתה דקימן ברומ(א)ותא וכל חרדין בישי
מעבדין ור(וס)זין וסני כל מני (11) מחבלין אס(י)רין
כלה(ו)ן מן מ(ה)פירוז בר הינדו ומן פנוי בת כוזיחרי ומן
ירתיה(ו)ן ומן ירתי ירתיה(ו)ן וכל דלארעא קריא וכל ד-
לישמיה (12) מציתא ש(מ)עת מן הדין עלמה קל איתתא דשר(א)
ולוטתא ושר אשפיתא מל.................................
ותקיפין

TRANSLATION OF TEXT FIFTY-EIGHT

Secrets of idols. Satans, idols, and curses will
go forth. All of them (2) are bound from MHPYRWZ the son
of Hindu--vows, curses, all male idols, (3) and female
curses, in the name of all the sons of man. All of them
are bound from MHPYRWZ the son of Hindu. (4) And they
will be overturned and go upon the ones who are working
them and upon the ones who are sending them. In the name
of HPKH, HPYKH, the Prince is his name.[2] (5) The stars
are overturned, the constellations are overturned, the
hour of all the sons of man is overturned--black-arts and
curses of father, of mother, of daughter, of daughter-in-

law, (6) and of mother-in-law. ŠDY' far and near, which
arises in the field and which arises in the town, which arises
in the field. ŠDYH which curses in the town. (7) ŠDYH which
has fallen on its nose and has sunk on its knees and curses
with its mouth. The earth has made heavy what (this) bond
has lifted. To seal the curses--(8) new and old--from MHPYRWZ
the son of Hindu by ŠMRYTK', the angel who has eleven names--
SSBB', SRYH, KKB', BPBB', (9) SYDRYH, HYDRYH, ^CZZH, BTQP',
'RQP, 'LSP', BMMRRYRY'. And to seal everyone who worked
against these [nam]es. Bound (10) and sealed are all vows,
curses, idols, goddesses, all evil spirits, which are estab-.
lished on high (?), all evil black-arts, (magical) practices,
secrets, hatings, (and) all species of (11) destroyers. All of
them are bound from MHPYRWZ the son of Hindu, from Pannoi the
daughter of KWZYHRY, from their heirs, and from the heirs of
their heirs. Everything which is the earth's calls and
everything which is heaven's (12) .... hears (?).
From this world. Hark! The wife of the prince and the curse
.... and powerful.

NOTES ON TEXT FIFTY-EIGHT

[1]For שרה?

[2]Or, "the Prince of the Heavens."

TEXT FIFTY-NINE

מזמנה קמיעה דנך מן שמיא חתיט ומחתים קמיעה ᵇ (2) דנך ביתא
⟨ד.....⟩ מירשותיה ליקרי {ליקרי} וליפוסיקיה ולכל מדידין
ביה (3) מן נידרא [ומ]ן שיקופתא ומן חרשי ומן לוטחא ומן
..........יא עריכי (4) ומן בעי מדוראאתא ומן כל ⟨מידעם⟩
ביש דעבידין ודלא עבידין ומן רוח רעה זכר ונקבה ומן עי{י}ן
(5) רעה ומן כשפים {כשפי} איש ואשה בשום בבנעא ניניכיעא
אמינאל הוי. אור .... היא (6) ....
אלין דבידיהון מסמין קבל קוס קוס וחושך ערפל אונק שימיהון
שס שס [אמן] אמן [ס]לא

TRANSLATION OF TEXT FIFTY-NINE

This amulet is designated--sealed and doubly-sealed from the heavens by this amulet (2) is the household ⟨of .....⟩ by his authority--for YQRY, for PWSYQYH, and for all who are dwelling in it--(3) from the vow[, fr]om the knocking, from black-arts, from the curse, from .... (magical) arrangements (?), (4) from emptiers of dwellings, from every⟨thing⟩ bad--whether it is being practiced or not being practiced--from the evil spirit--male or female--from the evil (5) eye, and from sorcerers--man or woman--in the name of BBNᶜ', NYNYKYᶜ', 'MYN'L .... (6) .... those who, by their power, are blinding. QBL, QWS, QWS, Darkness, Thick Mist, Choker are their names. ŠS, ŠS. [Amen]. Amen. [Se]lah.

TEXT SIXTY

מזמן הדין מילתא (2) לאפוכי חרשי ומעבדי מן (3) מירדבוך
{ו} מתקרי מירדא בר כוסיג הפיכא הפ{י}כא (4) הפיכא ארעא
הפיכא שמיא הפיכא כל מילי הפיכא לוטתא (5) דאימא וברתא
לכלתא וחמתא ודרחקתא ודקריבתא דקימא בדברא (6) ודקימא
במתא דקימא ביבשא על אפה נפלא ארעה תקפא וזידנא דברא
ופומא (7) לוטא אסירא וחתימי לוטתא וכל בני אדם והוא
מיניה[1] (sic) דמירדבל{ו}ך בר כוסיג טשחיאל (8) ויקתיאל
בישמך יורבא מלאכא דא{ית} ליה חד עשר שמהתא סטבא כרבא
כבכא מרוח סו (9) חעפניח כתיפא חלס סשפב כביבן בלורא כל
.... הלין שמהתא דמלאכא הדין עבדין האלין שמהתא אסירין
(10) וחחי{מ}ין כל שידין ודיירין סטנין ודיירן ופגעין
ושרבא ו..... [ד]שרי במירדא דמתקרי מירדבוך בר כוסיג כל
דלאו עחור{י}ה ויז .... (11) ....
[מיר]דבוך בר כוסיג אמן אמן סלה קל עורכיל ....
תרנגיל בנ..... קלהין דנשי זידניתא ריקדתא וצנפא ותנחא
ויליליא וילחת[א] .... (12) ש{י}ד{א} להת סטן .....
גברי ונשי דלטו לוטת{ה}ין בלין ודבקין ....
כביש .... דלטו ד.....חין נידריהין ואנשרי כין...
(13) ירורי כולחין איש וחומרין ושידין לוט[ח]ין {וא}
ולילין וחבלינין וענקינין ו[ד]יוא ושיד{א} וסטנין ופגעא
דשורי ב .... מירדבוך בר כוסיג ולא תקבל ...... (14)
לא כל{ו}חא .... כל .... וקודשן .... מן
ד...קום אנתא מירדא דמתקרי מירדבוך בר כוסיג ....
לחותם עלס ..... באלפא .... דלוטן אומרקא עע ....
אחרך חרשי ..... ומן .... (15) על טרטר ודלוטר אנבי{י}ן
אינקום יתה[ופכון] כל חרשין בישין על עבדיהון ועובדין
תקיפין על משדרנהון .... (16) ....
.... (17) יתהפכון כל חרשין בישין על עבדיהון
ועובדין תקי[פין על] משדרנהון שולא קבר דמוש בלחאט ויליד
מירדבו[וך] {דמית{ק{רי} [מירדא בר כוסיג ....[

TRANSLATION OF TEXT SIXTY

This word is designated (2) for the overturning of black-arts and (magical) practices from (3) Merdabuk who is called Merḍa, the son of Kosig. Overturned. Overturned.

(4) Overturned is the earth. Overturned is heaven. Overturned are all words. Overturned is the curse (5) of mother and daughter for (sic) daughter-in-law and mother-in-law, whether far or near, which arises in the field (6) or which arises in the town or which arises on the dry land. The powerful earth has fallen upon its nose and (likewise) the impious word and the cursing (7) mouth. Bound and sealed are the curses and (likewise) all the sons of Adam. And this is the word of Merdabuk the son of Kosig. Tashi'el (8) and Yaqti'el. In your name, Yorba, the angel who has eleven names--SSB', KRB', KBK', MRYH, SW, (9) HᶜPNY', KTYP', HLS, SSPB, KBYBN, BLWR'. All .... these names of this angel, these names are (magical) practices. Bound (10) and sealed are all demons, devils, satans, devils, plagues, the tribe .... [which] are dwelling in² Merda who is called Merdabuk, the son of Kosig. All who labored after him and .... (11) ......
.... [Mer]dabuk the son of Kosig. Amen. Amen. Selah. Hark! ᶜWRKYL .... a chicken .... the sound of women raging, dancing, shrieking, muttering, howling, and panting. (12) .... dem<on> ....
.... satan .... men and women who have uttered their curses are perishing, and clinging .... conquered .... who have cursed, of their .... their vows and .... (13) howlers, all of them. A man. And idols, demons, curses, lilis, injurers, necklace-charms, the Devil, a demon, satans, and the plague which dwell in ...
.... Merdabuk the son of Kosig. You will not receive .... (14) or the daughter-in-law .... all .... and the holy ones ...... from .... Arise, Merda who is called Merdabuk the son of Kosig .... for the sealing of the world .... with the thousand ...
.... curses, depths .... after you the black-arts .... and from .... (15) over drippings. And who have cursed the fruits .... Over-[turned] are all evil black-arts upon the ones who are practicing them and the powerful (magical) practices upon the ones who are sending them .... (16) .....
.... (17).
Over-turned are all evil black-arts upon the ones who are

practicing them and the power[ful] (magical) practices [upon] the ones who are sending them. Sheol is the grave of Mosh Bilḥaṭ the parent of Merdab[uk] ⟨who is ca⟩ll⟨ed⟩ [Merda the son of Kosig ....]

NOTES ON TEXT SIXTY

[1] For מיליה(?).

[2] For the idea of devils dwelling in another being, cf. Mark 5:12, where devils request of Jesus: πέμφον ἡμᾶς τοὺς χοίρους, ἵνα εἰς αὐτοὺς εἰσέλθωμεν.

TEXT SIXTY-ONE

הדין קמיעה לחסמה ולחתמתא ולנטרתא ולאסותא (2) לפרוך
כוסרו בר {א} סיסנוי ולמהדוך ולשישאי בני שהדוך וליאינקדו
וליכושיאג (3) בני מהמד ולשחין בר ש[בורדו]ך מן חרשי בישי
ומ<ע<בדי תקיפי ומן כוסי וקיבלי מן לוטתא ומן (4) שיקופתא
ומן עינא בי[ש]תא ומן סטני בישי ומן רוחי בישאתא ומן
חומרי זידנ<י<אתא ומן כל מידיעם ביש (5) ולא ליקרב ליה
לפרוך כוסרו בר סיסנוי לא ליה ולא לינש<י<ה ולא ליבניה
ולא לי[בנ]תיה ולא ליקיניניה ו־לא לקומתיה ד[ל]{פרוך] (6)
.... ויי מ<ע<בדין תקיפין ועינא בישתא וכוסא
וקיבלא וירורא וכל מידיעם ביש ותיהוי ליה תושבחתא לאלהא
חיא וקימא דקים (7) ליעלם ולעולמי עולמים אמן אמן סלה

TRANSLATION OF TEXT SIXTY-ONE

This amulet is for muzzling, for sealing, for guarding, and for salvation (2) for Parruk-Kosru the son of Sisnoi, for Mahduk and for Šišai the sons of Šahduk, for 'Anqado and for Kosig (3) the sons of Mahmad, and for Šahin the son of Ša[bordu]k, from evil black-arts and powerful (magical) practices, from (magic) bowls and counter-charms, from curses, from (4) knockings, from the evil eye, from evil satans, from evil spirits, from impious pebble-charms, and from everything bad. (5) Let it not draw near to Parruk-Kosru the son of Sisnoi, not to him, not to his wives, not to his sons, not to his [dau]ghters, not to his possessions, and not to the body of [Parruk] (6) .... and woe, powerful (magical) practices, evil eye, (magic) bowl, counter-charm, howler, and everything bad. And praise will become His, the living and abiding God who prevails (7) forever and ever and ever. Amen. Amen. Selah.

TEXT SIXTY-TWO

ולא ליתיבון לה שינתא לעניה ולא ליתיבון לה ניחא בפגרה
בחילמיה (2) ובחיזונה יחינהו⟨לן⟩ יקוצצ⟨לון⟩[1] לה וחיי לא
ניתכין לה בשמיש וסין ונבו ודליבת (3) ובִיל ונריג וכירון
מלכא רבא קרפדנא ומרתא דחרב{נ}⟨נ⟩א אנתי[2] חיילי[2] סחרא על
הדא (4) לוטתא דאחדר מההניש בר אמולאזד על ארנא בת גיית
ולא ליהוי לה לאונא בת גיית חקרנתא ולא (5) פשרתא לעלם
בשום שני לוטחיך בלבאי והוא שליטנא ובריגא דינא רבא
דנישמתא דמיתין[3] ותעבדין רעותי ושולטני (6) ליומא רבא
דדינא {דינא} וגבנא זכנא וזמנא שבעה נומרן ואסותא שלמתא
תיהו ליה למההניש בר מאולאזד (sic) ולא תיחטין {ולא}
ביה ולא באינתתיה (7) ולא בביתיה ולא בקיניניה אמן אמן
סלה

TRANSLATION OF TEXT SIXTY-TWO

[4]And let them not restore sleep to her eyes, nor restore ease in her body during her dreams (2) or during her visions. They will surround, they will cut her off. They will not establish life for her by Šameš, Sin, Nabu, Dlibat, (3) Bel Nereg, and Kewan.[5] O Great King QRPDN' and Lady of Destruction, you strengthen the enclosure against this (4) curse with which MHHNYŠ the son of 'MWL'ZD has surrounded 'WN' the daughter of GYYT. And there will be for her, for 'WN' the daughter of GYYT, no remedy forever and no (5) mitigation forever. In the name of ⟨....⟩ Abrogate your curses by my desire. And He is the Ruler and our Creator, the Great Judge of the souls of the dead. And you[6] will do my will and my command (6) to the day of judgment. WGBN' ZKN'. And they will adjure seven times. And there will be complete salvation for MHHNYŠ the son of M'WL'ZD (sic). And you will not sin against him nor against his wife (7) nor against his household nor against his possessions. Amen. Amen. Selah.

NOTES ON TEXT SIXTY-TWO

[1] Or, יקוצון.

[2] The feminine gender agrees with מרחא which is closer.

[3] The photograph is plainly דחיחין as Gordon notes in *Orientalia*, X, 1941, but מיחין is contextually necessary.

[4] The beginning of this text is unusual. However, the first lines of words and letters are clearly written and there is little doubt that the unique beginning is an authentic one.

[5] Cf. Amos 5:26.

[6] The form is a feminine singular, addressing the "Lady of Destruction" mentioned in line three above.

TEXT SIXTY-THREE

יגל 1 יגל י יגל ילחתא ואי ושׁו וחופסי וביסתרא סריאל אשׁבעית
עליכון (2) איסרי עלמא ד{תקון} ותיפקון מן הדין ביתיה
דישׁבון בר דודו ודבתי אנתיה (3) בישׁבועא רבה אשׁבעית
עליכון איסרי עלמא דתיפקרון חרשׁי בישׁי ועובדי תקיפי (4)
ואשׁפין וחומרין עזי{ב}זתא ולוטתא ונידרא ושׁיקופתא ואשׁלמתא
ומללתא וכוסי (5) ופנעי וירורי יסטנין (ו‹לל‹ליתא
ושׁ‹י‹נ{י}תא וחט{ט}יתא וסיגירית ודיוי בישׁין ורוחי
בישׁתא וחומרי זידניתא וחומר‹י‹ (6) עזיזתא ואפיהון יהון
אפיכון בעלידבבי 2 (blank space) תקיפי ופיריוטי בישׁי
ואיסורי ומסרין ועיקיימיקיו מעיק {יו}ריחו (blank space)
(7) דמשׁחדר בחרשׁין ושׁידי דשׁדרתא (blank space)
ובוקעי וסריתא וסוריגי וקגיריתא ובריחיתא וקשׁייתא וכל
זיקין ומזיקין

TRANSLATION OF TEXT SIXTY-THREE

.... and by the bond
of Sari'el I adjure you, (2) princes of the world, that
you go and go forth from this house of SBWN the son of
DWDW and of BTY his wife. (3) By the great adjuration
I adjure you, princes of the world, that you go forth--
evil black-arts, powerful (magical) practices, (4) en-
chantments, mighty idols, curses, vows, knockings, spells,
words, (magic) bowls, (5) plagues, howlers, satans, liliths, sleep, sins, SYGYRYT', evil devils, evil spirits,
impious amulet-spirits, mighty (6) idols--let even them
be overturned--the powerful enemies and evil PYRYWTY,[3]
and bonds and spells and ^{C}YQYYMYQYW are pressing RYHW (7)
which are sending against black-arts and demons of the
spine and BWQ^{C}Y and SRYT' and SWRYGY and Q?YRYT' and
BRYHYT' and QŠYYT', and all blast-demons and harmers.

NOTES ON TEXT SIXTY-THREE

¹These strange symbols, in shape not unlike the Arabic letter *Dal*, occur only in this text (cf. also line seven below), and there is no apparent reason for their use.

²For בעלדבבא.

³Perhaps "foes."

TEXT SIXTY-FOUR

אסותא מן שמיה לחיסדי בר אמה כל הרשין בישין ועובדין
[ח]קיפין ולוטתא ונידרי [ו]אשלמתא דרחיקין ודקריבין
דגברי (2) ודינשי דליליֹ{יֹ}ה ודימאמה דעבדו ליה ודעבדין
ליה מן יומה דנן ולעלם כלהון אילין {ואילין} משמתין
ומנידין ותבירין (3) ועקירין ומפקין מן גופיה ומן ביתיה
ומן מאתין וארבעין ותמניה הדמי קומתיה דחיסדי בר . (4)
אמה על אידה¹ חיציאל כוכביה דהוא נצח מן כל כוכביה דעליה
רכיבה אס‹י›פה .... דהיא מלפה (5) חרשי להרשתא ה‹א›
דעבדית ב[שמיה] דכרמסיס יה שמה רבה מפרשה אמן אמן סלה
....

Interior

ניחא וברחמי שמיה מן רוחא בישתא ומן מרעה (2) בישה ומן
כל מיניה חומרי דקימי‹ן› לקיבלי (3) דחיסדי בר אמה בטילין
ושביתין מיניה (4) אמן אמן סלה

TRANSLATION OF TEXT SIXTY-FOUR

Salvation from the heavens for Hisdi the son of 'Imma. All evil black-arts, powerful (magical) practices, curses, vows, and spells--whether far away or near, whether of men (2) or of women, whether of the night or of the day, whether they have worked[2] against him or will work[2] against him, from this day and forever--all of these are anathemitized, frightened,[3] broken, (3) uprooted, and expelled[4] from the body, from the house, and from the two-hundred forty-eight members of the body of Hisdi the son of (4) 'Imma, by the authority of Hisi'el his star who has conquered all the stars which are over him. Ridden down, gathered together is (the lady) who teaches (5) black-arts to witches. Behold what I have done in [the name] of KRMSYS. Yah is the great, the Ineffable name. Amen. Amen. Selah. ....[5]

Interior

Rest, and in the mercies of the heavens, from the evil spirit, from the evil (2) affliction, and from all species of idols which are rising up before (3) Ḥisdi the son of 'Imma. Banished and made to end are they from him. Amen. Amen. Selah.

NOTES ON TEXT SIXTY-FOUR

[1] For די with prosthetic א cf. Jastrow, *Dictionary*, p. 45 and p. 564.

[2] En réalité, il s'agit d'un accompli עֲבַדִי suivi d'un participe avec un sens futur, à traduire ainsi: ". . . qu'on a fait ou qu'on fera . . ." (Jeruzalmi, p. 28).

[3] ". . . nous devons, à cause de ce mem initial, lire au milieu du mot un yod et non un waw, considérant ainsi מנידין comme participe *passif* de la racine נוד qui, à l'*Afel*, a le sens d'effrayer, sursauter, faire peur." (Jeruzalmi, p. 29)

[4] "Obligatoirement un participe *Afel passif*, en dépit de tous les dictionnaires d'araméen et de syriaque qui ne signalent pour ce verbe aucune forme passive du Afel" (Jeruzalmi, p. 29).

[5] The bowl itself has eight dots here.

TEXT SIXTY-FIVE

כל חרשין בישין ועובדין תקיפין ולוטתא ונידרי ואשלמתא
ומללתא דרחיקין ודקריבין דליליא ודימאמא דגברי ודינשי
דעבדו ליה ודעבדין ליה לברחאוי ולחיותיה ולקיניניה
דביליחוי (2) בר לאלה מן יומא דנן ועד עלם וכולהון אילין
{ואילין} משמתין ומנידין גזירין ותבירין עקירין ומפקין
ומבטלין מן גופיהון {ומן כל הדמי קומתיהון} (3) ודברחואי
ומן מדרתיהון דחיותיה [1]
[ודביליחוי] בר לאלה על אידה חיצי(י){אל} כוכבא דהוא נציח
מכל כוכביא דעליה רכיבא אסי(י)פה ניחיא דהיא מלפא חרשי
לחרשתא (4) .... ית בישמיה דכרמסיס יה שמה
רבא מפרש אמן אמן סלה קה קה קה קה קה צצצצצצצצצצ ששש סס[2]

TRANSLATION OF TEXT SIXTY-FIVE

All evil black-arts, powerful (magical) practices, curses, vows, spells, and words--whether far away or near, whether of the night or of the day, whether of men or of women, whether they have worked against him or will work against him, against Bar H'WY, and against HYWTYH, and the possessions of BYLYHWY (2) the son of L'LH, from this day and forever--all these are anathemitized, frightened, cut off, broken, uprooted, expelled, and made to cease from the bodies {and from all the members of the bodies}, and from the dwellings of HYWTYH, (3) of Bar HW'Y (sic) [and of BYLYHWY] the son of L'LH, by the authority of Hisi<'el>, the star which has conquered all the stars which are over him. Ridden down, gathered together is NYHY', who teaches black-arts to witches (4) .... in the name of KRMSYS. Yah is the great, the Ineffable name. Amen. Amen. Selah. QH, QH, QH, QH, SSSSSSSSS, SSS, SS.

NOTES ON TEXT SIXTY-FIVE

[1]This line of three words is written directly under the phrase "and from all the members of their bodies," and

is evidently intended to be read in place of it.

[2]The photograph of this text published by Jeruzalmi on page 39 is unclear for this last line of the inscription.

TEXT SIXTY-SIX

אסותא מן שמיא לביתיה {ו} ולאיסקופתיה דאשתר (2) מהאד{י}וך
וכל שום דאית ליה בישמיה דיהוה קדיש אילאה (3) רבא דישראל
ד{ד}הוא אמר והוי הנה מיטתו שלישלומו{לה} שישים גיבׇורים (4)
סב{ב}י{ל}{ב} לח מיניבורי ישראל יברכך יהוה וישמימי{ךָ}[1] יאר
יהוה פני{י}ו אליך ויחונך ישא (5) יהוה פני{י}ו אלי{י}ך ויסים
לך שלום אמן אמן {מ} סלה מיפר אותות בית דין וקו{ס}מים
[יהולל]

TRANSLATION OF TEXT SIXTY-SIX

Salvation from the heavens for the house and for the threshold of 'ŠTR (2) SH'DWK and every person[2] who belongs to him. In the name of YHWH the Holy, the great (3) God of Israel, who spoke and it was. Behold his bed, which is Solomon's. Sixty mighty men (4) are around it from the mighty men of Israel.[3] May YHWH bless you and guard you. May YHWH make His face shine towards you and be gracious to you. May YHWH (5) lift His face towards you and grant peace to you.[4] Amen. Amen. Selah. (YHWH is) the one who breaks the omens of this house and [makes a fool of] the diviners.[5]

NOTES ON TEXT SIXTY-SIX

[1] The scribe first wrote וישמימי and then, realizing his mistake, wrote the letters ךָ over the incorrect ending.

[2] Lit., "name."

[3] Song of Songs 3:7.

[4] Numbers 6:24-26.

[5] Isaiah 44:25.

TEXT SIXTY-SEVEN

שיר תושבאחות למלך יהוה יהוה יהוה מלך יהוה (2) בצור עולם-
{ט} אהיה אשר אהיה מלך הממללבבאא דיבאישהא (3) ביאל הזק
וגיבור שלח ביד {שלח ביד} שלמיאל מיכאל רפאל (4) קנאל
למיסרה ולימחד ביתה דמ{ס}⟨הד⟩ט בר שברדוך בצרע וזקתרי וחלס
(5) וסרקא וסעלס שמיה עליביה רוח פנעא רס{א}⟨ט⟩נא שכבי
[על]יה בשום זיעס (6) חבריתא דשליט על זעקרא שלו חיגעו
בי⟨י⟩ה בית⟨י⟩ה דמהדט בו|ר] שברדוך

TRANSLATION OF TEXT SIXTY-SEVEN

A song of praise to the King, YHWH, YHWH, YHWH, King YHWH. (2) By the Rock of the World. I-am-who-I-am. King of the kings of the earth. (3) By God, strong and mighty, has he sent by the hand of ŠLMY'L, Michael, RP'L, (4) QN'L, "pour ouvrier"[1] and to close the house of M⟨HD⟩T the son of Šaborduk. By SR^c, ZQTRY, HLS, (5) SRQ', and S^cLS. His name is ^cLYBYH, the spirit of the plague and satans (which) are dwelling [over] him. In the name of ZY^cS (6) the wounder who rules over Z^cQR', so that you will not touch the house of MHDT the s[on of] Šaborduk.

NOTE ON TEXT SIXTY-SEVEN

[1]Jeruzalmi, pages 121-123, gives two possible explanations for the word למיסרה. It is cognate to the Arabic شَرَعَ; מיסרה is a mistake for מיפתח. In either case, "open" is the meaning demanded by the context.

TEXT SIXTY-EIGHT

אסותא ונטרתא (2) וחתמתא מן שמיא תיהוי (3) ליה לשירוי
{לשירוי} בר {בר} בורזוי וכל שום (4) ד[אית] <לשירוי> בר
בורזוי בריך מרי ביריחא בהדין פישרא (5) מפשרנא ובישמיה
דיציבא הדין מבטילנא לכל נידרא ולוטתא ושיקופ{י}תא (6)
ואשלמתא ודלי{י}ת ידין רצעיקית <ב>פומא ורתחית <ב>ליבא
ואנבטי<ר>ת <ב>עיני (7) ואפקית <ב>סיפתתא ולטו ואשלימו ואף
אישתקיפו ודלו ידיהון ורצעיקו בפומיהון ורת[חו] בל[יב]יהון
(8) ואפיקו בסיפתתהון ולטו ואשלימו ואף איש<ת>קיפו ודלו
ידיהון ורצעיקו בפומיהון ורתחו ב[ליביהון (9) וא[פיקו
בסיתתתהון[1] ולטו {ולטוטו} ית שירוי בר בורזוי בטולהון
בפומא דמרי{ת}הון ובלב כל מחב[רי]הון ובימעי ובימעי}
..... (10) ....<ב>שמא הדין מומינא עלי[הון] ריה
מטפר[2] ית נידרי אדם וגזר דין מלמעלה והא יבטול ית נידרי
אילין ....

Exterior

[אקטרו] ודלו ידיהון ורצעיקו בפומיהון ורתחו [בליבי]הון
ב{סיפ} <ואפיקו> (2) סיפתתהון ואב[ט]לון מיניהון כמא
דפקד כל עלמא וכמא דנברי ואינשי אבדין מן עלמ[א וכמא
אבטל]ון מיניהון (3) וכמא דנברי ואינשי אבדין מן עלמא
וכמא דנברי ואינשי מיתבעין ולא {מישכ} מישתכחי[ן ......]

TRANSLATION OF TEXT SIXTY-EIGHT

Salvation, protection, (2) and sealing from the heavens let there be (3) for ŠYRWY the son of Burzoi and every person[3] (4) which [belongs] <to ŠYRWY> the son of Burzoi. Blessed be the Lord of the Streets. By this counter-charm (5) I am disenchanting, and in the name of this true one I am causing to cease every vow, curse, knocking, (6) and spell. I have lifted (my) hands and I have cried <with> (my) mouth and I have been excited <in> (my) heart and I have looked <with> my eyes (7) and I have brought out from (my) lips.[4] They have cursed and they

have cast spells, but they have been driven off. They have
lifted their hands, they have cried with their mouths, they
have been exci[ted] in their hea[rts], (8) they have brought
out from their lips. They have cursed and they have cast
spells, but they have been driven off. They have lifted
their hands, they have cried with their mouths, they have
been excited in [their hearts, (9) and they] have brought
out from their lips. They have cursed ŠYRWY the son of
Burzoi. Stop them by the mouth of their lord and by the
heart of all their inj[ur]ers and by the belly ....
.... (10) .... <In> this name I adjure them.
And Yah is dismissing the vows of man and He has decreed
this from above. And Lo, He will bring these curses to an
end ....

Exterior

[They have disenchanted], they have lifted their hands,
they have cried with their mouths, and they have been excited [in] their [hearts]. <They have brought out> (2) from
their lips, and they have ce[as]ed from them. Just as he
commanded all the world, and just as men and people are perishing from the worl[d, just so they ceas]ed from them, (3)
and just so men and people are perishing from the world, and
just so men and people are searching but not findin[g ......
............]

NOTES ON TEXT SIXTY-EIGHT

[1]For בסיפתחהין.

[2]For מפטר.

[3]Lit., "name."

[4]Or, "spoken," and so throughout the text.

TEXT SIXTY-NINE

דין קמיעא דיהוי (2) לאסו⟨תא⟩ לשאלי בר חאתוי שיר תושבחות
(3) למלך צמלסד[1] עלמוא יהוה צבא⟨ו⟩ת צור עולמים אהיה (4)
אשר אחיה יה מלך ממליל ⟨ו⟩⟨בר⟩⟨א⟩ יב⟨ר⟩ ישתא אסיא ק{י}ר⟨י⟩א
דורפס פודודפא (5) דרוחי אסיא ⟨יסי⟩ ית שאלי בר חאתוי מן כל
מדעם ביש מן יומא דין ולעלם מן רוח פגעא (6) בשום יהוה יהוה
יהוה יחו יחהחחו אהחייה יה אהה ההו חהר יה הה הה יהה אהה יההו
החו (7) ההו חוה אהה יהו אל אל יהו בשום לליזפת אנרגוס אנד
נבת בשום יהוס יהוס יהוש ואהושא ואנריבט (8) קומיאל קותיאל
יהו סבהו אמן אמן סלה אנא כתביח ואלהא מארי כולא יסי. ית
[שאלי בר חאתוי]

TRANSLATION OF TEXT SIXTY-NINE

This is an amulet which will be (2) for salvati⟨on⟩ for Š'LY the son of Hâtoi. A song of praise (3) to the King of the world, YHWH of Hosts, the Rock of the worlds, I-am- (4) who-I-am, Yah, the King who speaks ⟨and⟩ creates dry land, the Savior who is called DWRPS, PWDWDP' (5) of spirits. The Savior ⟨will save⟩ Š'LY the son of Hâtoi from everything bad, from this day and forever--from the plague spirit--(6)[2] in the name of YHWH, YHWH, YHWH, YHW, YHHHHW, 'HHYYH, YH, 'HH, HHW, HHW, YH, HH, YH, HH, HH, YHH, 'HH, YHHW, HHW, (7) HHW, HWH, 'HH, YHW, 'El, 'El, YHW. In the name of LLYZPT, 'NRGWS, 'ND, NBT. In the name of YHWS, YHWS, and 'HWŠ' and 'GRYBT, (8) QWMY'L, QWTY'L, YHW, SBHW, Amen. Amen. Selah. I have written, but God, the Lord of All, will save [Š'LY the son of Hâtoi].

NOTES ON TEXT SIXTY-NINE

[1]Note that the diagonal line was drawn through this word by the scribe. This is the only place in these texts where a scribe attempts to strike out a mistake.

²I have simply re-copied the readings of Jeruzalmi from line six to the word "I" in line eight because his photograph for these lines (page 127) is unclear.

TEXT SEVENTY

לישמך אני עושה חדין כתבה (2) יחוי לאסו לביתא דכנרכשוד
בר טאטא (3) לחיל אתתלי>ה ובנה ולביתלי>ה ולכל אינשי דאית
בלי>ח אנתח הא (4) א}י{פרדי .... יוח
ששעו כדי תלד שכל חנשים (5) מזלא ו{תלד} שתלד [בימים] ש-
[לא] תלד בלילול חלליוח חתים עולוך בשום¹ [צידקי>) צדק (6)
צדקי]¹ אל בחרב כפיפה בקלע פשיטח בקלע פשיטה בחרב כפיפה
¹[שלא תבאו (7) ושלא תיראו]¹ בידמות בני חוה בישתח בכל מקום
בין <בימממא> ובלי>ן בלילא חלליוח חתים¹ [על יד צידקימלך]¹
(8) <צידקי>מלך צידקימלך אמן אמן סלה

TRANSLATION OF TEXT SEVENTY

I am acting for Your name. This writ (2) will become salvation for the household of KNRKŠWD the son of Ṭ'Ṭ', (3) for ḤYL his wife, his sons, for his house, and for all the people who are in it. O woman, Lo, (4) separate yourself .... who looks when (a woman) gives birth, who is the Star of all (5) the women who give birth [in the daytime], who do [not] give birth at night. Hallelujah! It is sealed against you in the name of [ṢYDQY, (6) ṢDQ, ṢDQY]'L ṢDQY]'L. With a sword is she conquered, with a rope is she flayed. With a rope is she flayed, with a sword is she conquered [so that she will not come (7) and so that she will not appear] in the likeness of the sons of Eve. (She is) the evil one in every place, whether ⟨by day⟩ or by night. Hallelujah! Sealed [by the authority of ṢYDQYMLK], (8) ⟨ṢYDQY⟩MLK, ṢYDQYMLK. Amen. Amen. Selah.

NOTE ON TEXT SEVENTY

[1] [...........] are the readings according to Jeruzalmi (page 141). His photograph is unclear for all the words included in these brackets.

TEXT SEVENTY-ONE

מ[נטר] מן לותא {ו}דיקבא מן לותא דירכא מן לותה ראחקא[1]
(2) וקרבא מן לותתא דרע להההה אאא מן לותא אמה וברה מן
לותתא אמה וברה מן (3) {מן} לותא רבתה וביךלתא מן לותא
רב[ת]א [ובי]רתא מן לותא ראבתא ובלי‹רתא מן ל‹ו›‹חא ראבתא
וריבתא[2]

TRANSLATION OF TEXT SEVENTY-ONE

Gu[arded] from the curse of QB', from the curse of RK',[3] from the curse far away (2) and near, from the curse of evil LHHHH, ''', from the curse of mother and her son, from the curse of mother and her son, from (3) the curse of great ones and the fort, from the curse of grea[t] ones and the [fo]rt, from the curse of great ones and the fort, from the curse of great ones and the fort.

NOTES ON TEXT SEVENTY-ONE

[1] Note that, both here and throughout this text, the ד can be omitted.

[2] The scribe first wrote ריבתא instead of בירתא. He then added the ו between the ב and the ת.

[3] Cf. Matthew 5:22. However, a true parallel to the New Testament word should be ריקא.

TEXT SEVENTY-TWO

אסותא מן שמיא קדשיא לבת מה ... ש..ש דתיתסי ....
(2) שמיא מן לילִיתא [דכ]רא וניקבת(א) בשם איסרא רבא (3)
.... בשם אגן ....
....

TRANSLATION OF TEXT SEVENTY-TWO

Salvation from the holy heavens for BT, MH .....Š, so that she may be saved .... (2) heaveńs from liliths--[ma]le and female--in the name of the Great Prince .... (3) .... In the name of 'GN ....
....

GLOSSARY OF ARAMAIC WORDS

    The GLOSSARY is an attempt to list all of the words which are written in the seventy-two texts of this dissertation. The numbers following each entry refer only to those texts which appear in this dissertation. The reader is directed to the "Glossary" of William H. Rossell (*Handbook*, pp. 121-153) which was the pattern used in the compilation of the present list.

    In the INDEX OF PERSONAL NAMES which follows the GLOSSARY, the personal names are listed according to the order of the Aramaic/Hebrew alphabet.

א

1.	אבא	father -- 53.1; 14.4; passim.
2.	אבד	to perish -- 15.7; 68.2,3 (*exterior*).
3.	אבדא	destroyer -- 8.2.
4.	אבהו	divine name -- 3.9.
5.	אביל	Abel.
6.	אברא	lead -- 21.10; 43.4.
7.	איברא	arm, limb -- 53.9.
8.	אבר	"Mighty One," epithet of God -- 12.12.
9.	אברסכס	Abraxas, a (destroying) demon -- 53.4; 3.9; 4.4.
10.	אגזריאל	angel/deity -- 21.11.
11.	איגרא	roof -- 47.2; 53.2; 41.10; 11.7.
12.	אגרביס	"the holy Agrabis" -- 9.2.
13.	אגרתא	letter, (personified) letter, written curse -- 19.7; 12.13; 56.4.
14.	אדמא	mankind -- 60.7.
15.	אודנא	ear -- 43.1.
16.	אדניאל	angel name -- 41.11; 43.5.
17.	אידרונא	inner room -- 23 (*case*).
18.	אה	Oh! Ha! -- 15.7; 16.1. This may be a spelling of the divine name Yah, Ah.
19.	או	or -- 2.5, passim.
	או ... או	either ... or -- passim.
20.	אונא	a disease -- 32.2.
21.	אוץ	to squeeze -- 1.11.
22.	אור	(BH) to shine -- 66.4.
23.	אורחא	a road, a way.
24.	אוריתא	The Law -- 50.3,7; 51.1.
25.	אות	an omen -- 66.5.
26.	אזזיאל	angel name -- 21.18.
27.	אזל	to go -- 7.1,4,10; passim.
28.	אופא	deity name -- 21.7.
29.	אחא	brother -- 5.3; 53.1.
30.	אחד	to close, to hold -- 17.4; 35.3; 67.4.
31.	אוחר	to be behind.
32.	אחור	behind (prep.) -- 12.3. Cf. 60.10.
	אחור ל-	backward -- 52.8.
33.	אחרמתא	a ban -- 2.6; 7.9.
34.	אחרוניתא	strong herb (for a love potion) -- 36.3.

35.	איבול	deity name -- 21.5.
36.	איבולית	feminine of #35 -- 21.5.
37.	אינון	they (m. pl. personal pronoun) -- passim.
38.	איסרא	a prince -- 49.11; 56.13; passim.
39.	אית	there is/are -- 49.5,7; 1.14; passim.
40.	אכל	to eat -- 56.2; 19.9.
41.	אכלא	food -- 20.6.
42.	אלאל	deity name -- 25.7.
43.	איליאל	angel name -- 16.2.
44.	איליה	Elijah.
45.	אל פנים	'El Panim -- 12.13.
46.	אילישבא	Eliševa -- 50.1. Cf. Exodus 6.23.
47.	אל שדי	'El Šaddai -- 7.17; 48.4; 12.11, passim.
48.	אילשוע	Elisha.
49.	אילא	but, except -- 35.5; 36.2.
50.	אלדדביה	mystical name -- 10.3.
51.	אלהא	God -- 40.3; 56.8; 3.4; 25.6; 9.1.
52.	אלף	to teach (Afel) -- 64.4; 65.3.
53.	אלף	one thousand -- 60.14.
54.	אם	if -- 2.3.
55.	אימא	mother -- 12.4, passim.
56.	אומוקא	depths -- 60.14.
57.	אמר	to say, speak -- 2.3; 7.5,7, passim.
58.	מימרא	a word, command -- 25.8; 49.10.
59.	אמתא	cubit -- 53.3.
60.	אמתא	handmaiden -- 49.7.
61.	אנא/ה	I (personal pronoun) -- passim.
62.	אנבא	fruit -- 60.15.
63.	אינגע	plague -- 37.9.
64.	אנגרוס	deity name -- 21.7.
65.	אנד	deity name -- 21.9.
66.	אנחנא	we (personal pronoun) -- 1.14.
67.	אסף	to gather together -- 64.4; 65.3.
68.	אפא	face/nose -- 58.7.
	באנפי	"before" -- 25.5.
69.	אינשא	man; plural: people -- 47.2; 48.7; 53.3.
70.	איתתא	wife, woman -- passim. Plural: נשין.
71.	את	you (sg.). Feminine: אנתי. Masculine plural: אתון. Feminine plural: אתין.

72.	אסא	myrtle -- 25.11.
73.	אסא	to save, heal -- 1.15, passim.
74.	אסותא	salvation -- 46.1, passim.
75.	אסיה	savior, healer -- 57.5, passim.
76.	אסנא	thorn-bush -- 53.17.
77.	איספלידא	hall -- 23 (case).
78.	אספנדס דיוא	jinnee of King Solomon -- 50.4.
79.	איסקופ/בתא	threshold -- 19.3, passim.
80.	אסר	to bind -- 1.12, passim.
81.	איסורא	bond -- 10.2, passim.
82.	מסרתא	binding -- 61.1.
83.	איסתר/תא	god/goddess (Istar) -- 40.4; 47 (case), passim.
84.	אף	so, also, even -- 63.6; 3.14.
85.	אפך	see הפך.
86.	אפסוס	Abyssos -- 52.3.
87.	אוקינוס	Okeanos -- 21.18.
88.	ארא	copper -- cf. Akkadian $er\hat{u}$.
89.	ארבע/ה	four -- passim.
	ארבעין	forty -- passim.
90.	ארגושנסף	demon name -- 56.4.
91.	ארדיסבא	deity name -- 21.9.
92.	ארזן	deity name -- 21.12.
93.	אריאל	angel name -- 21.12; 43.4.
94.	אריון	deity name -- 21.13,17.
95.	ארמאין	Aramaeans -- 49.9.
96.	ארמיס	Hermes -- 2.2; 3.8; 6.5; 7.3; 52.3.
97.	אריס	'Iras son of Ḥanas (demon?) -- 21.11.
98.	ארעא	earth -- passim.
99.	אשלמתא	a spell -- 23.9; 24.10; 33.1.
100.	אשרנא	time, a moment.
101.	אשף	to enchant -- 2.3; 7.6.
102.	אשפא	enchantment -- 2.3; 7.6; 63.4.
103.	אשרת	Queen of the Demons -- 53.12.
104.	אישתא	fire/fever -- 8.6; 9.7; 32.2.
105.	אישתקופתא	a blow, a knock -- 24.10; 48.6.
106.	אתא	to come, arrive -- 49.11.
107.	אתרא	a place -- 23.8.
108.	אתרוס	'Atros -- 52.2.

ב

109.	ב/בי	in, against, from -- 2.4; 7.4; passim. Cf. "as" -- 53.6.
110.	בד	separate, single ("by yourself") -- 39.7.
111.	באלבי	bâlbê, a class of demons -- 47.3.
112.	ביש/חא	bad, evil -- passim.
113.	בבא	a door, a gate.
114.	בגדנא	King of the Devils -- 17.5; 18.4; 19.2; 20.4; 21.6,10,13; 22.2.
115.	בדר	to scatter -- 52.2; 56.11.
116.	בהל	to hurry off (Ethpe.) -- 46.4.
117.	בזא	to break, tear -- 52.4; 39.7.
118.	ביזא	spoil -- 10.3.
119.	בחר	to choose -- 43.5.
120.	בטל	to annul -- 52.1; 49.10; 19.5; passim. to banish -- 64.3 (*interior*).
121.	ביל	Bel -- 62.6.
122.	ביסס	Byssos -- 52.3.
123.	ביתא	house -- 1.6, passim.
	בית משכבא	bedroom -- 16.7; 4.3.
124.	בכין	therefore, then -- 34.1.
125.	בכיר	angel epithet -- cf. Rossell, *Handbook*, p. 126.
126.	בלי	to perish -- 60.12.
127.	בלם	to muzzle -- 1.11.
128.	בלע	to swallow -- 8.7; 15.6.
129.	בין	between -- passim.
130.	בינינא	building -- 24.6.
131.	בסרא	flesh -- 19.10.
132.	בוסתנא	garden -- 51.1.
133.	בעא	to search, ask -- 5.6; 68.3 (*exterior*).
134.	בעי	to empty (a dwelling) -- 59.4.
135.	בועותא	a request.
136.	בעלא	lord, husband -- 19.2, passim.
137.	בעלדבבא	enemy, for -- 2.3; 7.5.
138.	בעירא	cattle -- 49.7.
139.	ברא	to create -- 69.4; 7.4.

140.	ברא	son. Plural: בנין passim.
	בר איגרא	roof spirit.
	בר מיט	cripple.
	בר כומא	maimed person.
	בר אינש	anyone.
141.	ברתא	daughter. Plural: בנן/בנתא passim.
	בת ברתא	granddaughter -- passim.
142.	בר	apart -- 21.15.
143.	בראי	foreigner -- 37.8.
144.	בירִיא	creature -- 7.11.
145.	בירכא	knee -- 58.7.
146.	בירתא	fort (?) -- 71 (three times).
147.	בירִיתא	streets -- 68.4.
148.	ברינון	demon who shakes the left limb -- 53.9.
149.	ברדא	hail -- 9.3.
150.	ברך	to bless -- 48.4.
151.	ברלא	Beryl -- 19.1,2.
152.	בורסף	Borsip.
153.	ברק	to shine -- 23.8.
154.	ברקא	lightning -- 23.8.
155.	ברקיאל	angel name -- 43.5.
156.	בחולתא	young woman -- 25.9.
157.	בחוקפא	angel epithet.
158.	בתר	after, behind (prep.) -- 1.10; 7.16.
159.	בתרוס	Batros -- 52.2.

ג

160.	גבב	to draw (a bow) -- 7.8; 2.4; 6.7.
161.	גבל	to knead -- 23.5.
162.	גיבור	(BH) mighty man -- 66.3,4. Cf. 67.3.
163.	גוברא/גברא	strong, mighty (one) -- 50.3; 8.2; 19.4.
164.	גברא	man -- 52.6; 49.10.
165.	גבריאל	Gabriel -- passim.
166.	גדריאל	angel name -- 9.5.
167.	גוא	belly, midst -- 9.7; 25.10.
168.	גובא/גופא	body, back -- passim.
169.	גוד	to tie, bind -- 37.10.
170.	גונא	color, form -- 3.15.
171.	גונבא	tail.

172.	גונדא	band, troop -- 3.13.
173.	גזר	to cut, cut off, decree -- 3.13; 14.1; 65.2.
174.	גזירתא	law, decree -- 1.9; 7.9.
175.	גיטא	bill of divorce -- 17.8; passim.
176.	גידא	sinew, cord.
177.	גינאה	jinnee (of Solomon) -- 50.4; 51.
178.	גיסא	neighborhood, side -- 11.2; 53.4.
179.	גלא	to reveal -- 53.17.
180.	גלגלא	wheel, sphere -- 11.11; 12.13; 34.7.
181.	גלל	to unfold, roll -- 34.7.
182.	גלף	to engrave -- 17.9.
183.	גמלא	camel -- 49.13.
184.	גרמא	bone -- 3.17; 52.5.

ד

185.	ד/די	of, which -- passim.
186.	דבא	to lurk -- 1.6; 11.4; 20.6.
187.	דביה	epithet of Hermes? -- 7.3; 2.2; 6.5.
188.	דבק	to cling -- 60.12.
189.	דברא	field, desert -- 13.3; 58.6; 60.5.
190.	דהן	to drip, be fat.
191.	דויד	David -- 48.5; 50.4, passim.
192.	דובא	place.
193.	דור	to dwell.
194.	דירתא	dwelling -- 7.16; 47.4; 52.8; passim.
195.	דוש	to thresh, tread -- 43.2; 57.8.
196.	דחל	to fear, be afraid -- 54.7; 1.12; 8.7.
197.	דיבא	gonorrhoea -- 53.8.
198.	דיוא	demon -- 7.17; 22.2; passim.
199.	דינא	law, judgment, religion -- 5.5; 21.8; 33.4; 53.1.
200.	דכיא	pure -- 6.4; 7.3; 43.5.
201.	דכר	to pronounce, record -- 7.11; 14.6.
202.	דיכרא	male -- 47.3; 48.5; 11.2; passim.
203.	דלא	to lift -- 7.15; 52.5; 68.6.
204.	דליבת	Dlibat, goddess of love -- 36.5; 62.5.

205.	דמא	to appear (Ethpe) -- 1.12; 11.4; 53.5.
206.	דמותא	likeness -- 1.12; 11.4; 19.8; 23.15.
207.	דמע	to weep, shed tears, drip -- 53.8.
208.	דנן/דין	(masculine) this. דא (feminine), passim. Enclitic pronominal forms.
209.	דנאיל	angel name -- 43.4.
210.	דנחיש	demon name -- 21.14,16.
211.	דיקולא	basket -- 52.3.
212.	דרא	generation -- 13.1.
213.	דרומא	south -- 46.3.
214.	דרדקא/חא	boy/girl -- 22.4; 40.4; 55.4; 57.4; 20.6.
215.	דרך	to walk, tread -- 43.2.
216.	דריסת	certified, confirmed -- 25.8.
217.	דשא	door.

ה

218.	הא	Oh! Lo, behold -- 20.8; 22.5; 64.5.
219.	הדמא	member (of body) -- 39.6; 44.8; 46.5; 53.14.
220.	הוא	3rd. sg. masc. personal pronoun -- passim. היא (f).
221.	הַהוּא	masc. demonstrative pronoun -- 57.1; 7.4; 56.2. ההיא (f); הנהון (pl., "those").
222.	הוה	to exist, be -- 8.5; 11.12; 46.1; passim.
223.	היכלא	temple -- 9.3.
224.	הינדואין	Indian (m. pl.) -- 49.9.
225.	הכדין ... הכדין	just as ... so.
226.	הכין	thus, so -- 12.8.
227.	הלך	to walk -- 43.2.
228.	הלין/אילין	these (demonstrative pronoun) -- 11.4; passim.
229.	הימנותא	faithfulness -- 37.12.
230.	הנה	(BH) behold -- 66.3.
231.	אפך/הפך	to overturn, upset -- 52.2,8; 33.3; passim.
232.	הפכיאיל	angel name ("The Overturner") -- 33.2.

233.	הרהורא	imagination -- 7.8; 19.8.
234.	השתא	now -- 5.1; 8.9.

ו

235.	ו	and, but (conjunction) -- passim.
	ו ... ו	whether ... or -- 59.4; passim.
236.	ואי	Oh! Woe! -- 1.9; 7.5; 61.4.

ז

237.	זח	to move, depart -- 25.7; 43.6.
238.	זוטא	young, small.
239.	זויתא	corner -- 5.2.
240.	זוע	to move, tremble -- 3.5,12; 35.5; 46.2,4; 53.3; passim.
241.	זידנא	impious -- 7.10; 48.7; 53.7.
242.	זיוא	glory -- 3.5.
243.	זיפא	honey -- 23.5.
244.	זיפא	eyebrow -- 3.13 (cf. also note eight).
245.	זיקא	blast -- 1.9; 42.8; 52.1.
246.	זלף	to pour -- 23.5.
247.	זמם	to resound -- 11.11.
248.	זמן	to designate -- Pael: 47.1; 53.1; passim.
249.	זמנא	time -- 62.19.
250.	זנד	father of 'Aryon -- 21.13.
251.	זעוז	Zeus -- 21.17.
252.	זעירא	small, young -- 49.7.
253.	זרז	to equip, arm (well) -- 5.6; 21.13.
254.	זרחיציאל	a "star" -- 41.2.
255.	זרני	name of a lilith -- 17.6; 22.3; 31.3.
256.	זרע	to sow.
257.	זרעא	seed, offspring -- 1.8; 43.1; 53.5.

ח

258.	חבב	to love -- 19.10; 25.4,9.
259.	חדיאל	angel name -- 25.3.
260.	חבל	to destroy (Pa) -- 1.10; 3.16; 25.9; 53.4,9.
261.	חבלא	injury, destruction -- 3.16; 24.6; 42.8.
262.	חבלס	name of a lilith -- 17.5; 20.5; 22.3; 31.3.
263.	חבק	to embrace -- 25.4.
264.	חבר	to enchant -- 11.6.
265.	חבריתא	a wounder -- 67.6.
266.	חד	one, a certain (one) -- 11.7; 41.11.
	חד עשר	eleven.
267.	חדאקוק	angel name ("one is 'Aqoq") -- 52.5.
268.	חדמקוק	angel name ("one is Maqoq") -- 52.5.
269.	חדפכיר	angel name ("one is Pekir" or "bound") -- 52.5.
270.	חדר	to return -- 12.15; 22.6; 52.8. to surround, turn back (Afel) -- 5.6; 44.9.
271.	חדתא	new, fresh -- 25.11; 58.8.
272.	חוש	quickly -- 9.4; 25.9.
273.	חזא	to appear (Ethpe) -- 11.9; 15.3; 19.8.
274.	חזיון	vision -- 39.3; 38.5; 44.8.
275.	חזק	strong -- 67.3.
276.	חטא	to sin -- 2.3; 7.12,16; 54.3; 43.3.
277.	חטף	to seize, snatch, rob -- 12.2.
278.	חטפיתא	ravager -- 12.2; 13.4.
279.	חטרא	village.
280.	חיא	to live -- 19.2; 23.3.
281.	חיתא	beast -- 3.14.
282.	חיאל	deity name (?).
283.	חיל	to strengthen -- 2.2; 7.4; 62.8.
284.	חילא	strength -- 7.1; 2.1.
285.	חלבס	variant of חבלס.
286.	חולין	sick persons -- 39.7.
287.	חלחולא	poisoning -- 53.2,7.
288.	חללתא	profane (one) -- 19.7.
289.	חולמנא	soundness -- 46.1.
290.	חילמא	a dream -- 11.10; 14.2; 39.5.

291.	חלף	to pass over, to pass by.
292.	חליץ	to arm -- 21.13.
293.	חומיחיאל	angel name.
294.	חמס	to do violence -- 1.10.
295.	חמצא	leaven -- 25.12.
296.	חמרא	donkey -- 49.6; 55.4.
297.	חמרא	wine -- 19.10
298.	חומרא/תא	pebble-charm, talisman -- 5.1; 7.10,12; 47.3; 53.7; passim.
299.	חמש/א	five -- 12.3; 13.4; 14.3.
	חמישיתא	fifth -- 11.8.
300.	חמתא	mother-in-law -- 48.7.
301.	חניניאל	angel name -- 25.3.
302.	חנק	to strangle -- 19.4; 20.6.
303.	חנקתא	strangler -- 19.7; 55.4.
304.	חיסדא	grace, kindness -- 25.6.
305.	חסם	to muzzle -- 61.1.
306.	חסמתא	envious -- 42.9. Cf. חאסמיתא in 38.4.
307.	וצבא	a stone pitcher.
308.	חקיתיאל	deity name (?).
309.	חקק	to hollow out, engrave, mark, inscribe -- 12.14. Cf. חוק.
310.	חרב	to be dry, to destroy -- 53.5.
311.	חרבא	a sword -- 70.6.
312.	חרבונא	destruction -- 62.2.
313.	חרין	excrement -- 52.3. Root: חרא.
314.	חורם	to ban (Pa) -- 14.1.
315.	חרסורא	leprosy -- 37.9.
316.	חריפא	sharp -- 3.17.
317.	הרר	to burn -- 40.1.
318.	חרשין	black-arts -- 45.3; 46.2; 49.8,9,10; passim.
319.	חרשא/תא	a witch, magician -- 52.4; 53.1; 64.5.
320.	חרשתא	bewitching -- 57.7.
321.	חשך	to be dark -- 48.7.
322.	חשכא	darkness -- 24.6; 44:5.
323.	חתם	to seal (Pe), to double-seal (Pa) -- 7.14; 21.19; passim.
324.	חתמא/תא	a seal, sealing -- 7.11; 47.1; 49.3; 50.2.

ט

325.	טבא/תא	good -- 3.9; 41.5,10; 42.6.
326.	טהר	to be pure -- 23.7.
327.	טוס	a peacock -- 53.15.
328.	טופנא	flood -- 16.5.
329.	טורא	a mountain -- 7.9; 15.6; 53.10.
330.	טיטינוס	demon name -- 48.8; 54.3; 55.5.
331.	טיאעין	Arabic, Ṭayyite -- 49.9.
332.	טילא	shade -- 37.9.
333.	טולניתא	Ghul.
334.	טילאכטיל	deity name -- 21.6.
335.	טורמאה	uncleanness -- 37.7; 47.3.
336.	טעא	to lead astray (Af) -- 57.3.
337.	טופרא	toe/finger (nail) -- 21.19.
338.	טרד	to drive away (Af) -- 3.17.
339.	טרטר	drippings -- 60.15.
340.	טרף	to knock down.
341.	טרפסא	membrane, pericardium -- 17.7; 18.4. Cf. טופרי (19.4,11) and טפרס (22.5).
342.	טרש	to be deaf -- 43.1.

י

343.	יא	Oh! -- 9.6,7.
344.	יאסוס	Jesus -- 52.3.
345.	יבשא	dry land -- 60.6. יבישתא in 69.4.
346.	ידא	hand, power, authority -- 43.2; 59.6; 64.4. With prosthetic א -- 64.4.
347.	יהב	to give -- 19.6.
348.	יהודאין	Jewish (m. pl.) -- 49.9.
349.	יהושע	Joshua son of Peraḥia (the famous Rabbi/wonder-worker) -- 12.6; 13.8,10; 15.2.
350.	יומא	a day -- 19.8; 33.4; 47.4; 52.8; passim.
351.	יונאין	Greek (m. pl.) -- 49.9.
352.	יופיאל	angel/deity name -- 34.4.
353.	יחזיאל	angel name -- 33.4.
354.	יחיאל	angel/deity name -- 34.4.

355.	ילד	to beget, to father (Af) -- 1.8; 25.5,9.
356.	יוליד	a parent -- 60.17.
357.	ילדא	a child -- 53.3.
358.	ילל	to howl -- 60.11.
359.	ימא	sea -- 2.4; 3.12; 7.6; 9.2; 39.2.
360.	ימא	to swear, adjure (Af) -- 8.3; 12.6; 39.6; 43.4; 53.2; 62.19.
361.	ימינא	right (hand) -- 11.10; 53.4.
362.	ימן	"faithful" (Hafel passive participle) -- 19.6; 42.7. מהימן.
363.	יסף	sorcerer name (?), Son of Gòʼel -- 57.2.
364.	יציבא	true one -- 68.5.
365.	יקידתא	burning, glowing -- 8.6; 9.7.
366.	יקרא	glory -- 12.6.
367.	ירודא	howler (demon class) -- 26.6; 47.2,3; 53.2; 61.6.
368.	ירחא	month -- 11.5.
369.	ירתא	heir -- 56.11.
370.	ישראל	Israel -- passim.
371.	ית	sign of direct object. (Cf. Hebrew את.) 8.7; 19.5; 53.3; passim.
372.	יתב	to sit -- 44.7; 53.8.
373.	יתרא	string (of a bow) -- 2.5; 7.8.

כ

374.	כ/כי	as, like -- 23.8; 25.11.
	כד	when, as -- 8.7; 23.5; 25.7.
	כדנא	likewise, in the same way -- 24.8.
	כמא	as, like -- 19.6.
375.	כאב	to feel pain.
376.	כביבן	angel epithet.
377.	כבכא	angel epithet.
378.	כבש	to conquer -- 5.1; 7.9,11,12; 11.6; 43.2; 49.14.
379.	כיבשא	a press, throne-step -- 11.1; 23.6; 36.2.
380.	כבשיאל	angel name -- 43.4; 49.14.
381.	כובא	thorn.

382.	כוכבא	star -- 41.2; 44.3; 52.7.
383.	כול	to contain, hold -- 5.1.
384.	כומרא	priest -- 21.10.
385.	כיון	deity name -- 62.6.
386.	כלא	to cease, perish -- 43.7.
387.	כול	all -- 33.2; 17.2; 47.4; 49.5; passim.
	כל מדעם	everything -- 10.5; 42.9; 46.5; passim.
388.	כלילא	a crown, garland -- 25.11.
389.	כלתא	daughter-in-law -- 48.7; passim.
390.	כין	thus, so -- 8.11.
391.	כנואתא	colleagues, associates -- 21.9.
392.	כנפא	wing, corner -- 49.14.
393.	כסא	bowl, cup -- 3.13; 61.21; 63.4.
394.	כסא	to conceal, cover (Pa) -- 25.6.
395.	כסותא	a cloak, robe, covering -- 25.6.
396.	כסדאין	Chaldaeans -- 50.3,7; 51.1.
397.	כסדיאל	angel name, "Prince of the Chaldaeans" -- 50.3; 51.1.
398.	כען	now -- 19.11; 49.7.
399.	כפא	sole/palm -- 43.4.
400.	כפן	to be hungry, to hunger.
401.	כיפסא	menstruation (cf. Syriac) -- 37.7.
402.	כפף	to conquer -- 70.6.
403.	כורהנא	a sickness -- 3.11.
404.	כרך	to curl around (Af).
405.	כרכא	a city, a fortified place.
406.	כורסיא	a throne -- 24.7; 49.11.
407.	כשפא	a sorcerer -- 59.5.
408.	כשירא	an evil curse (?) -- 37.7.
409.	כיתין	Romans (often in Rabbinic literature) -- 49.9.
410.	כתב	to write -- 1.15; 19.11; passim.
411.	כתבא	a writ -- 70.1.
412.	כתיש	angel epithet ("fighter").

ל

413.	ל	to, for -- passim.
	לות	ל plus sign of direct object (cf. Syriac).
	לרע	below, (ארעא plus ל) -- 49.14.
414.	לא	no, not -- passim.
415.	לאי	to labor -- 60.10.
416.	ליבא	heart -- 19.4; 17.7; 21.18.
417.	לבש	to be dressed -- 7.3; 14.3; 12.3; 13.5.
418.	לבושא	a garment -- 7.3; 25.6.
419.	להי	to annoy -- 53.3.
420.	לוא	to cling to, to join -- 11.3; 56.12.
421.	לוט	to curse -- 56.4.
422.	לוטתא	a curse -- 27.3; 44.3,6; 47.2; 48.6.
423.	לחמא	bread, food.
424.	לחש	to whisper, charm -- 10.1.
425.	לחת	to pant -- 60.11.
426.	לטבין	evil, no-good ones -- 15.7; 39.3; 47.3.
427.	לויתון	Leviathan -- 2.4; 7.7,9.
428.	ליחנין	bowls [cf. Akkadian laḫan(n)u] -- 53.2.
429.	ליליא	night -- 19.8; 27.4; passim.
430.	לילי/תא	lili/th, night demon(ess) -- 1.8,9; 47.2,3; 53.2; passim.
431.	לעם	to swallow (Saf) -- 53.6.
432.	לשנא	a tongue, language -- 5.1; 7.10; 49.10.

מ

433.	מאה	one hundred. Dual: מאתן two hundred -- 39.5; 44.8; 46.3,5; 53.3,14.
434.	מבדרא	scattering -- 56.3.
435.	מבכלתא	a monster -- passim.
436.	מגלא	a sickle -- 3.17.
437.	מדנחא	east -- 46.3.
438.	מדינתא	a province -- 46.3.
439.	מוחא	brain -- 53.8.
440.	מוט	to waver, flee -- 13.11; 14.6.
441.	מוך	to make (a bed).

442.	מומא	a cripple, a maimed (person) -- 14.7.
443.	מות	to die -- 34.1.
444.	מותא	death -- 8.6; 54.7; 56.2.
445.	מזלא	a constellation -- 52.7; 57.8.
446.	מזונא	food -- 7.13,16; 49.14.
447.	מחא	to smite -- 11.4; 17.7; 19.4; 20.7.
448.	מחותא	a blow -- 24.6; 54.1.
449.	מחיא	sorcerer epithet, "the smiter" -- 22.1.
450.	מחגת	the daughter of ṢYL who shakes the entire backbone of man -- 53.10.
451.	מחץ	to smite -- 53.7.
452.	מוט	to be crippled.
453.	מטא	to bring (Af) -- 34.5.
454.	מטה	(BH) a bed -- 66.3.
455.	מטול	on account of, for the sake of; with -ד: because -- 2.6; 5.3; 7.11,16.
456.	מטטרון	Metaṭron, the protecting angel -- 34.4; 49.11; 56.12.
457.	מיטלין	covers -- 5.1.
458.	מטללן	an herb used in a love potion -- 36.3.
459.	מיא	water -- 1.11; 3.13; 53.12.
460.	מיכאל	angel name, Michael -- 3.8; 15.11; 44.10.
461.	מינא	species, genus, sort -- 1.8; 2.3; 58.10.
462.	מלא	to fill, be full -- 19.4; 23.7.
463.	מלאכא	an angel -- 33.2; 52.4; 54.7.
464.	מלויאשין	zodiac signs -- 5.4.
465.	מלכא/תא	king/queen -- 17.18; 21.6; 53.12.
466.	מלל	to speak -- 53.11.
467.	מלמעלה	from above -- 68.10.
468.	מלתא	a word. Plural: מלין -- 11.7,9; 40.1.
469.	ממללא	Mamlala, מְמַלְלָא: "The Talker" -- 2.2; 6.5; 7.3.
470.	מומתא	an oath -- 19.11; 14.6; 43.6.
471.	מנטרנא	a guardian -- 3.9.
472.	מן	who? what? -- 2.2; 11.11; 17.4.
473.	מין	from, more (or less) than -- passim.
474.	מידעם	something, anything -- 2.3,4; 7.5,7.
475.	מנא	to arrange -- 26.5.
476.	מנדינסן	deity name -- 21.11.

477.	מנירנש	deity name -- 21.11.
478.	מסא	to melt -- 15.6.
479.	מיסכינותא	poverty (cf. Akkadian *muškēnu*) -- 24.10.
480.	מעבדא	(magical) practice, a spell -- 46.2; 53.1; 61.7.
481.	מעבדנא	a wizard, a magician.
482.	מעה	belly -- 68.9.
483.	מעילא	a cloak, a robe -- 25.6.
484.	מעק	to oppress, beat -- 53.13.
485.	מערבא	west -- 46.3.
486.	מפרש	ineffable -- 64.5; 65.4.
487.	מיצואה	(divine) Command (?) -- 37.11.
488.	מיצעא	midst -- 19.12.
489.	מיצרא	a corner -- 57.7.
490.	מקום	(BH) a place -- 70.7.
491.	מריא	a lord -- 7.11; 23.6; 36.5; 50.5; 53.17.
492.	מרתא	a lady, mistress -- 21.5; 62.2.
493.	מרד	to rebel -- 1.9.
494.	מרכבתא	a chariot -- 9.2; 44.4.
495.	מרומא	height -- 15.7.
496.	מרמוצא/תא	lad/lassie -- 19.4; 57.4; 20.6.
497.	מרניתא	lance, spear -- 22.5; 40.4; 17.7.
498.	מרעה	an affliction -- 64.1 (*interior*).
499.	מרעאיל	angel name -- 44.10.
500.	מרירא	strong, bitter -- 2.3; 5.4; 7.5; 57.2.
501.	מרתיתיאל	demon name -- 53.3.
502.	משה	Moses -- 53.17.
503.	מישחא	oil, fat.
504.	מתא	town -- 58.6; 60.6.
505.	מותבא	a residence -- 19.6; 49.4.
506.	מתרוס	Mithras, a guarding power -- 52.3.

נ

507.	נאלא	incubus -- 24.9; 47.3; 53.7; 57.4.
508.	נבו	demon/deity name -- 47.2; 62.5.
509.	נבט	to look (Af) -- 67.6.
510.	נגע	to touch, injure -- 19.2; 24.4; 67.6.

511.	נדר	to vow -- 40.1; 56.4.
512.	נידרא	a vow -- 33.1; 40.1; 53.3; passim.
513.	נהורא	light -- 7.2.
514.	נהריאל	angel name -- 9.5.
515.	נוד	to frighten (Af) -- 64.2; 65.2.
516.	נוח	to lie, rest -- 2.6.
517.	ניחא	rest -- 24.7; 62.2; 64.1 (interior).
518.	נורא	fire -- 9.3; 12.13; 26.7; 50.4.
519.	נורייא	pepper (used in making a love potion) -- 36.3.
520.	נוריאל	angel name -- 48.1.
521.	נזל	to depart, flee -- 12.1; 17.2; 10.1; 8.2; 34.1; 43.6; 54.2.
522.	נזק	to harm (Af).
523.	נזקא	a blast-demon, damage -- 28.2; 30.2.
524.	נהר	to stab, pierce.
525.	נחשא	bronze -- 5.6; 11.11.
526.	נחת	to come down, rest -- 2.6; 7.9; 12.7; 23.5.
527.	נחתיה	angel epithet.
528.	נטר	to guard -- 16.3; 42.7; 46.5; 49.11.
529.	נטרתא	protection -- 42.2; 47.1; 67.1. Cf. also מטרתא in 3.13.
530.	נסא	to lift -- 58.7. Cf. BH נשא in 66.4.
531.	נסב	to take -- 5.6; 7.16; 36.3.
532.	נפח	to blow (away) -- 48.7.
533.	נפל	to fall -- 7.11; 37.7; 44.3; 53.11,12; 57.4.
534.	נפק	to go out -- 3.12; 8.11; 39.5; passim.
	אפק	'Afel: to bring out -- 68.7,8,9.
	מפקין	'Afel passive: "expelled" -- 64.3; 65.2.
535.	נפשא	life, self -- 7.1.
536.	נצח	to conquer -- 64.4; 65.3.
537.	ניצחנא	glorious -- 44.5.
538.	נקב	a perforation -- 15.6.
539.	נקבחא	female -- 11.3; 12.8; 38.4; 47.3; 48.5; 49.13; passim.
540.	נקט	to grasp, seize -- 3.17; 5.6; 24.8.
541.	נקרדוס	deity name -- 21.8.
542.	נרזבא	a roof-spout -- 53.3.

543.	נריג	Nereg. Nergal (?) -- 62.3.
544.	נשמא/חא	breath, spirit -- 53.8. "Soul" -- 62.5.
545.	נשף	to blow -- 23.8.
546.	נשקא	a weapon -- 43.4.

ס

547.	סאב	to be unclean, filthy -- 1.10.
548.	סבב	I. to turn away -- 12.13.
549.	סבב	II. to be around, surround -- 66.4.
550.	סגא	I. to fortify -- 48.2,5.
551.	סגא	II. to walk -- 23.6.
552.	סדום	Sodom -- 2.6.
553.	סידרא	order, a row -- 2.7; 7.10.
554.	סדריאל	angel name -- 26.9.
555.	סחרא	an enclosure -- 62.3.
556.	סום	to blind (Pa) -- 59.6.
557.	סוף	reed (in "Sea of Reeds" or "Red Sea") -- 9.2,3.
558.	סחנודמוך	deity name -- 21.6.
559.	סחף	to cast prostrate (Pa) -- 3.17.
560.	סטא	to go astray -- 1.9.
561.	סטנא	Satan, a satan, an enemy -- 7.4; passim.
562.	סיטרא	side (of a person) -- 11.10.
563.	סים	to grant, place, put -- 66.5.
564.	סין	The Moon God, Sin -- 62.2.
565.	סיכתא	a peg -- 52.5. Pl: סיכין -- 53.15.
566.	סכל	to commit offense, injure -- 5.2,5; 7.12,13.
567.	סכר	to shut, close -- 25.1; 43.1.
568.	סוכרא	bolt (of a door).
569.	סיליתא	a bread basket -- 21.10.
570.	סלא	a basket.
571.	סלק	to go up -- 15.7.
572.	סמאל	evil angel name -- 42.8.
573.	סמולא	left (hand) -- 11.10; 53.4,9.
574.	סנא	to hate -- 2.3; 39.3.
575.	סיפתא	a lip -- 68.7,8,9; 68.2 (*exterior*).

576.	ספרא	a book, document -- 12.13; 19.7.
577.	סערא	hair -- 14.3.
578.	סרא	a prince, chief -- 3.17; 57.5; 58.4,12.
579.	סוריאל	angel name -- 26.9.
580.	סרח	to open -- 67.4.
581.	סריא	rebellious, bad -- 24.9.
582.	סרסמיאל	angel name -- 9.5.
583.	סרף	to burn -- 22.4.
584.	סרפיאל	angel name -- 9.5; 21.8.
585.	סרתיה	angel epithet.
586.	סתר	to disarrange, be disarrayed -- 12.3, 14.3.
587.	סיתרא	destruction -- 24.6.
588.	סתר	to hide, conceal -- 34.2.

ע

589.	עבד	to do, work (magic) -- 7.5; 15.2; 23.6; 46.4; 48.5,8; 49.10; 52.2,6,8; passim.
590.	עבדא	a slave -- 49.6.
591.	עובדא	(magical) practice -- 15.1; 46.4; 48.5,6; passim.
592.	עבר	to remove, pass -- 1.9; 11.11; 12.9; 33.4; 43.6.
593.	עבר	across -- 12.9; 13.10.
594.	עברא	a bolt, bar -- 43.4.
595.	עגלא	speed, swiftness -- 42.2.
596.	עדא	to remove (Pa) -- 3.17.
597.	עד	until, to -- 5.4,5; 49.8.
	עדמא	same. On this form, cf. Rossell, *Handbook*, p. 57, and Gordon, *Orientalia*, XX, 1950, p. 311.
598.	עידנא	a time, an occasion -- 11.6; 35.5.
599.	עופא	a bird, fowl -- 3.14.
600.	עוק	to press (Af) -- 25.12.
601.	עור	to blind -- 43.1; 53.11.
602.	עזיזא	strong, powerful -- 36.5; 57.2.
603.	עזא	angel name -- 49.11.
604.	עז(י)אל	angel name -- 41.7; 49.11.

605.	עזקא/חא	a signet-ring -- 12.11; 13.12; 18.8; 21.17; 47.1; 48.4. Cf. איזקתא in 51.2. Pl: איזקין 28.3; 29.3; 30.3.
606.	עזריאל	angel name -- 12.14; 41.7.
607.	עינא	eye -- 10.5; 42.9; 43.1; 48.6,7; 54.2,3.
608.	א/עיכורין	shrine-spirits (Cf. Sumerian É.KUR) -- 7.10,11. Cf. also note seven to Text 7.
609.	עכורי	angel epithet (?).
610.	על	on, upon, against -- passim.
611.	עילא	above -- 21.10; 49.14.
612.	עלל	to come in, enter -- 21.20; 25.5.
613.	עלמא	world, universe -- 15.7; 19.2; passim.
614.	עלפת	demoness name -- 53.6.
615.	עלקא	a leech.
616.	עמא	a people, a race -- 25.1.
617.	עים	with -- 1.3,13; 11.3; 25.7.
618.	עמורה	Gomorrah -- 2.6.
619.	ענני שימשא	species of herb used in a love potion -- 36.3.
620.	ענקתא	necklace (charm) -- 3.11; 44.4,6. Cf. אנקתא in 60.13.
621.	עסיאל	angel name -- 3.8.
622.	עשר/עסר	ten. Cf. חד עשר eleven; תרי⟨ן⟩ עשר twelve -- 5.4; עסרין twenty -- 46.3.
623.	עפרא	dust.
624.	עקר	I. to take flight -- 12.15; 15.6; 19.4,7.
625.	עקר	II. to uproot -- 64.3; 65.2.
626.	עקרתא	(spirit of) barrenness -- 17.3.
627.	עקריאיל	angel name -- 12.15; 33.4.
628.	עקרבא	a scorpion.
629.	עריכי	(magical) arrangements -- 58.3.
630.	עריחא	chills.
631.	ערטילא	naked -- 12.3; 13.5; 14.3.
632.	ערסא	a bed -- 3.17.
633.	ערפל	(BH) thick mist, demon epithet -- 59.6.
634.	ערק	to flee -- 8.7; 54.7.
635.	ערתא	enmity -- 56.7.
636.	עשר	angel name -- 41.7.
637.	עתקא	old, ancient -- 58.8.

פ

638.	פ	and (common as conjunction in Arabic and found in Ugaritic and other dialects of Aramaic). Cf. Rossell, *Handbook*, p. 144.
639.	פגם	to mutilate -- 1.10.
640.	פגע	to confront, meet -- 7.4,10; 19.8.
641.	פנעא/חא	plague, stroke, class of evil spirits -- 24.10; 53.2,7,8.
642.	פגר	to break -- 1.11.
643.	פגרא	body -- 7.13,16; 48.8,9.
644.	פומא	mouth -- 25.1; 43.1; 52.4.
645.	פורא	bowl -- 15.1.
646.	פזר	to scatter -- 12.2.
647.	פטר	to dismiss -- 15.9; 19.5,11; 68.10.
648.	פטרחא	separation, dismissal -- 13.12.
649.	פטרגינוס	Patragenos, deity name -- 21.18.
650.	פכר	to tie, bind -- 43.1.
651.	פכרפס	angel epithet.
652.	פלגא	dissension -- 53.7.
653.	פלחדד	lilith name -- 12.4; 13.6,11; 14.4.
654.	פלחס	demon name -- 12.4; 13.6,11; 14.4.
655.	פלניני	deity name -- 21.11.
656.	פלסא פליסא	wizard/genius name -- 12.7.
657.	פסס	to break (Af) -- 3.17.
658.	פסק	to sever, cut -- 36.5.
659.	פקד	to command -- 68.2 (*exterior*).
660.	פיקדין	pledges -- 53.7.
661.	פקע	to burst, split -- 11.11.
662.	פרגוס	lilith name (sent against Saul) -- 53.2,6.
663.	פרד	to scatter -- 3.16; separate oneself -- 70.4.
664.	פרזלא	iron -- 7.2; 43.4.
665.	פרח	to fly -- 1.10; 19.11; 43.7.
666.	פרנגין	Parnagin (the son of Parnagin), wizard name -- 3.12.
667.	פרס	to sprinkle -- 36.4.
668.	פרסאין	Persian (m. pl.) -- 49.9.
669.	פרק	to remove -- 13.13. Cf. 57.2.
670.	פורקנא	deliverance, redemption -- 7.15; 5.5.

671.	פרר	to break -- 66.5.
672.	פשט	to stretch (a bowstring) -- 2.5; 7.8; to flay -- 70.6,6.
673.	פשר	to disenchant -- 68.5.
674.	פישרא	a counter-charm -- 68.4.
675.	פשרתא	release, mitigation -- 44.9; 62.5.
676.	פתח	to open -- 49.13.
677.	פתחא	a door, entrance -- 11.6.
678.	פתכרא	an idol, image-spirit (Persian loanword) -- 40.4; 47.2; passim.
679.	פתר	to undo -- 56.9.
680.	פתרוס	Petrus -- 52.3.

צ

681.	צבא	a swelling -- 53.8.
682.	צבאות	deity epithet -- 12.5; 12.13; 15.11.
683.	צוח	to cry.
684.	צור	"Rock," deity epithet -- 12.12; 67.2; 69.3.
685.	צוריאל	angel name -- 9.5; 43.4,5.
686.	צור	I. to bind -- 11.6; 37.5.
687.	צור	II. to carve -- 17.9.
688.	צורתא	figure (stamped on a seal) -- 26.7.
689.	צות	to obey -- 12.4.
690.	צותא	society -- 14.6.
691.	צחא	to be dry, to thirst.
692.	צטר	to burst -- 11.11.
693.	ציחרת	"the evil spirit that speaks with a powerful tongue" -- 53.11.
694.	ציצא	splendor -- 3.5; 23.7.
695.	צירא	fluid -- 53.8.
696.	צלחתא	headache -- 53.12.
697.	צילמא	figure -- 54.1; 55.2.
698.	צלף	to scourge -- 1.10.
699.	צנף	to shriek -- 60.11.
700.	צעק	to cry -- 68.6,7,8; 68.1 (*exterior*).
701.	צער	to lose. יצערי: "losses" -- 3.11.

702.	ציפונא	north -- 46.3.
703.	צפעסק	demon name -- 8.2.
704.	צפרא	morning -- 35.5.
705.	צרא	to split, burst -- 11.11.

ק

706.	קבל	to receive, accept (Pa) -- 11.11; 19.11.
707.	קיבלא	counter-charm -- 11.2; 19.10; 61.6.
708.	קבקביאל	angel name -- 12.15.
709.	קברא	a grave -- 60.17.
710.	קדח	to flee -- 19.7,12.
711.	קדם	before -- 8.7,9; 16.3; 44.7; passim.
712.	קדישא	holy -- 5.1; 48.1; 56.12.
713.	קום	to stand, rise, be established -- 7.10; 14.2; 49.12; passim.
714.	קומתא	body -- 2.1; 7.1,2; 21.3; 46.5; 53.3.
715.	קוסא	"Qosa," divine name -- 21.18.
716.	קטל	to kill -- 8.4; 19.4; 53.3; passim.
717.	קטר	to tie (in knots) -- 10.1.
718.	קיטרא	a (magic) knot -- 36.5; 46.4; 50.1,5.
719.	קלא	a voice, sound, Hark! -- 11.11; 24.10; 25.9; 60.11,11.
	בת קלא	a (mysterious/angelic) voice from heaven -- 24.10.
720.	קלא	to burn -- 57.4.
721.	קלילא	fleet, swift -- 41.10.
722.	קללא	dishonor, a curse -- 10.3.
723.	קלעא	a rope -- 70.6,6.
724.	קמיעא	an amulet -- 1.6; 16.1; 42.1; passim.
725.	קנינא	property -- 43.1; 48.4. "Possessions."
726.	קסם	(BH) to divine -- 66.5.
727.	קסרבא	angel epithet.
728.	קפא	"Qapa," divine name -- 21.18.
729.	קצפיאל	evil angel name -- 42.8.
730.	קציצתא	a beam, bar -- 2.1; 6.3; 7.2.
731.	קרא	to call, read -- 53.5; 57.5.
732.	קריתא	an invocation -- 42.9; 48.6; 57.7.

733.	קרב	to approach, come near -- 11.10; passim.
734.	קריבא	a relative, "near" one -- 53.1.
735.	קרח	to flee -- 20.9.
736.	קוריא	a town -- 53.2.
737.	קרנא	a horn -- 23.5.
738.	קרפדנא	the "Great King" -- 62.3.
739.	קרקפא	a skull, head -- 2.1.
740.	קש/יא	hard, strong -- 42.11; 43.2; 57.1.
741.	קשישא	old, elder, ancient -- 21.9.
742.	קשתא	bow, rainbow -- 7.7.
743.	קתרוס	Qatros (a protecting spirit) -- 22.5; 19.4.

ר

744.	ראשא	head -- 7.15; 5.5.
745.	רבא/תא	great -- 5.5; 7.6; 43.6; 49.7; 53.17.
746.	רברבא	great, great (person) -- 24.8; 49.13.
747.	רוגזא	anger -- 24.7.
748.	ריזלא	a foot -- 23.7; 43.2; 52.6; 53.9.
749.	רדטייייאל	(sic!) angel name -- 43.5.
750.	רוחא	wind, spirit -- 12.16; 24.9; 38.3.
751.	רום	to be high -- 9.4.
752.	רמא/תא	height -- 15.6.
753.	רזא	a mystery, a secret -- 2.7; 11.11.
754.	רזזום	"the evil spirit that is silent and does not speak, and falls upon the sons of man" (Cf. Rossell, *Handbook*, p. 148) -- 53.10.
755.	רחבא	greed -- 53.8.
756.	רחם	to love -- 19.10; 25.4.
757.	רחמא	love, mercy -- 14.1; 53.1; 57.5; passim.
758.	רחמיאיל	angel name -- 25.3; 33.4; 36.5; 43.5.
759.	רחק	to be far away -- 8.3; 9.2; 19.5; passim.
760.	רחיקא/תא	(one) far away, distant.
761.	רחיקיה	a destroying angel name.
762.	רחת	to be excited -- 68.6,7,8. 68.1 (*exterior*).

763.	רטבי	"the evil spirit that sits on ṬQYN mountains and shakes the right arm" -- 53.9.
764.	ריבא	a law-suit -- 34.3.
765.	רכב	to ride down, overcome -- 64.4; 65.3.
766.	רכן	to sink -- 58.1.
767.	רכשא	a steed -- 49.13.
768.	רמא	to throw, cast down -- 3.17; 9.7; 11.4; 12.3; 14.3; 15.1; 19.4; 21.10.
769.	רימזא	a gesture -- 21.8.
770.	רמס	to trample -- 1.10.
771.	רימסא	a creeping thing, a reptile -- 3.14.
772.	רמיריר	angel epithet ("spittle thrower").
773.	רמשא	evening -- 35.5.
774.	רעותא	will, desire -- 23.6; 62.5.
775.	רעיונא	a thought, desire -- 53.4,7.
776.	רופין	physicians -- 2.7.
777.	רע	bad, evil -- 44.5; 71.2.
778.	רפאל	angel name (the "healer") -- 3.8; 15.11; 56.13.
779.	רפד	to camp, encamp -- 2.7.
780.	ריפסא	shaking -- 53.8.
781.	רקד	to dance -- 60.11.
782.	רקדא	a dance -- 23.8.
783.	רקיעא	firmament -- 12.9; 44.6.
784.	רשע	to harm -- 53.6.
785.	רתק	to knock.
786.	רתת	to shake, be terrified -- 43.4; 53.6.
787.	רתתנא	the BRBWRY demon -- 53.4.

ש

788.	שאל	to ask -- 5.6.
789.	שאול	Saul, son of Kish -- 53.6.
790.	שאול	Sheol -- 11.12.
791.	שבב	to burn -- 36.1.
792.	שבח	to praise -- 23.6.
793.	שובטא	band (of spirits) -- 14.2; 23.4; 53.2.

794.	שבע	to swear, adjure (Af) -- 8.3,4; 19.3; 39.6; 43.6; 53.2; passim.
795.	שבועא	an adjuration -- 63.3.
796.	שבועתא	a promise, an oath -- 43.6.
797.	שבע/ה	seven -- 5.4; 7.15; 31.3; 46.3; passim.
	שבעין	seventy -- 49.10.
	שביעיתא	seventh -- 11.8.
798.	שבק	to forsake -- 13.2; 19.6; 41.1.
799.	שיבוקא	a dismissal, release -- 12.13; 15.5; 19.7.
800.	שבת	to rest, make to end -- 49.10; 64.3 (*interior*).
801.	שגר	I. to dissolve -- 1.11.
802.	שגר	II. to burn -- 36.1.
803.	שגש	to confuse -- 1.11; 32.4; 53.4,7.
804.	שידא	a demon -- 7.17; 47.2; 48.1; passim.
	שידניתא	a demoness -- 3.14.
805.	שדא	column -- 43.2.
806.	שדי	Shaddai, deity epithet -- 3.4; 12.12.
807.	שדר	to send -- 43.7; 53.6.
808.	שדרא/תא	column (i.e., of the spine) -- 43.2,4; 53.10; 63.7.
809.	שוחאה	lust -- 36.4.
810.	שונקא	deity name -- 21.8.
811.	שוף	to rub.
812.	שורא	a wall -- 5.6.
813.	שושלתא	a chain -- 43.4; 44.3.
814.	שחן	to be inflamed (with passion) -- 36.1.
815.	שחקא	heaven -- 37.11.
816.	שחרתא	slumber -- 3.16; 12.11.
817.	שיבא	a circle-spirit -- 26.6.
818.	שיקא	a type of demon -- 26.5.
819.	שירא	a song -- 69.2.
820.	שירא	a ring -- 31.3.
821.	שכב	to lie down -- 17.8; 53.14.
822.	שכח	to find -- 12.7; 34.2; 68.3 (*exterior*).
823.	שכן	to dwell, reside -- 43.7.
824.	שלהיבתא	a flame -- 9.7.
825.	שלומה	Solomon (spelled various ways) -- 7.18; 47.1; passim.

826.	שלח	I. to send -- 49.10; 67.3.
827.	שלח	II. to strip bare, make naked -- 12.3; 13.5; 14.3.
828.	שלט	to prevail (over), rule -- 33.3; 67.6.
829.	שליטא	ruler -- 17.7; 22.2; 31.3; 62.5.
830.	שולטנא	a command -- 62.5.
831.	שלם	to cast a spell, perform (magic) (Af) -- 40.1; 56.7; 68.7,8.
832.	שלמא	peace -- 25.12.
833.	שלניתא	a ghost -- 12.2; 13.4; 19.7.
834.	שמא	a name, a person -- 7.11; 1.14; passim. Construct: שום. Plural: שמהתא.
835.	שמיא	heaven, the heavens -- 7.4; 49.2; passim.
836.	שמע	to hear -- 12.3,4,7; 14.4; 43.1.
837.	שמר	(BH) to guard -- 66.4.
838.	שמש	to officiate, make use of (Ethpa) -- 41.10.
839.	שמשא	the sun -- 38.2.
840.	שמיש	Šameš -- 62.2.
841.	שמת	to ban, anathematize -- 23.9; 64.2; 65.2.
842.	שמתא	a ban, curse -- 2.6; 12.6; 24.7; 47.2.
843.	שנא	to bewilder -- 3.16.
844.	שסנגיאל	angel name -- 34.4.
845.	שנק	to strangle -- 53.4,6.
846.	שתא	a year -- 11.5. Plural: שנין.
847.	שינתא	sleep -- 11.10; 62.1.
848.	שעה	to look -- 70.4.
849.	שערתא	fever -- 17.3. Cf. also note two to text seventeen.
850.	שעתא	an hour -- 5.5; 33.4; 35.5; 58.5.
851.	שפל	to lower (Af) -- 52.5.
852.	שיפורא	an excommunication -- 47.2.
853.	שקל	to take, take away -- 17.8; 19.7; 35.6.
854.	שקע	to sink -- 15.1.
855.	שקף	to knock, strike -- 19.4; 56.4.
856.	שיקופתא	a knocking, a blow -- 23.9; 33.2.
857.	שיקצא	vermin -- 3.14.
858.	שרא	to dwell (Af) -- 9.3; 33.2; to release, be untied (Ethpa) -- 43.4; 50.5.
859.	שירא	a (signet)-ring -- 31.3.

860.	שרבא	a tube -- 60.10.
861.	שריאל	angel name -- 9.5.
862.	שרירא	reliable, true -- 8.1; 25.8; 54.7.
863.	שושירא	a twisted chain -- 50.2.
864.	שתא	to drink.
865.	שתיתא	sixth -- 11.8.
	שיתין	sixty -- 21.8. Cf. BH ששים in 66.3.
866.	שתק	to be silent -- 53.10.

ת

867.	תבר	to break -- 21.5; 50.5; 64.2; 65.2.
868.	תברא	destruction -- 14.5. Cf. Rossell, *Handbook*, pp. 152-153, and his citation of Gordon's article in *Archiv Orientální*, IX, 1937, p. 106.
869.	תיבותא	an ark, a chest -- 16.5; 19.10.
870.	תגמא	a legion -- 25.1.
871.	תוב	to return, restore -- 62.1.
872.	תוב	again, furthermore -- 43.6; 22.6; passim.
873.	תורא	an ox -- 49.6; 55.4.
874.	תחות	under -- 53.3.
875.	תכלתא	an abortion -- 17.4.
876.	תלא	to hang -- 52.5.
877.	תלת/א	three -- 12.3; 13.4; 14.3; 52.4; 56.1.
	תלתין	thirty -- 56.1,1.
	תליתיתא	third -- 11.8.
878.	תמן	there -- 9.7; 21.14.
879.	תמני/א	eight -- 21.4; 39.5,6; 46.5; 53.14.
	תמנן	eighty (feminine) -- 21.9.
880.	תנה	to mutter -- 60.1.
881.	תנין	jackals.
882.	תנינא	leviathan -- 2.4; 7.7,9.
883.	תקן	to attach, make secure (Pa) -- 21.10; 37.11.
884.	תיקא	safety -- 41.12.
885.	תקנתא	a remedy -- 62.4.
886.	תקף	to make heavy (Af) -- 58.7.

887.	תקיפא	strong, powerful -- 53.5,11; 57.2.
888.	תריך	תרתין two -- Cf. Rossell, *Handbook*, p. 153.
	תרי⟨ן⟩ עשר	twelve -- 5.4.
	תינינא/תא	second -- 11.8; 21.15.
889.	תרך	to banish (Pa) -- 13.3; 43.6.
890.	תירוכא	a dismissal -- 19.7; 35.6.
891.	תרסין	"the demon that shakes the right foot" -- 53.9.
892.	תרעא	a gate -- 49.14.
893.	תרנגולא	a chicken -- 60.11.
894.	תושבחא	praise -- 12.7; 29.12; 61.6; 69.2.

INDEX OF PERSONAL NAMES

א

'Aba -- 13.12.
'Ibai -- 55.5.
'Abanduk -- 10.1.
'Abn -- 40.1.
'Abuna -- 2.3,4,5,7; 5.5,7.
'Abraham -- 23.11; 24.3,13.
'Adaq -- 11.3,9; 31.1,3,4.
'Adon -- 54.3.
'WN' -- 62.4,4.
'Aḥat -- 8.4,7,9,12; 11.3,9; 28.1,3; 29.1,3; 30.1,3,4; 34.1; 36.2,4; 48.2,3; 54.3.
'Aḥata -- 33.4,5; 47.3,4.
'Aḥi -- 32.5.
'Akarkoi -- 45.3.
'Elišeba -- 50.1,6; 51.1.
'Imma -- 19.1,2,3,5,8; 48.3,3; 62.1; 64.4,3 (*interior*).
'Imma Salma -- 19.1,2,3,5,7,11,12.
'Immi -- 40.2; 56.11,12.
'Amṭur -- 43.1,3,7.
'Oni -- 27.1,4.
'Anqado -- 61.2.
'Anur -- 36.1,4.
'Asmanduk -- 23.1,10; 24.1,12.
'Ispandare/id -- 18.3; 35.4; 38.2.
'Ispandoi -- 20.2,10.
'Aspenaz -- 4.1,3.
'Ispiza -- 38.1.
'Astroba -- 37.8.
'Apila -- 33.2,3,4.
'Epra -- 1.1,3,5,7,15; 20.1,9.
'Arazniš -- 47.1,3.
'Ardoi -- 4.1,3,5,9; 8.2,4,7,9.
'Argušnasp -- 56.4,10,12.

'Arḥa -- 38.1.
'Artašriḥa -- 13.7.
'ŠTR -- 66.1.
'Itay -- 7.6,7,8,13,14,15,17.
'Atyona -- 48.3

ב

Babanoš -- 15.4,8.
Bahmanduk -- 1.4,5,7; 18.3,6,8; 25.2,4.
Bahrad -- 18.3.
Bahram-Gušnasp -- 57.5,6,7.
Buzmandad -- 54.3.
BHLYḤWY -- 65.1,3.
Banai -- 3.10,15; 6.8.
Burzoi -- 68.3,4,9.
Burzin -- 39.1. Cf. also 22.1.
Brîk-Yah-b^e-Yah -- 35.4; 52.6,7.
Brîk-Marya -- 41.5,8,9,11,13; 42.1,5,7,11.
Beryl -- 19.1,3,3,5,7.
Bar Ḥ'WY -- 65.1,3.
Bar-Šibebi -- 26.3,8.
BT -- 72.1.
BTY -- 63.2.

ג

Goi -- 4.1,3,5,9.
Geyonai -- 12.1,4,10,13.
GYYT -- 62.4,4.
Geribta -- 2.3,4,5,7; 5.5,7.
G/Qurdas -- 7.8,13,14,15,6,7,14,17.
Guroi -- 34.1,7.
GRYGNY -- 47.4.

ד

Dadai -- 39.1,2.
Dada -- 23.2,11; 24.2,12.
Dadbeh -- 23.1,10; 24.12.
DWBR -- 53.1.
Dodā -- 34.1.
DWDW -- 63.2.
Dodai -- 22.4,7; 42.2,7,11; 44.2,8,9; 46.2.
Dodi -- 26.2,8,9; 28.1,2; 29.1,3,4; 30.1,3,4.
Dahabai -- 21.4,15,16,18,19.
Dustai -- 42.2,7,11.
Dipši -- 48.2.
Darši -- 37.8.

ה

Hindu -- 32.1; 33.3,5.
Hormiz -- 26.2,8.
Hormizdad -- 46.2,5.
Hormizduk -- 8.2,4,7,9; 9.1.
Hormisduk -- 56.10,12.
Hormisdar -- 27.2.
Hotdora -- 35.4.

ו

Warzin -- 40.2.

ז

Zebinta -- 49.4,6,8,11,12,14,15.
Zadoi -- 14.1,5; 16.1,3,5.
Zidin -- 50.1,6.

Zidin Šabor -- 51.1,1.
Zawita -- 2.3,5.
Zarhiṣiya -- 41.2.
Zarinkaš -- 32.5,5.
Zaraq -- 49.5,6,8,11,12,14,15.

ח

Ḥ'WY -- 65.1,3.
ḤYWTYH -- 65.1,2.
ḤYL -- 37.8.
Ḥalipai -- 37.8.
Ḥisdi -- 64.1,3,3 (*interior*).
Ḥâtoi -- 11.3,9; 23.11; 24.2,12; 69.1,5,8.

ט

Ṭ'T -- 70.2.
Ṭati -- 34.1,7; 40.2.
Ṭardi -- 27.1,2,4.

י

Yazdid -- 13.12.
Yezidad -- 3.3,6,7,10,15; 6.2,7,9,10.
Yanai -- 48.2.
Yandundišnaṭ -- 38.1.
Yasmin -- 23.11; 24.2,12.
YQRY -- 59.2.

כ

Komeš -- 13.2,7,11,12.
KNRKŠWD -- 70.2.
Kosig -- 60.3,7,10,11,13,14,17; 61.2.
Kapnai -- 14.1,5.
Kapni -- 16.1,4,5; 17.1,3,5,7,8.
Kup/fitai -- 2.1; 5.2,6,7; 23.11; 24.3,12.

ל

L'LH -- 65.2,3.

מ

Maduk -- 9.1.
Mehoi -- 26.9.
MHDṬ -- 67.4,6.
Mahduk -- 23.11; 24.3,12; 61.2,3.
MHHNYŠ -- 62.4,6.
MHPYRWZ -- 58.2,3,8,10.
MWL'ZD -- 62.4,6.
Mazdewai -- 19.1,2,3,5,7,11,12.
Maḥlapta -- 13.2,7,11; 21.15,16,18,19; 31.1,3,4; 32.1,3,5;
         33.2,3,5; 40.2.
Meḥišai -- 22.4,7.
Meḥiši -- 40.1.
Malki -- 48.2.
Mama -- 26.2,8; 44.1,8,9; 45.3.
Mamai -- 12.1,4,10,13; 40.1; 55.5.
Mami -- 31.1,4; 35.4.
Marai -- 7.6,7,8,13,14,15,17.
Maraba -- 47.4.
Merda -- 60.3,10,14,17.
Merdabuk -- 60.3,7,10,11,13,14,17.
Merduk -- 3.10,15; 6.8.

Miriam -- 47.3.
Marat -- 12.5,10,13,17; 52.7.
Marta -- 26.3,8.
Mosh Bilhat -- 60.17.
Maškoi -- 4.1,3,5,9.
Mešaršia -- 21.3,4,15,16,18,19.
Metaniš -- 37.2,5.

נ

Newanduk -- 10.1,3; 14.1,5; 16.1,3,4; 17.1,3,5,7,8; 18.3,6,8.
Nukrayta -- 40.2.
Nanak -- 7.6,7,8,13,14,15,17.

ס

SBWN -- 63.2.
SH'DWK -- 66.2.
SYWTW -- 53.1.
Salma -- 19.1,2,3,5,7,11,12. Cf. also 'Imma Salma.
Sama -- 1.4,6,7; 25.2,5.
Simoi -- 4.1.
Simkoi -- 38.2.
SMT -- 56.10,12.
Sisnoi -- 61.2,5.
Saradust -- 15.4,9.

ע

cAwirti -- 40.1,2.

פ

Pabak -- 2.1,5; 5.2,5,7.
Pannoi -- 23.11; 24.3,12.
Parkoi -- 8.4,7,9,12; 36.1,4.
Parsa -- 40.3.
Parruk -- 10.1,3; 47.1,3.
Parrukdad -- 49.4,5,8,11,12,14,15.
Parruk-Kosru -- 61.2,5.
Pušbi -- 10.1,3.

ק

Qayomta -- 15.4,8.
Qamoi -- 49.5,6,8,11,12,14,15.
Qaqai -- 47.3.
Qaqi -- 32.3.
Qarqoi -- 48.3,3.

ר

Rurzil -- 40.1.
Rešan -- 37.3,5.
Rišinduk -- 41.6,8,9,11,13; 42.2,5,7,11.
Rašnoi -- 12.4,10,13,17.

ש

Š'LY -- 69.1,5,8.
Šabor -- 50.1,6.
Šaborduk -- 1.2,3,5,.7; 61.3; 67.4,6.
Šahduk -- 61.2.
Šaḥin -- 61.3.
ŠYRWY -- 68.4,9.

Šili -- 23.11; 24.3,13.
Šilta -- 43.1,3,7; 48.3.
Širin -- 15.4,9.
Šarqoi -- 14.1,15; 16.1,4; 23.1,10,11; 24.2,3,12,13.
Šišai -- 61.2.
Šišin -- 37.8; 40.2.

ת

Teshiharazad -- 26.3,8.

LIST OF QUOTATIONS FROM SCRIPTURE

Numbers 6:24-26 -- 66.4-5.

Numbers 9:23 -- 35.1-2; 55.9-10.

Deuteronomy 6:4 -- 35.1.

Isaiah 6:3 -- 33.5.

Isaiah 44:25 -- 66.5.

Amos 5:26 -- 62.3.

Zechariah 3:2 -- 8.12; 10.6; 24.14; 35.2-3; 42.10-11.

Psalm 91:7 -- 52.9.

Psalm 91:10 -- 52.9.

Psalm 121:7 -- 23.12.

Psalm 125:2 -- 19.10.

Song of Songs 3:7 -- 66.3-4.

BIBLIOGRAPHY

BOOKS

Belot, J. B. *Vocabulaire Arabe-Francais*. Beyrouth: Imprimerie Catholique, 1899.

Brown, Francis; Driver, S. R.; and Briggs, Charles A. *A Hebrew and English Lexicon of the Old Testament*. Oxford: The Clarendon Press, 1968.

Burton, Richard F. *The Book of a Thousand Nights and a Night*. Burton Club, n.d. Vol. I.

Buttrick, George Arthur (ed.). *The Interpreter's Dictionary of the Bible*. New York: The Abingdon Press, 1962. Vol. IV.

Chwolson, A. *Corpus Inscriptionum Hebraicarum*. St. Petersburg, 1882.

Gordon, Cyrus H. *Adventures In the Nearest East*. London: Phoenix House Ltd., 1957.

_____. *Evidence For the Minoan Language*. Ventnor: Ventnor Publishers, 1966.

_____. *Ugarit and Minoan Crete*. New York: W. W. Norton and Company, Inc., 1966.

_____. *Ugaritic Textbook*. Rome: The Pontifical Biblical Institute, 1965.

The Greek New Testament. Aland, Kurt; Black, Matthew; Metzger, Bruce; and Wikgren, Allen (eds.). New York: The American Bible Society, 1966.

Hamilton, Victor. *Syriac Incantation Bowls*. Ann Arbor: University Microfilms, Inc., 1971.

The Hebrew Bible. Jerusalem: Koren Publishers Jerusalem, Ltd., n.d.

Jastrow, Marcus. *A Dictionary of the Targumim, the Talmud Babli and Yerushalmi, and the Midrashic Literature*. New York: Jastrow Publishers, 1967.

Jean, Charles F., and Hoftijzer, Jean. *Dictionnaire des Inscriptions Sémitiques de l'Ouest*. Leiden: E. J. Brill, 1965.

Jeruzalmi, Isak. *Les Coupes Magiques Araméenes de Mésopotamie.* Paris: The Sorbonne, 1964.

Lane, Edward W. *The Modern Egyptians.* London: Ward, Lock and Company, Ltd., 1835.

Layard, Austen. *Discoveries In the Ruins of Nineveh and Babylon.* London: 1853.

McCullough, W. S. *Jewish and Mandaean Incantation Bowls.* Toronto: University of Toronto Press, 1967.

Montgomery, James A. *Aramaic Incantation Texts From Nippur.* Philadelphia: The University Museum, 1913.

Moore, George Foot. *Judaism In the First Centuries of the Christian Era.* New York: Schocken Books, 1971. 2 Volumes.

Myhrman, D. W. *Hilprecht Anniversary Volume.* Leipzig, 1909.

Rosenthal, Franz. *Die Aramäistische Forschung Seit Th. Nöldekes Veröffentlichen.* Leiden, 1939.

Rossell, William H. *A Handbook of Aramaic Magical Texts.* New Jersey: Shelton College, 1953.

Stübe, Rudolph. *Jüdisch-Babylonische Zaubertexte.* Halle, 1895.

Wallis, Wilber B. *Aramaic and Mandaean Magic and Their Demonology.* Unpublished Ph.D. dissertation. Philadelphia: Dropsie College for Hebrew and Cognate Studies, 1956.

Yamauchi, Edwin Masao. *Mandaean Incantation Texts.* Ann Arbor: University Microfilms, Inc., 1964.

_____. *Mandaic Incantation Texts.* American Oriental Series 49. New Haven: American Oriental Society, 1967.

ARTICLES

Gordon, Cyrus H. "An Aramaic Incantation," *Annual of the American School of Oriental Research,* XIV, pp. 141-143. New Haven, 1934.

_____. "Aramaic Incantation Bowls," *Orientalia,* X, pp. 116-141; 272-280. Rome, 1941.

_____. "Aramaic Magical Bowls in the Istanbul and Baghdad Museums" (with 6 plates), *Archiv Orientální,* VI, pp. 319-334; 466-474. Prague, 1934.

_____. "Aramaic and Mandaic Magical Bowls" (with 13 plates), *Archiv Orientální*, IX, pp. 84-95. Prague, 1937.

_____. "His Name Is 'One,'" *Journal of Near Eastern Studies*, 29, No. 3.

_____. "Leviathan: Symbol of Evil," *Biblical Motifs*, ed. Alexander Altmann (Cambridge: Harvard University Press, 1966), pp. 1-9.

_____. "Two Magic Bowls in Teheran," *Orientalia*, XX, pp. 306-315. Rome, 1951.

Halévy, J. "Observation sur un vase judéo-babylonien du British Muséum," *Comptes rendus de l'Académie des Inscriptions et Belles-Lettres*, V, pp. 288-298. Paris, 1877.

Hyvernat, Henri. "Sur un vase judéo-babylonien du musée Lycklama de Cannes (Provence)," *Zeitschrift für Keilschriftforschung*, II, pp. 113-148. 1885.

Isbell, Charles D. "Some Cryptograms In the Aramaic Incantation Bowls," *Journal of Near Eastern Studies*, 33, 1974, pp. 405-407.

Kaufman, Stephen A. "A Unique Magic Bowl From Nippur," *Journal of Near Eastern Studies*, 32, 1973, pp. 170-174.

Lacau, P. "Une Coupe d'Incantation," *Revue d'Assyriologie et d'Archéologie Orientale*, II, pp. 49-51. Paris, 1894.

Levine, Baruch. "The Language of the Magical Bowls," in Jacob Neusner, *A History of the Jews in Babylonia V: Later Sassanian Times* (Leiden: E. J. Brill, 1970), pp. 343-387.

Lévy, M. A. "Epigraphische Beiträge Zur Geschichte der Juden," *Jahrbuch für die Geschichte der Juden*, 1861.

_____. *Über die von Layard aufgefundenen chaldäischen Inschriften auf Topfgefässen. Ein Beitrag zur hebräischen Paläographie u.z. Religionsgeschichte, Zeitschrift d. Deutschen Morgenländischen Gesellschaft*, 1885.

Lidzbarski, M. "Ein mandäisches Amulett," *Florilegium ou recueil de travaux d'érudition dédies à M. Melchior de Vogüé* (Paris: Imprimerie Nationale, 1909), pp. 349-373.

Macuch, R. "Altmandäische Bleirollen I," *Die Araber in der Alten Welt*, ed. F. Altheim and R. Stiehl (Berlin: W. de Gruyter, 1967), IV, pp. 91-203; *idem*, V, pp. 34-72.

McCown, C. C. "The Christian Tradition as to the Magical Wisdom of Solomon," *Journal of the Palestine Oriental Society*, 2, 1922, pp. 1-24.

Montgomery, James A. "A Magical Bowl-Text and the Original Script of the Manichaeans," *Journal of the American Oriental Society*, 32, 1912, pp. 434-438.

Narqis, M. "שבעה ארמית," *Tarbiz*, 6, 1934, pp. 106-107.

Neusner, Jacob, and Smith, J. "Archaeology and Babylonian Jewry," *Near Eastern Archaeology in the Twentieth Century*, ed. James Sanders (Garden City, New York: Doubleday and Co., 1970), pp. 331-347.

Obermann, Julian. "Two Magic Bowls," *American Journal of Semitic Languages and Literatures*, LVII, pp. 1-31. Chicago, 1940.

Rodwell, J. M. "Remarks Upon a Terra-Cotta Vase," *Transactions of the Society of Biblical Archaeology*, ii, pp. 114-118. London, 1873.

Schwab, Moise. "Les Coupes Magiques et L'Hydromancie dans L'Antiquité Orientale," *Proceedings of the Society of Biblical Archaeology*, XII, pp. 292-342. London, 1890.

Schwab, Moise, and Babelon, E. "Un vase judéo-chaldéen de la Bibliothèque Nationale," *Revue des études juives*, IV. Paris, 1882.

Wohlstein, J. "Über einige aramäische Inschriften auf Thongefässen des Königlichen Museums zu Berlin," *Zeitschrift für Assyriologie und verwandte Gebiete*, VIII, pp. 313-340; IX, pp. 11-41. Berlin-Leipzig, 1893 and 1894.

Yamauchi, Edwin Masao. "Aramaic Magic Bowls," *Journal of the American Oriental Society*, 85, 1965, pp. 511-523 (also three photographs and a hand copy of an Aramaic bowl).

www.ingramcontent.com/pod-product-compliance
Lightning Source LLC
Chambersburg PA
CBHW060606230426
43670CB00011B/2001